A

VERY

POLITICAL

FAMILY

Note for Librarians: A cataloguing record for this book is available from Library and Archives Canada at www.collectionscanada.ca/amicus/index-e.html
ISBN 1-4251-1402-4

Printed in Victoria, BC, Canada. Printed on paper with minimum 30% recycled fibre. Trafford's print shop runs on "green energy" from solar, wind and other environmentally-friendly power sources.

TRAFFORD
PUBLISHING™

Offices in Canada, USA, Ireland and UK

Book sales for North America and international:
Trafford Publishing, 6E–2333 Government St.,
Victoria, BC V8T 4P4 CANADA
phone 250 383 6864 (toll-free 1 888 232 4444)
fax 250 383 6804; email to orders@trafford.com

Book sales in Europe:
Trafford Publishing (UK) Limited, 9 Park End Street, 2nd Floor
Oxford, UK OX1 1HH UNITED KINGDOM
phone 44 (0)1865 722 113 (local rate 0845 230 9601)
facsimile 44 (0)1865 722 868; info.uk@trafford.com

Order online at:
trafford.com/06-3161

email: verakrist@dccnet.com

10 9 8 7 6 5 4 3 2 1

A VERY POLITICAL FAMILY

Vera Kristiansen

(nee Sharko)

"Oh, what a romance my life has been"

TABLE OF CONTENTS

Page

TABLE OF CONTENTS – continued

PREFACE

"Success is not a destination; it is a journey."

I started writing these memoirs in the early 1980s, when Lyle was first elected Member of Parliament for Kootenay West. In particular, I was made aware of the need to explain to future generations what life was like, how changes took place – with the hope they will appreciate what they inherited.

During that time, we had a couple of Korean students living with us. One day they told us that day was a holiday at home in Korea. They called it "Heritage Day". It was a day when they remembered they ancestors. In fact, they could name their relatives for seven generations back, including what their occupations were, where they lived, and where they were buried.

I looked at my life and realized I could only go back one generation – my parents! It was like everything started with them. I could not even picture my grandparents or where they lived. This book will be available for my grandchildren, and their children.

As I wrote, friends and relatives read my chapters, enjoyed them, laughed at them, and commented on things they did not know before. Many encouraged me to get it printed. I have done this, and hope that others will share these feelings.

I would like to thank my husband, Lyle, for all the editing he did. He helped remember events, and corrected many misconceptions.

Our daughter, Haida, has been most helpful, being a budding writer herself. A dear friend, Amanda Offers, in Sechelt, has been invaluable in helping me with the computer. Even more importantly, she took my independent, rambling chapters that I had written over twenty years, and pulled them together to form a book. This has been most helpful, and I am deeply indebted to her.

What I wanted to portray, also, was that changes in society, in people's lives, happened because tens of thousands of individual people banded together to work for these changes. Ordinary people, with ordinary lives, faced with every day family problems, take time to work toward improvements. The men and women sitting in parliament or city hall don't initiate changes – they respond to demands from their electorate. People can beat money – most of the time.

This book outlines some of these activities, by so many people, in so many ways, in so many organizations. And the four generations of this family were involved in so many different venues.

WE WON!

Sitting on a plane, in the first class compartment, heading back to Nelson, I reminisced about events that brought me to this point in life. Politics. So many elections. Federal, provincial, municipal – losing most - but the few that were won made up for all the losses.

This was my first experience flying first class, seeing how the other half flies. This would be very easy to get used to. I had been bumped up to first class because of over-booking, but I was not complaining. It will be harder to sit in economy now. I had a glass of wine in my hand before we took off. Delicate canapés were served as soon as we were in the air. Delicious dinner, drinks before, after, and during the whole trip. And so much more room – wider seats, room for feet, room between aisles – this was classy.

I was returning home from Ottawa after attending an orientation session for spouses of newly elected members of parliament. My husband, Lyle, had just been elected Member of Parliament for Kootenay West. In Ottawa we were treated like royalty. Having doors opened, limousines provided, reporters requesting interviews. We were taken to a reception at Ottawa's city hall, and welcomed by the NDP mayor, Marion Dewar. The clerk of the House of Commons circulated amongst new Members, familiarizing himself with names, faces, and constituency names so he could assist the Speaker when Parliament opened.

I was somewhat familiar with the House of Commons because I worked there between 1963 and 1965, when Lyle was federal secretary of the New Democratic Youth. I worked for MP Dr. William Howe from Hamilton. In those days, the offices were dingy; two

Members shared an office and a secretary, in a cramped, dark room. This time, 1980, Lyle had two rooms: one for himself (I had a desk in that room), and an adjoining office for his three staff members. The furniture was posh: beautiful desks, carpet on the floor, and a sofa. These were major changes.

When one runs for political office, all one thinks of is the campaign. You work flat out to win; you don't consider "what if we win." Then you win. Then reality sets in. Lyle will have so much to learn. I too will face challenges: where to live, how to adjust children to new circumstances, how to juggle my time between family and politics. We had already been told by our oldest child that he wouldn't move to Ottawa. Ah, but winning is definitely more fun than losing!

We won the federal election February 18th, 1980. The next morning Lyle phoned former MP Bob Brisco, to see when we could get his (government-owned) furniture for our office. His wife answered and was very pleasant. She said it would be nice to have him home again. She didn't move to Ottawa. However, when he returned to Trail, he brought with him a woman and 2-year-old child. His wife divorced him.

The next few days were spent setting up an office in Castlegar, moving furniture from Brisco's office, writing thank you letters. Gerald Rotering was hired as constituency assistant, which was the best thing we did.

Friday, before we left for Ottawa, our whole family was invited to KC Restaurant by its owner, Cameron Mah, and treated to an elaborate Chinese dinner. We were treated royally. This special treatment would be repeated many times, in many situations.

Because the weather was so uncertain and the airport at Castlegar was sopped in, Lyle and I drove to

Cranbrook (about 150 miles) to catch the plane. However, the plane then went back to Castlegar and was able to land. Thus, we were introduced to the uncertainty of commuter air travel to our riding. Arriving in Ottawa, we were met with cold and windy weather. We nearly froze walking the three blocks to the House of Commons. Noel Duignan, who had been Lyle's campaign manager, quit his job at Comico's lead plant, and came ahead as executive assistant.

Vic Althouse, a farmer MP from Saskatchewan, had the office next door. Lyle and Vic called themselves the "Farmer-Labour" caucus. Both Vic and his wife Cecily were very amiable and we enjoyed their company throughout the years. Cecily and I found two apartments within walking distance of the House, and helped the guys move in the next day.

Sitting on the plane I went over the election campaign. It was winter, but most enjoyable. Everything went well. People wanted to talk issues. People came out to meetings to hear the candidates. These are the kinds of campaigns where the NDP shines. Every election our challenge has been to get issues discussed. The only other campaign that matched this one was the 1972 provincial election in which the NDP and Dave Barrett won.

But before I get to that, I want to note how truly satisfied I am with my life. How very full and useful I feel. Perhaps it was the royal treatment in Ottawa, or returning first class. However, I feel happy, content, satisfied, fulfilled - every worthwhile feeling a woman - nay, a human being - could have.

Me, Vera (Sharko) Kristiansen, third daughter of immigrants Leo (Levonti) and Pauline (Pavlina) Sharko, from Coolidge, Alberta, born and brought up on one of the most backwoods homesteads in Canada. A childhood of dreaming. Working my way through

3

Business College, and getting good at my profession as a legal secretary, in Edmonton and Vancouver.

Then marrying Lyle Kristiansen in 1961, into a family I love dearly. Through him getting the best mother and father-in-law, and grandmother and grandfather in the country. I never knew my own grandparents (only saw a photo of one), so I cherish them.

Throughout my life, whatever I was doing, I was guided by the words of wisdom of my dear father, whom I lost in 1969. I loved him dearly. For a man with a grade three education, he was wise beyond words. He was honest and forthright, and always concerned about those less fortunate. At all times I have tried to follow his example of being sincere and truthful, not only in word and deed, but in my heart. He was the best example of what a civilized human being should be.

Working in the political arena, as a volunteer, I had many disappointments, heartaches, devastations. But there were also pleasures and fulfilment. Whatever happens in the future, I can truthfully say I did my best, I worked hard, I left my mark on the history of the Kootenays. I influenced the course of history - just a little - in the right direction, hopefully leaving this world a little better than I found it.

Then there is my husband, Lyle, the recently elected Member of Parliament for Kootenay West. We've had our ups and downs. Lyle has always treated me with respect. He taught me to enjoy life. He gave me confidence; and (in the words of Anne Murray's song) when I lost it, got it back for me. I appreciate the kind of sincerity and concern he has for the ordinary people of his country - nay, of the world. His deep feelings, his knowledge and ability, are only matched by that of my dear father.

4

IT ALL STARTED

Well, when do political events start? Perhaps it started in 1905 when Lyle's grandmother, Augusta Moreland, carrying her 2-year old daughter, left the train at Swift Current, Saskatchewan, and stepped into mud in her dainty shoes. She watched as men loaded her piano and fine china and linen into a home-made buckboard wagon. She then climbed up onto the wagon (which would not have been easy as she was only 4'11"), and rode, with her husband, George, the 13 miles to their homestead.

George had come ahead two years earlier to set up a home. As they arrived on the buckboard, Grandma saw the sod-covered shanty she would be living in. I can only imagine her thoughts.

They had come from a middle class English background. George had been planning on joining the army to fight in the Boer War. Augusta had been training to be a concert pianist. Instead, they met, fell in love, married and moved to Canada to become farmers. Their love and humour sustained them through so much early hardship and through their 70 years of married life.

Their first winter together was bitterly cold. Their two Clydesdale horses died. Still they carried on. They were high Anglican and Conservatives. Every Sunday Grandpa loaded the piano onto the buckboard and hauled it to the school where church services were held for Grandma to play.

They suffered through the droughts, locust invasions, and crop failures. But when the preacher started recruiting for the army for World War I, from the pulpit, it was the last straw. They quit going to church and became atheists and socialists.

Grandpa knew nothing about farming. He built a new house on the highest spot on the farm, because of the lovely view. The winds howled around it unmercifully. One day Grandma was standing at the window and saw the wind toppled their horse into the ravine.

They participated in many political and social movements: the United Grain Growers, the Progressive Party, the Saskatchewan Wheat Pool, Saskatchewan Farmer-Labour Party, and the Co-operative Commonwealth Federation (CCF – both attending the founding convention in 1933).

In 1934, their youngest child, Hilda, (Lyle's mother) left to work in B.C. In February, Grandma went to visit her. What she saw in Vancouver astounded her: cherry trees in bloom, lush green lawns, mild weather. When she got back to Saskatchewan, she said, "Pack up, Pa, we are moving to Vancouver." And she did exactly that. Grandpa, of course, couldn't do that. He continued putting in the crop and reaping it for another five years.

Lyle's father, Thorvald (called "Denny") immigrated from Denmark in 1923. He had no family in Canada. He taught himself English by copying the Saturday Evening Post. He worked in Nelson hauling bricks to build the Hume school, and then as a waiter on the sternwheelers, and a cook's flunkey in logging camps. Once when he was down to his last dime, he bought himself a ten cent cigar, and before he finished it, he had a job. This was quite different from what my father did in the same circumstances.

In the early 1930s he moved to Vancouver and worked on the CPR coastal ships. Dad participated in the Progressive Arts Club and acted in their play "Waiting for Lefty" when it won the best-in-English award at the Dominion Drama Festival in Ottawa. He also wrote a number of plays, some of which were broadcast on the new CBC radio network.

In 1935 relief camps were set up to house the thousands of unemployed, single, homeless men. They were given shelter, food, clothing and paid twenty cents a day for 44 hours of public work per week. Dissatisfied with these conditions, 1,500 men left these relief camps, marched to Vancouver, and threatened to storm the Vancouver Police Station. CCF leader, Harold Winch, stood with one foot on a lamp post and one on Dad's shoulder to address and halt the men. There was a machine gun set up inside.

Mom and Dad (Kristiansen) met at a Vancouver Centre CCF social evening. Dad proposed to mother on their first date. They married in 1936, and Lyle was born May 9th, 1939. (He was named after Dr. Lyle Telford who was their doctor, and MLA. Later he was Mayor of Vancouver and a socialist lecturer on radio.) Hearing his yells, the floor nurses labelled Lyle the yodeller of St. Paul's Hospital – an ominous title for a future politician.

Grandpa and Grandma Moreland

Hilda and
Denny
Kristiansen
1958 –
with dog
Judy

LIFE ON A HOMESTEAD

My parents immigrated from the Ukraine. They were held up because of Dad's weak eyes, and missed the first ship going to Canada. He had gone blind, as a teenager, from malnutrition. Someone informed him that urine would "wash the red away." It did. They caught the last ship going to Canada in 1928. The Great Depression set in after that and all immigration ceased for some time.

I thought they suffered great hardships and were very brave to move half way round the world to a country where they didn't know the customs or the language. But these were people who knew hardships and deprivation. They also knew farming, and were self-sufficient in building their own homes.

My father had two brothers in Canada, who wrote many letters describing a country that had forests filled with deer, moose and elk, and lakes filled with fish. Most important, of course, was that anybody could hunt and fish as it was not reserved for a tsar and his minions. Dad thought that was heaven.

The most difficult part must have been when Dad and Uncle Harry Woytovich took their ten dollars to the Land Titles Office and asked for a quarter section (160 acres) of homestead. They were given a description and pointed north. The two men walked north for 75 miles, then west 15 miles. There, in a myriad of plots, they found their land.

Each was equipped with a saw, hammer and axe. They cut down trees, squared off the logs, chipped the grooves, and put up Uncle Harry's house. They then sent for the women and children – Mother had two daughters, and Aunty Calishka had four sons. Later they would build our house the same way.

There was deprivation and much hard work. But Dad enjoyed the hunting and fishing, and this provided us with food. On light rainy days, Dad would take my sister Nena and I fishing. Dad rowed while we dropped our heavy cords and hook and watched the big jacks grab on. In a couple of hours we would have all we needed. Mother was on shore, cleaning the fish.

What they didn't expect was that 160 acres would produce such poor crops. Their three acres in the old country could produce so much. And they never imagined so many stones could exist in one spot.

During harvest Dad would walk back toward Edmonton, taking whatever work was available. Once he walked for several days without work. When he was down to his last dime, he went to a Chinese cafe in a small town, told them he was hungry and all he had was a dime. He was brought a big bowl of soup with lots of meat in it. We always felt warmly toward the Chinese because they were known to never turn away anybody who was hungry.

When our schools held Christmas concerts, Dad would hitch the horses to a sleigh. The back was filled with straw, and Mother piled feather quilts on top to snuggle into. At school we participated in a concert with songs, recitals and skits, got a bag of candy and an orange. Then home again, happily snuggled in the quilts, listening to the jingle of bells on the horses, and the sharp crunchy sound the runners made on the glistening snow. We'd be fast asleep before we reached home.

As we grew older we attended dances at our school. They were so much fun. Parents and all the children attended. Everybody danced. When the children got tired, they just fell asleep in a corner on a quilt. Those of us dancing would do square dances, schottisches, polkas, and ladies' choice waltzes.

Some times we held box socials to raise money. Women decorated a shoebox with crepe paper. Inside were sandwiches and a pie. Old bachelors were willing to bid high just for the food. But the intrigue came when a fellow had to find his heartthrob's box. He would bribe her brothers, or ask her mother, or sneak around watching her bring it in. It was not cricket telling him. Of course, when the other fellows found him bidding on a certain box they bid up the price.

We preserved vegetables for the winter, made a barrel of sauerkraut, with heads of cabbage in the middle for cabbage rolls. The root cellar was filled with potatoes, beets, carrots, turnips, and onions. Our parents would buy a couple of boxes of crab apples and plums in the fall and we preserved them in jars and used them as dessert all winter.

Evenings were spent tearing goose feathers in half (discarding the bone) for quilts and pillows. Mother would buy wool, wash it, card it, make thread, and knit our socks, mitts and scarves. Dad spent the evenings reading his newspaper out loud to us.

Recently I was telling Haida that there was a contest in a magazine I could easily win. They were asking people to describe events that made them the poorest in the country. "I would describe the way Mother sewed all our clothes by hand." I told her. "What made it unusual was that she never discarded the tail ends of thread. She re-threaded the needle, over and over, until the very last bit of thread was used up."

Later, Haida and I were making dinner. As she whipped the cream, she said, "I guess you never had cream when you were young." I replied, "Yes, we had cream, every day." She queried further, "Then you didn't have meat?" "No," I said, "We had lots of meats: beef, pork, chicken, fish, venison." "Well, what were you lacking?" I thought about it for a while, and answered, "We wanted peanut butter, Cheez Whiz, and bologna."

Let's face it; poverty in the country is different than poverty in the city. What made us feel deprived was the lack of entertainment activities. The difference between Lyle's childhood and mine was he spent his weekends going to movies, roaming through shops, going to the beach. I had responsibilities from the age of five: "feed the chickens", "bring in wood", "take this to the pigs", "watch your little sister", "herd the geese to the lake and then bring them back." To him, Spike Jones (the band) was neuvo music; to me it was a bunch of crazies playing with cowbells and beating a barrel.

I was to remember all this when Haida got married at Camp Narnia, where she used to work. I was so glad her former boss let her have the ceremony and reception there, because I would finally see what a "children's camp" was. I was green with envy when I heard of people sending their children to camp. It sounded so exciting! At last I would see a camp, sleep the night there, and partake of their activities! Well, was I ever brought down to earth!

What I found was that my whole childhood was spent at a children's camp. At Camp Narnia children were allowed to pet the calves and horses, feed the pigs, the chickens, and the cow. Wow!

When my parents came to visit us in Nelson, my father stood in the windows and looked at the mountains all around, and said, "How ugly! Look at that. Nothing but rock. You couldn't grow anything here." In later years, when Lyle and I were driving to Ottawa, Lyle looked out at the wheat fields of Saskatchewan, and said, "How ugly. Nothing but flat land and the same crop for hundreds of miles." I loved both sceneries."

At Easter, we painted and decorated eggs - Ukrainian design. Mother made the most intricate designs with a homemade stile. Eggs were coloured with onionskins. On Easter morning a hard-boiled egg was eaten by each person, because that was the first thing Christ ate during the Last Supper, we were told.

On February 18, 1939, my sister Nena was born. The midwife attended the birth while we played all around the bed. Finally we heard the baby cry, and she announced, "It's a girl."

I ran out to tell Dad. He didn't stop working, just called back, "Boy or girl?" I said, "It's a girl!" He just groaned, "Another girl!" This stunned me. I was very upset. I remember kicking a stone all the way back to the house, thinking, "It's not her fault she's a girl. What's wrong with being a girl?"

I like to say that was my first stirring of feminism. And I never let it go. I would plough the fields, stook the grain, drive the binder, or work at whatever needed doing. Throughout my life I felt, if it can be done, I can do it. No matter what it was. I remember ploughing late into the night once, expecting to get praise from my father. Instead he just said, "Your furrows are crooked."

However, during one of my visits home in the 1960s, I had the pleasure of hearing my father say, "I was probably better off having daughters than sons. With our poor land we had to make a living from chickens, geese, turkeys, cattle, and pigs. The girls could handle them. And I would have had to provide each son with a quarter section when he married." It made me feel good.

Life was hard. Trees were chopped down by hand, and Dad would pull the roots out with horses. Our fields were full of rocks. Every spring more rocks were pushed up by winter frost, so we had to take time off school to pick them. Horses pulled a stoneboat up and down the field while we loaded it, then unloaded along the fence. Our hands were like sandpaper. We made fortresses all over our property with these stones.

George Ryga (an author from Athabasca, whom I dated for a while) described it better in his book *"Ballad of a Stonepicker"*.

"They call us 'dirt farmers' here in the backlands. Not because we're dirtier than farmers anywhere else, but because we've got to keep our hands closer to the soil to keep going. Winters are cold here. Spring turns up fresh blisters of stone which weren't there the summer before. Then comes heat, and the dust and the mud when it rains...

"Once I read a book on American prisoners working on chain gangs busting rocks for roads. Compared to stonepicking here, a chain-gang was a holiday. There's no hotter, harder or dirtier work going. It stoops your back and turns your hands into claws..."

Others would have left that land and moved on, but not our parents. They said only irresponsible people moved from place to place.

We built up a herd of cows, milking 10 to 15 by hand, selling the cream every week. We would have to go out to the community pasture between Birch Lake and Long Lake for the cows (the lead cow wore a bell). Sometimes I would ride my horse Judy. She had a habit of darting under trees. I swore she was trying to wipe me off her back.

After milking, we would turn the milk through the separator, put the cream in the dry well (which was filled with snow every winter for refrigeration), and give the skim milk to the pigs. On Saturday a truck would come from Forfar, and pick up the cream cans people placed at the side of the road. The driver delivered them to the dairy in Athabasca, and a cheque was sent to the owners. That, plus sale of eggs, was what we lived on from week to week, until we sold a load of pigs or calves.

People would also catch a ride with the truck to shop. Occasionally one of us kids would go along. I had to go to the dentist quite often, which was dreadful, but it meant going to town. We would eat pork sausages, potatoes and gravy in the Chinese restaurant. It was so good. We would bath, wash and curl our hair, and wear our best clothes. Then riding on the back of the truck we'd get covered with dust.

I hated making hay. We mowed the grass in the wilderness beyond Long Lake. Lunch and supper, mostly hard-boiled eggs and salt pork, were packed, and after travelling about eight miles, we worked in the hot sun piling the hay into huge stacks, with hay falling down the back of our clothes. If work wasn't finished, we stayed the night, sleeping in the open.

But threshing time was exciting. My father would cut the grain with the binder. We stood these bundles up into "stooks", one against the other, six in a bunch, so the grain dried well. When thrashing started, about four farmers worked together.

The men would load these bundles onto the rack, pull up to the threshing machine, and drop the bundles, one by one, onto the machine. The machine would separate the straw and chute the grain into the granary. When it was nearly full, a kid would be sent in to shovel the grain away from the chute. I hated this job, as I felt claustrophobic. I'd be up near the roof, the grain would be pouring in, I'd sink walking and feel like I was going to get buried. The dust would plug up the nostrils and throat. It was scary!

However, as I got older I did the cooking. The hungry young guys would arrive in the house for lunch, smelling of grease and sweat.

When I was ten, in 1943, another child was born and this time IT WAS A BOY! Wonder of wonder, a boy was born. Dad was elated. Mother felt her purpose in living was fulfilled. I went to school and told the teacher all about it, and announced proudly what I heard said at home: "And Dad was the doctor." They named him Arthur (Arkadi). I hardly got to know him as I left home when I was 15 and he was 5.

My education started at 5 in a little granary on Manasterski's farm. During the winter our neighbours, the Sams, would take their dog sled to school. They usually picked me up. It felt so cosy, low down on the ground, covered with fur blankets, smoothly running over the snow, pulled by the dogs.

The next year we moved to a school, further away from home, but a proper building. There was a teacherage next to it, with such luxuries as a separate kitchen, living room, and bedroom. What comfort! We had lived in one room until my brother was born. Then Dad built an extension. We had a wood heater. In the winter Dad would be the first one up to stoke the fire. We didn't get out of bed until the room was nice and warm.

Our school was staffed with "normal" teachers; that meant they were still in school, but had to get some classroom experience. Sometimes we had four different teachers in one year. We did correspondence courses and the teacher was on hand to help us out. It wasn't until Grade 8 that we got a regular teacher, David Pearce. He taught me to enjoy learning, which I did all my life. He helped me pass government tests in Grade 9, and I went on to Athabasca High School for Grade 10. Later in life, still thirsting for more formal education, I attended the University of Montreal through the Canadian Labour College, wrote the equivalency test at Selkirk College in Castlegar (which gave me a High School Equivalent Diploma), and attended many seminars.

I passed Grade 10, but didn't want to go back to school. Mother was upset. I went to Edmonton and attended a private secretarial college. However, this part of my life is a blank. I can't remember it.

Spring arrived and Anne and I left for the farm to help with the work. By now my sister Neta was married to Peter Ballas. I knew I had to break away from this routine. In that part of the country, girls married at 15-16 (my compatriot, Annie Zachoda, was already married). There had to be more to life than farming and having babies.

One day when I was 14, mother came home to announce she found a husband for me. There was a man, 30 years old, with a good farm, looking for a wife. I was petrified. After worrying a couple of days, I asked my father if mother could force me to marry him. He said, "No." And then added: "Don't rush into marriage. When you marry you're married for a long time." It was good advice and I took it to heart. I didn't marry until I was 27.

In the fall I went back to Edmonton and worked as a waitress. I still wanted to be a secretary, but at $18.00 a week, how long would it take to save for business college? When springtime arrived, Anne and I headed back to the farm. I gave Dad enough money to buy me 50 turkey chicks when he ordered his own.

The summer went and fall came. We had 250 turkeys to kill and pluck. Chickens could be dunked in hot water, which made removal of feathers easy. But turkeys had to be plucked dry. It had to be done quickly because there was no refrigeration. Fingers would bleed by the end of the day, but we couldn't stop. We worked late into the night for three days.

We got a good price for them. Dad announced proudly he had enough money to buy a tractor. I asked for my share. He said, "No. No. I need the money for the tractor. You can earn more through the winter and then go to college next year." I stopped working and eating for 3 days, demanding my share of the money. I heard Mother tell Dad to give me my money. He did.

Next year Dad got a tractor, and then a truck. But my parents would never have electricity, telephone or running water until they moved to Edmonton.

I had paid for 5 1/2 months college, and at the end of that time had to look for a job, even though I hadn't completed my shorthand course, and would always be at a disadvantage because of it. I got a job with Lindsay, Emery & Co., lawyers.

I had to be the worst secretary who ever lived; scared out of my wits, with limited shorthand. Mr. Jamieson was so patient. I would watch the best secretary in the office and try to determine what made her good. Later, in Vancouver, I entered a Best Secretary contest, and was picked as one of Vancouver's six best.

I worked for Mr. Jamieson for a year until I saw an ad for a legal secretary for P.G. Davies at Clyde, which was only fifty miles from the farm. I applied and got the job. Mr. Davies always called me "Veracity" because of my preponderance for truth. This was a very small town, and I was much happier. I went home most weekends by taking the bus to Rochester. There would usually be a dance Friday night somewhere, and someone from our neighbourhood would give me a ride home.

At one of these dances, I saw the handsomest guy walk in. My heart flipped. He asked me to dance and we danced together all night. His name was Danny Lys. It was love at first sight. We were inseparable. Every weekend I took the bus to Rochester. We went dancing or spent time in the beer parlour. This went on for a couple of years, and we planned to marry. In 1956 Danny wanted to put it off for another year. I didn't. We quarrelled and parted.

I heard of two girls in Edmonton who were planning to go to Europe in the summer. It was something I always wanted to do. I went to Edmonton to meet Lydia Hudyma and Eva Strachan and asked if I could join them. They agreed to include me. Their route was already picked. All I had to do was get a passport. We had a wonderful 3 months in Europe.

By the time I returned from Europe, Dan's best friend's sister was pregnant, and she and Dan got married. He died before age 50, of sclerosis of the liver – a drunkard's disease. I swear I have always had a guardian angel watching over me.

I moved back to Edmonton and got a job. I moved into a one-room suite with a partitioned kitchen and common bathroom. My sister Nena graduated from business-college and moved in with me after she started work. Later our oldest sister, Anne, did too.

A year later we bought a house, with a little help from Mom and Dad. Again we had to penny-pinch. Nena and I walked the two miles to work to save a dime. We worked in a neighbourhood cafe for extra money. We furnished the house nicely and were so proud of our home. It was our first decent home. In 1966, when Dad got his pension, Mom and Dad moved into the house.

However, life was not good. Every weekend we drove home to the farm with Anne. We worked all weekend at whatever needed doing outside. We cleaned the house and scrubbed the wooden floors. Sunday night we drove back to Edmonton. The next two days were spent resting up from the weekend. We had no money; we had no social life; and I was 25 years old. Life seemed to be passing me by.

One weekend I refused to drive home to the farm. When Anne left, I packed my things, took the Greyhound bus, and headed for Vancouver. I knew I would never get my parents approval to leave. I like to say I ran away from home at 25. As I crossed the mountains I felt myself becoming my own person. I would have no one to report to, nothing to do but entertain myself, nothing to spend money on but me.

I moved into a furnished suite at a women's hostel on Thurlow Street. I spent every evening at Sunset Beach, made lots of new friends, went dancing three times a week. A few months later Nena joined me. We had a wonderful year together. Nena was working for a law firm - Shulman, Tupper, Worrall and Berger. There was an opening when I quit working for Rocky Myers, my first job. I applied and got the job, working for Tom Berger. He was a wonderful person, boss, and lawyer. Just out of college, but making headlines with the cases he undertook and won.

One of the best cases he won was for Louis Bataglia, a miner and member of the Mine, Mill Union. Louis had a crippling miner's disease, silicosis, or black lung. Workmen's Compensation would not acknowledge it as an occupational disease. Miners that got it died from pneumonia or heart failure, not silicosis. The fact that silicosis contributed to their getting these other diseases didn't count. We took the case all the way to the Supreme Court of Canada; every court deciding in our favour.

When we finally won in the Supreme Court of Canada, Workmen's Compensation decided to award Louis' pension from the day of the operation that established he had silicosis, not from the day he was disabled. This didn't set a precedent that silicosis was a compensable disease for other miners.

We start all over again. We won again in all the courts, and within a couple of weeks of learning this, Louis Bataglia died. He clung to life until a precedent was established for other miners. It was a big contribution by Louis as well as Tom Berger.

When I attended the Canadian Labour College at the Montreal University in 1963, one of the professors spoke about this case, and praised the young lawyer who fought it so eloquently. After class I told him I worked for Tom Berger during this case. He was in awe; he said as a young law student he and other fellow students admired Berger immensely, and wanted to emulate his career. He said he followed Berger's career throughout the years, watching for his cases and reading his court presentations.

I became a prolific letter-to-the-editor writer. I could fill a book with these letters. It started with having a letter printed in 1974 by Allan Fotheringham (in his Vancouver Sun column). Fotheringham did not print many letters, and usually only partial, so getting my whole letter printed was a major accomplishment. I had many compliments from friends across the province, including Tom Berger. It spurred me on to write more. I quote part of it:

"*With reference to your column of May 17 Canadian Labour Congress' convention … "First: You say 'Could they (the trade unionists) please give the slightest impression that they are looking over the shoulder at those beneath them'.*

"Who do you think led the fight, both during elections and in briefs presented to governments, for universal education, pensions, hospital insurance, medicare, denticare, compensation for industrial injuries, insurance against unemployment?

"But if that isn't direct enough a show of concern, then consider the following very rough figures: In 1973 the CLC budgeted $275,000 specifically for white collar organizing. Besides that, they had a staff of 39 working part or full time on this organizing. Their ranks were increased by some 71,000. ...

"In addition, unions across Canada spent hundreds of thousands of dollars on political and legislative action to secure social and economic benefits for all Canadians, especially those less fortunate.

"They are the only major economic interest group in Canada that does give a damn about other than themselves, and have proved it – time and time again.

Getting organized has been the only way to improve the wage scale and working conditions, with one exception: The one major increase in the pay of those at the very bottom of the wage scale was with the increase in minimum wages, an action long demanded by organized workers and their political allies.

"In any case, pray tell, how would a 'lowly clerk in a dingy office' be helped by a construction worker holding the line on his own wages?

"You point out that 12 of the delegates (and spouses?) chartered a $400-a-day luxury yacht. Really, Frothy, what is the point? This works out to $33 each. When have you had a night on the town for so reasonable an amount? Surely you know that many delegates came from other provinces. Many delegates plan their annual vacations around this trip. You may have noticed the number of wives present.

"Chartering such a boat would only be an extension of union principles: pooling money and effort together to enjoy *what could never be possible on an individual basis."*

Those were wonderful days. Nena and I spent all our money on clothes and entertainment. One winter we took part time jobs at Grouse Mountain Ski Hill on weekends, as waitresses. Nena took up skiing, spraining an ankle soon thereafter. I never thought I'd learn to ski, but I did at age 40.

By 1966, my parents retired from farming and moved to Edmonton to live in the house the three sisters bought. Dad was receiving a pension and felt he never had it so good. He finally got everything he didn't have on the farm: electricity, running water, central heating, telephone – and financial security!

When Lyle and I visited them in Edmonton, Dad was like a kid: he was interested in everything. We sent Lyle and Dad to the Laundromat to wash clothes. Lyle said Dad took pleasure even in that. He said, "Look, I put the clothes in here, then put my money in here and push this. Presto, the water starts, the clothes get turned, and then automatically the water drains, fresh water comes in, and when the machine stops, the clothes are clean. It's wonderful!"

And it was wonderful, especially remembering how we washed clothes on the farm. We would haul a barrel of water from the lake. We heated it on a wood stove. The water was poured into a huge tub, and each piece of clothing was scrubbed on a washboard. Clothes were rinsed in a second tub, wrung out by hand. It was an all-day affair for several women.

But Dad only had two years in the city before he died. It was so unfair. I was planning on having a longer visit and ask about his life. My father left me with many gems of wisdom which I relied on heavily throughout my life.

The best was this: "Every new experience adds to your character. But if all your experiences were pleasant one, think of what a shallow person you would be. So if you are hurt or unhappy about something, just remember, it is adding to your character." I took comfort from that adage many times. And I had the pleasure of hearing my daughter quote it and take comfort from it.

He also told us that lying was not acceptable. He said, "Lying was cheating. Cheating was stealing. Therefore, lying was stealing." However, when I moved to Edmonton I was furious with my father. I found I was the only person in the world who thought lying was shameful.

Our father taught us that honour was the most important quality a person can have. Even if you were the only person that knew, it was important. He told me about one winter when we were running out of feed for our cattle. He asked around the neighbourhood if someone had extra hay or straw. One neighbour said he did. Dad paid him the $3.00, and went to pick it up. He found the straw was several years old and completely rotten. He went to get his money back, but was told "Too bad. You should have looked before you paid." Dad couldn't believe it. Someone he would have to live along side, someone who would have to look him in the eye, would stoop so low as to cheat for a mere $3.00.

That year my sisters bought me a lovely ring. My first piece of jewellery. I loved it. I wore it to school, and Annie Zachoda loved it, too. She begged and pleaded with me to let her take it home to show her sister. After a long time, I relented. That evening my father noticed I didn't have the ring. I told him what I had done. He said, "You'll never see that ring again." And I didn't.

He encouraged me to read all political opinions, from the far right to the far left. "After a while" he said, "a thin line of truth will come through, and you will be able to decide for yourself what you believe"

His best comment, "The people in power urinate in the peasants' faces. The peasants call it rain and give thanks." After I got involved in politics, I was to recall this and witness it many times.

My mother and father with their first two daughters, Anne and Neta

I am stooking wheat with my sister Neta. Her son, Ronnie, is supervising

LOVE AND MARRIAGE

Lyle's earliest memories are of political meetings held in their living room, listening to the voices of CCF leaders, Helena Gutteridge, Dorothy Steeves, Laura Jamieson, Grace and Angus McInnis, Grant MacNeil, Ernie and Harold Winch, M.J. Coldwell and many others, filtering through the swinging door of his adjoining bedroom.

When Lyle was 18 he had been active in the CCF for two years, and was elected president of the Vancouver Centre CCF Constituency. He attended UBC for two years, and "majored in political activity."

I met Lyle in 1959 when I was working for Tom Berger. Tom was one of those people who was a socialist by nature, always on the side of the underdog. A number of people called on him and urged him to join the CCF and become their candidate in the 1960 provincial election. After some soul-searching, he did.

A year later my sister Nena and I joined. I wrote my father about it, thinking he would be proud of us. Instead, he wrote back immediately, asking us to drop our membership. When pressed for an explanation, he said, "Because you are peasants. You can work, struggle, take the bullets, and who knows? You might win. But if you do, the bourgeoisie will step in and say, "Thanks very much. You did a good job. Now we'll take over." I wondered if he participate in the Russian Revolution. I wish I had asked him before he died. After the NDP won in 1972, I watched Lorne Nicolson, the new MLA, appoint his teacher friends to every government post in the riding and I was to recall Dad's words.

In 1960 Tom Berger won the CCF nomination and went to his first campaign strategy meeting. The next morning he told me he met a wonderful young man, Lyle Kristiansen, who was so informed and experienced in politics, Tom wished he was the candidate.

On the way home that evening I passed an office on Robson Street, and noticed the sign "CCF campaign headquarters". Busy putting up posters was a handsome young man with beautiful blue eyes. I asked if he was Lyle Kristiansen. He said he was, without stopping his work. We talked for a while, but he was so engrossed in what he was doing, he was insulting. I wasn't used to being ignored. In fact, Lyle doesn't even remember this meeting.

I worked in that campaign and enjoyed it very much. There were people working selflessly for a common cause without saying, "what's in it for me." It was a community of intelligent, caring people. I had tried to find this in the different churches I attended but couldn't. Nena and I canvassed several polls.

But the voters turned my candidate down; Tom lost the election. The CCF was expected to win, but on Election Day the Vancouver Province came out with huge headlines: "10,000 JOBS LOST TO BC IF CCF WINS." The Province was a morning paper, so this headline blared on every street corner. I was so angry, hurt, astonished. It was so unfair. I couldn't believe this could happen in our democracy. After all, we were taught in school, "Of the People, By the People, For the People." Surely, nobody would abuse the democratic system. I was to learn in time how much unfairness there was. Anyway, the CCF lost. And there were no 10,000 jobs.

After the election, Nena and I were at loose ends. I missed the camaraderie of the election. One

Saturday, John Motiuk and Harvey Smith, whom we met in the election, dropped in to visit. They told us a group of young people were meeting at Lyle Kristiansen's house that evening.

Nena and I went over and enjoyed seeing many of the people we met during the election. Later that evening a group of us went to a jazz club. Lyle and I danced and talked all night. Before the evening was over Lyle told me he was going to marry me. I laughed. I was five years older than him: I was 26 and he 21. But he was insistent. He said statistics showed women outlived men by five years. This made us just about even. (Lyle didn't know it then but his father had also proposed to his mother on their first date.)

I liked Lyle very much, but felt I was much too old for him, although I had to admit he was very mature for his 21 years. Before long we were dating regularly. Most of our courtship took place at political meetings and protest marches: Ban-the-Bomb, Hands-off-Cuba, union picketing. By Christmas we were engaged, and married on July 26th, 1961.

B.C.'S NEW DEMOCRATIC YOUTH

The New Democratic Youth (NDY) movement was formed in 1960, in B.C. and across Canada. At the first meeting of the Vancouver club I was elected vice president. I knew nothing about chairing meetings or parliamentary procedure. However, Lyle was encouraging and assured me I'd learn. When I first spoke at meetings I memorized what I'd say, say it, and sit down trembling. It took years before I could speak confidently.

The Party and the Youth movement were plagued with "Trotskyites". These were people who were followers of Leon Trotsky who had been banished from the USSR by Stalin. Trotsky and his followers formed the 4th International, which regarded itself as the only true vanguard of the international working class. It rejected the idea of building "socialism in one country" and saw its role as fomenting and guiding a worldwide revolution, either openly or clandestinely operating within other working class movements.

Trotskyites organized in Canada under the name of Revolutionary Workers Party (RWP). Unsuccessful on their own, in the mid 1950s, they, as outlined in a secret memo, officially disbanded their party and instructed their members to infiltrate the CCF and organize their movement from within. Their stated goal was to divide the CCF into factions and, at a future time of their choosing, split away and re-form their own party again. They were disruptive and divisive wherever they appeared.

When Lyle and a few friends started to reorganize a B.C. and national youth movement during the last year of the CCF, some party leaders had warned them that a youth section could be disruptive and subject to infiltration – but no solid information was shared.

In the B.C. NDY, the "Trots" (as we would call them) were small in number but they could keep us hamstrung for hours. They knew parliamentary procedure very well and could use this knowledge to keep a turmoil going, upsetting new members, and frustrating the rest beyond words. However, this forced all of us to sharpen our skills and knowledge. Their tactics would tend to bore to death all but the most dedicated members and, as attendance at club meetings fell, they often won votes and control by a combination of deceit and exhaustion.

As a result of our naivety, the Trots and their often-unknowing allies won majority control of the B.C. NDY executive at its founding convention.

Lyle, as NDY Federal Vice President, appointed a Federal Organizing Committee for B.C., which also functioned as an NDP loyalist caucus. It was a parallel organization internal to the B.C. NDY, and the next year it simply outgrew, out-educated, and out-organized the opposition. All Committee (caucus) votes had to be unanimous, thus everyone involved (almost 50 by year's end) was fully committed to implementing decisions. B.C. NDY membership expanded from about 250 to over a thousand.

Slowly we regained control of one club after another. We worked hard at establishing and winning over rural clubs - holding camping trips in every region, featuring folk singing, lectures, discussion groups, and recreational activities. Those among our committee (it had reps from every club) whom we had unanimously agreed would stand for provincial executive, were required to attend each camp.

Years later a member from Duncan would tell me that, when she attended her first NDY convention, she was surprised to find she knew at least one person running for every executive position. Many shared her experience. Victory was complete and B.C. ended up with the largest, best organized, and self-sustaining NDP Youth Section in Canada.

After this exhausting, albeit exhilarating experience, we collectively determined (in light of what to us was new information) that the B.C. NDY and the NDP should never have to suffer deliberate internal sabotage from "another political party" again.

At the time of the NDP's and the NDY's founding, the retiring CCF provincial secretary had shown our friend, Bill Piket, (first NDY Federal Secretary), a copy of the secret RWP "memo" referred to earlier. Anyone reading the memo could have no doubt that the RWP's successor organizations – the League for Socialist Action (LSA) and the Young Socialist Alliance (YSA) constituted "another political party" as proscribed in the constitution and membership oath of the New Democratic Party and CCF before it.

Keeping a pledge of confidentiality, Bill made a copy of the "secret" memo for himself before returning the original. Later, in Ottawa, Lyle and Bill printed and mailed some 3,000 copies of the lengthy RWP memo – each stamped 'CONFIDENTIAL' – to individual members of the NDY across Canada – complete with a yellow cover featuring the Webster's Dictionary definition of "parasite". You could hear the screams all across Canada – confidentially, of course.

Despite protest from a few 'timid souls' and others in the 'adult party', the B.C. NDY executive and council moved to expel a very limited number of NDY members on the grounds that they were "members of another political party or organization ancillary thereto."

What an ordeal! I don't even want to think about it. After a lengthy trial, complete with evidence, defence counsel, and a verbatim transcript (which I typed), all the accused were either expelled outright or suspended on condition that they deny such membership before reinstatement.

The only humorous note was that, on the very day that we expelled them, a newspaper reported that the Young Communist League had expelled all but one of the same people the day before. C'est la vie!

This action freed us to undertake other activities. We could sponsor speakers, social activities, fund raisers. We formed a Bowling League, which was fun, and something to bring potential members to. From the NDY many members went on to be MPs, MLAs, cabinet ministers, mayors, councillors, school trustees, labour leaders, organizers, and activists in community and professional organizations. It was a good training ground.

About this time Canada's most important legislation was under consideration: Medicare. Ten years earlier the Saskatchewan CCF government brought in Hospital Insurance, which other provinces emulated. The 1960 provincial election was fought on Medicare. The Liberals and Conservative, as well as the province's doctors financed by U.S. doctors, went all out to defeat the CCF.

The CCF won, and Premier Tommy Douglas immediately moved to implement Medicare. This is a well-known story. However, what isn't so well known is how the rest of Canada got it.

Prime Minister Diefenbacher set up a commission to study how the federal government could assist in setting up Medicare in Canada. He appointed Justice Emmett Hall, to head it. The same pressure was on then as still is in the U.S: private companies would provide the basic coverage for most citizens, with governments picking up the tab for low-income people.

In the middle of these hearings, Emmett Hall turned 65 years of age, and immediately got a letter from his medical insurance company informing him his policy was cancelled because of his age. He took the letter to a large gathering of people and read it out. He added further that in all the years he paid premiums, he only used it once! That cinched it!

By the time the federal government got involved, the Liberals were elected. Thus every party claims some credit. However, Canadians know it was the CCF/NDP that made it possible. In 2005 there was a contest on CBC to name "The Greatest Canadian", and Tommy Douglas won! Now the buzzwords across the country are that we can't afford to keep Medicare. It is proven that our Medicare, which covers every citizen, is cheaper than the U.S. system which excludes 40 million. This is ignored and the elite of the country are still trying to get rid of Medicare.

In October, 1962, there was the Cuba crises. After Cuba installed a pro-communist government, the U.S. attempted to overthrow Castro by sending in troops (the Bay of Pigs fiasco), which was repelled. U.S. planes continued flying over Havana in a threatening manner. A plane got shot down, and that seemed a reason to have a full all-out invasion.

To forestall this, Cuba asked the USSR to install missiles that would give them some protection. Now the United States really had reason to invade Cuba. They said it was a threat to their security as the missiles could reach American soil.

When the Soviet missiles were on ships heading for Cuba, President Kennedy informed the Soviets they would bomb the ships. This would have culminated in an all-out nuclear war.

I remember leaving work on Friday night and having everyone saying "Hope to see you Monday." On the elevator people looked at each other, wondering what the world would be like by Monday. At home, Lyle collected all our camping gear, put together canned food and water, and packed the car.

However, over the weekend, hard negotiations took place, as documented in a movie, and the Soviets agreed to turn the ships around if the U.S. dismantled their missiles, pointing at the USSR, in Turkey. This was agreed to and the threat of war averted. (The Turkish dismantling took place six months later in order not to influence an election coming up.) For a few days the threat of a nuclear World War III hung over the world. This was the closest the world came to such a war.

Lyle and his mother in a parade with former Speaker of the Legislature and MLA Emery Barnes.

One of the many protest marches.

NEW DEMOCRATIC PARTY

In 1961 the CCF and Canadian Labour Congress met to form a new political party, the New Democratic Party. We spent our honeymoon at it. The dumbest thing we did at the convention was back Hazen Argue for leader. Tommy Douglas won. Years later we had to face the wrath of our son, Colin, who had written an essay for a school project on Tommy Douglas. On questioning us, he found we had not supported Douglas for the first leader of the NDP.

After the convention we went to Toronto and stayed with a school chum of Lyle's. He let us use his car to drive to Niagara Falls for the "conventional" part of our honeymoon. And then it was home, back to work, back to political activity.

We organized, publicised, raised money, and held innumerable meetings. Many were held at our apartment. Lyle and I were one of the few married couples in the NDY. Some weekends we had ten to fifteen people staying the night. It was wonderful. I enjoyed the family-community feeling.

The most outstanding event we participated in was the 1962 federal election. These were hot "Ban-the-Bomb" days. The U.S. was pressing Canada to place nuclear warheads on Canada's BOMARK missiles. Most people opposed this, including Mike and Marion Pearson, the Liberal Opposition leader and his wife.

However, during the campaign, the Pearsons suddenly changed their position. (The Liberals were expected to form the government.) When Pearson was scheduled to speak in Vancouver, many people were determined to let him know they did not approve of his switchover. These were the days of huge rallies; each political party out-doing the other. The NDP had nearly 10,000 at their rally a week earlier. It was essential for the Liberals to top this.

They had to do something to make the rally look good, if only for the T.V. audience. They issued invitation cards to Liberal members, asking them to arrive an hour early and sit near the podium. Thus, the microphones and cameras would not pick up heckling or other antics of the protestors.

However, someone got hold of one of these cards and printed a couple hundred more, passing them on to a youth movement. They in turn passed them to other Ban-the-Bomb groups. When Lyle and I arrived, an hour early, the guy at the door recognized Lyle. He had been the Liberal leader at UBC when Lyle was the CCF leader. He asked Lyle if he had an invitation. Lyle handed it to him, and he said "Something's wrong here." However, he let us in.

When we entered the hall, it was like old home week: every New Democratic Youth, Young Communist, Young

Conservative and Ban-the-Bomber was there. We sat close to the podium. Pearson arrived, piped in with fife and drum, and started his speech.

Every now and then we stood up and turned to face the back of the hall. At the back, high up in the bleachers, a group of young communists had organized two rows of seats; the upper had persons with one huge letter printed on a white T-shirt. Together they spelled "Ban the Bomb". The row in front of them had powerful flashlights, which they shone on these letters, making them very visible to everyone in the hall and the T.V. cameras.

When we turned to look at them, Liberals would also turn to see what we were looking at, which meant that for a few minutes Pearson would be speaking to the backs of people. We did this over and over again before the Liberals stopped joining us.

We were interspersed throughout the hall, so their henchmen could not throw us out. Liberals sitting near us were frustrated and angry. A protestor got hit with an umbrella. Fights broke out. It was chaos! It was good organization. Marion Pearson told the press she would never come to Vancouver again!

OTTAWA - FIRST TIME

In 1963, Lyle took the job of federal secretary of the New Democratic Youth in Ottawa. We packed our car, drove to Regina to attend the NDP convention, and then on to Ottawa. I worked for Dr. Howe, an NDP M.P. from Hamilton. He was one of a few doctors who supported Medicare, which was a burning issue at the time. He was asked to run in Hamilton, and won where no New Democrat had before. But he had no other political interest, and set up a medical practice in Ottawa. I had a free hand in running the office.

During this time I attended the Canadian Labour College at McGill University in Montreal, taking four courses: Sociology, Economics, History, and Political Science. Because I only had Grade 10, I always felt inadequate. This experience was tremendous; it felt like getting a base for my philosophy to build on. I soaked up the learning like a blotter. I passed with Great Distinction, averaging 84%.

By 1964 I was 30 years old, and if we were going to have a family, we had to do it soon. We decided that perhaps we should have one child - more as a civic duty than any great desire. I got pregnant.

I had morning sickness all day and for the whole nine months. The doctor prescribed Thalidomide for me. However, I wouldn't take any alcohol, wouldn't smoke, and I wouldn't take any medication. I refused this drug as well. The doctor was very angry with me.

Instead, to control my nausea I had to eat every hour on the hour. That kept the acids under control. Had I succumbed, I might have had a baby with no arms or legs caused by that drug. When I see my beautiful Eric, and picture him without his arms or legs, I thank my lucky stars for my determination.

I hated being pregnant. I kept asking how could I do this to myself. Lyle was so patient and understanding. Finally the time arrived. At the hospital the doctors advised Lyle to go home as this was a face-presentation birth and would take a long time. Every half-hour a nurse would arrive to ask if I wanted a drug to put me out. I resisted for hours, but by mid-morning gave in and took it.

When I awoke the baby had been born and Lyle was in to see me. We walked together to see the baby, and when I saw him, motherhood hit me like a ton of bricks: the feeling of love was overwhelming. In the first glimpse of that little redheaded baby I saw Lyle's face. It was a tremendous feeling.

Two months later we were heading back to BC. Lyle's term as federal secretary was over. It took us a month to get home, travelling slowly, camping all the way. Near Thunder Bay we "baptized" Eric by dunking him in Lake Superior – so he would grow up big and strong. It worked. We stopped at Athabasca to visit my parents.

BACK TO VANCOUVER - 1965

Lyle was the NDP candidate in Vancouver Centre in the 1965 federal election. This was not a constituency we could win. It was good experience, but that was all. He lost to Liberal Jack Nicholson.

We had to reconstruct our lives somehow, outside the political arena. I worked in temporary jobs through Office Overload. Lyle looked at different lines of work, including learning the computer or selling life insurance, but that was not what he wanted to do.

Finally he decided he was going where his heart was. A friend in the IWA, Del Pratt, had asked Lyle if he was interested in working in the labour movement. The answer was yes. Del suggested moving to either the Sunshine Coast or West Kootenay to work in the pulp or lumber industries. We weighed the alternatives and, in late January of 1967, Lyle headed out by car for the Kootenays. When we retired, we took up residence in the Sunshine Coast.

Arriving in Castlegar at the end of a long day's drive, Lyle picked up a local paper, and saw an ad for the annual meeting of the Rossland-Trail NDP in Trail. He decided to go and meet some locals.

Arriving at the meeting, he discovered that - as they had no guest speaker - and as he was a member of the NDP Provincial Council - he would be it. He made some friends - and enemies - immediately.

Among the best of these new friends were Tom and Jean McKenzie. Tom, a former senior officer of the IWA during the Red vs. White bloc days, was maintenance superintendent at the Castlegar sawmill. He proved to be a great source of information and advice - on West Kootenay politics. He was also helpful to me in the Kootenay Country Co-op.

After several days of job hunting and applications at Castlegar and Trail area mills, Lyle moved on to Nelson. When he left Vancouver, he had a letter of introduction to Kootenay IWA Local president Jack Munro, who had been an unsuccessful NDP candidate in the 1966 B.C. election. There had been 6 members at the nomination meeting. Jack and another man flipped a coin to determine the candidate – whoever lost got the nomination. With the help of active IWA members and $1.00 donations, Jack increased the vote from 20% to 30% but he lost to 24-year veteran Socred cabinet minister, Wesley Black.

Lyle called on Jack, introduced himself, and received a list of the many woods products companies and mills, both union and non-union, in the area. Munro warned him that the Interior IWA was in the final stages of very difficult negotiations – and that a strike was imminent. (It was to be an historic strike – achieving wage parity between coast and interior woodworkers – and lasted 7 1/2 months).

For the next six weeks, Lyle covered hundreds of miles, making repeated calls to the many mills and company offices throughout the West Kootenay. Nobody would hire him. They called him a pencil pusher. Finally, a small non-union mill at Harrop, Stafford Brothers, hired him. Beldon Stafford bet him $20.00 he wouldn't last two weeks.

Lyle started work at 1 pm on a Friday afternoon. His job was loading green rough 6x6 and 8x10 lumber, up to 24 feet long, into railway boxcars. He had to lift pieces onto a jack, lever up and push them into the boxcar from an elevated platform. This was hard on the stomach. Every few minutes he would stop and vomit. But he carried on. He lasted the half-day and had the weekend to rest.

On Monday morning he got a slightly easier job. He lasted the week, and another, and collected the $20 bet. That's how he broke into the lumber industry.

In late March, Eric (at 21 months) and I took the bus to join Lyle. We lived in a tiny fisherman's cottage in Balfour on Kootenay Lake. It was not insulated, so the dampness of the winter weather seeped in through the walls. All we did was eat and try to stay warm. Lyle would often spend long periods soaking his hands in a sink of hot water, trying to limber them up. They were stiff like claws after pulling planks from the green chain all day in cold winter weather.

I was expecting our second child. I wanted a daughter so badly. Mother (Hilda) came early to care for Eric when I went to the hospital. On May 16th I went in. I was in labour for two days.

It was a horrible experience. After two days in labour, I was reduced to a whimpering child. I became convinced that midwives should be used during childbirth, and campaigned actively for it later. A mid-wife would have sat with me, encouraged and assisted. Instead, I was alone for hours. A nurse dropped in once in a while, and a doctor once a day. Finally, the nurse decided I was ready for delivery. She led me into the delivery room and laid me flat on a very narrow hard bed, with a glaring light in my face, and left me. I couldn't turn over or move because the bed was so narrow.

I lay like that for a couple of hours, with the nurse poking her head in now and then. Finally she decided I wasn't ready and told me to go back to the other room. In the middle of doing this, I was seized with a contraction, and bent over to relieve it. The nurse jerked me by the arm and told me to hurry up; she didn't have all day. There was no sympathy or empathy. There wasn't even time for civility.

Finally, at 5 a.m. on May 18th, I was ready to deliver. The doctor wasn't there; the nurse told me to stop pushing and wait for the doctor. I thought, go to hell, after all this time I am not waiting for anybody. The baby was delivered without the doctor. In fact, ten babies were delivered while I was there, and only one had a doctor actually present. A nurse delivered the rest. If that wasn't evidence that a doctor wasn't needed, I don't know what is.

IT'S A GIRL! I have a daughter. I was so happy. It was 6 o'clock in the morning, and I wanted a cigarette and a cup of coffee. Whenever I got pregnant I could neither smoke nor drink coffee but, the minute the baby was born, it was like I hadn't stopped at all. And even more, I wanted to tell Lyle he had a daughter. I couldn't stand the thought he would go to work at 7 a.m. and work all day without knowing. I forced myself to stay awake until 6:30 and phoned our landlord. He was awake and agreed to go over and give Lyle the good news. Then I slept.

We named her Haida Carmen. We went through thousands of names, but were unable to agree on one. She was our 1967 Canadian Centennial project and Lyle wanted to give her an Indian name. He suggested Shoshone. I agreed to Haida.

I was right in wanting a daughter. She inherited a "liberated" society, and made full use of it. She is the one who is most politically and environmentally conscious, did the most world travelling, carries on traditions I inherited in gardening and preserving foods, and cooking ethnic food. She quotes my father's sayings and gets comfort from them. Everything a mother wants.

That was it. We had our son and daughter – and a dog. There would be no more children. We were quite flippant with our friends: no reason not to have a planned family. Just set your mind to it. We got exactly what we wanted; boy first, girl second, both born in the spring.

Well, were we in for a surprise! Two years later another son was born, whom we named Colin Aneurin. We used to introduce him as our unplanned baby – or our accident - until he was five years old, when he said to me: "But, you still love me, don't you?" I stopped saying it. He has been such a joy in our life.

Eric, Haida and Colin

POLITICS IN WEST KOOTENAY

In the spring of 1968 we moved to Nelson and bought a three-apartment revenue house at 702 Mill Street. We became part of the Nelson community and immediately started political activities.

This was an area where Social Credit was born, and nobody expected to elect a New Democrat. In the two largest provincial ridings that made up the federal riding of Kootenay West, no New Democrat or CCF candidate had ever been elected.

However, federally, we held the seat with 'Bert' Herridge for some twenty-five years. Lyle looked at statistics and became convinced we could win provincially as well. Federally, there had usually been three or four parties running: Liberals, Conservatives, Social Credit, and NDP (CCF earlier). Herridge always won in a pretty close three or four way split (often with about 35% support).

While most people, including Herridge, insisted this federal NDP vote was Herridge's personal support, figures showed that there was a solid and not dissimilar NDP vote in all three component provincial ridings. With that in mind, we proceeded to organize a proper party, and proper campaigns.

When we moved there, the NDP had 28 members in Nelson-Creston, about 100 in Rossland-Trail, and a handful in Kaslo-Slocan. In Nelson-Creston, there was no executive and no membership meetings since six members met the year before to nominate Jack Munro. Herridge's federal campaign budget in 1965 had been about $700 – paid mostly by himself.

We began organizing. We called on each member throughout the riding, and asked for ten names of potential members. As each of these potential members was called on, we asked for ten more names.

Thus, we built up a long list of potential members throughout Nelson-Creston.

A leadership convention was coming up. Bob Strachan resigned as NDP leader and the three main contenders for the position were my former boss, Tom Berger, MLAs Dave Barrett and Bob Williams. I was frustrated staying at home, and appreciated a reason to get out of the house to sign up members.

While I strongly supported the rights of mothers to work, I could not bring myself to leave my children with a babysitter and seek full-time work. There were no part time jobs available. Anyway, Lyle said there was no need for me to go to work. Unions fought for liveable wages, so one parent could stay at home and care for the children.

What we preferred, and tried to raise at union conventions, was to provide an opportunity for fathers to take a year or two off work, (retaining seniority and perhaps medical coverage). This would give the woman a chance to work, and give the father an opportunity to get to know his children. But until then, the children were my responsibility; they would get my values.

We worked non stop, utilizing the interest in the leadership convention to recruit new NDP members and build an organization. Every evening after dinner I called on three or four possible members. Lyle put out an information bulletin regularly to our growing list of members, and organized towards a 're-founding convention' of the Nelson-Creston NDP.

The members knew our personal preference was Tom Berger, but no pressure was applied. Straw votes were held at each zone meeting as a non-binding guide to our 18 delegates, who were elected without a slate. Interestingly, their votes at the leadership convention matched our straw votes almost exactly. Tom Berger won the NDP leadership. However, that same weekend I learned that my father had died.

I learned of my father's death in an awkward way. The children and I had caught a ride to Vancouver with another delegate, Ron Jacobson. When we arrived at Ron's relative's home in Coquitlam, I phoned Lyle's parents to pick me up. Grandpa Moreland answered the phone, and said, "I'm so sorry to hear about your father." I screamed, "What about my father?" He didn't realize I didn't know, so had to tell me that Dad died earlier that day.

I suffered through the convention crying constantly. But I couldn't leave. Nena arrived from California, on the way to the funeral. She waited until the convention was over and the two of us took the train to Edmonton. Berger won the leadership, only to lose his seat and the election two years later.

FIRST FEDERAL ELECTION

In 1968, Bert Herridge retired as Member of Parliament. A number of us convinced "Ran" Harding (MLA for Kaslo-Slocan) to run. It was a break to get him as a candidate as he was very well respected, and had been elected for many years. His wife, Frances, was a relentless canvasser and a great asset to the campaign. Lyle became his campaign manager, and for the first time there was an organized campaign. Up to now Herridge ran his campaign like a personal business. He couldn't drive, so he hitchhiked around the riding. He'd phone a friend to hire a hall for a certain day, and put up a notice announcing a meeting.

This election we had more than 1,000 members. A proper nominating convention was held with a good turnout. Bert Herridge was the keynote speaker and, to our surprise, he criticized those who had been organizing. He said membership wasn't everything. He hoped we weren't disappointed if we didn't win. He told the crowd that he had won the seat through a personal following. We were so angry with him.

We worked hard in that 2-month election. Lyle quit his job at Staffords, and worked full time. He and I did practically all the central campaign work. Many mornings I came downstairs and found him asleep at his typewriter. He worked on press releases and advertisements. In the daytime he set up canvassers in zones throughout the huge riding: Creston, Riondel, Kaslo, New Denver-Silverton, Nakusp, Castlegar, Trail, Rossland, Fruitvale, Salmo- Ymir, and Nelson. He also set up public meetings, scheduled the candidate, and co-ordinated the area campaigns.

In the meantime, I did office work (with the help of neighbour, Ruth Hufty) in the morning, worked on silk screening lawn signs in the afternoon, and in the evening canvassed a poll. And, of course, I had two little children. I can't remember what I did with them. Sometimes I carried one-year-old Haida on my back as I canvassed, going up and down stairs, up and down the hills of Nelson. I canvassed 10 of the 20 city polls, three times each. I just kept at it. I was sure someone would turn up to take over, but nobody did. Helen Hecker canvassed another five or six.

We had lawn signs, but very few would take them. Many of our own members refused. We had to encourage them to be proud of their politics. They might find that their neighbours were New Democrats as well. In many cases that was exactly the case. But in that election not many people took lawn signs (50 in Nelson; 250 in all).

However, we blundered through. Not only did Lyle and I do the lion's share of the work, but we also had to pay many of the expenses. One day Ran phoned to ask if Lyle would meet him for lunch at the Hume Hotel to hold a short meeting. I begged Ran to meet at our home instead. I would make the lunch, and he could pay me, so I could buy milk that day.

Election night: 200 people turned out to watch the results come in. They kept saying, "We did it!" "We did it!" I was livid. I wanted to scream, "Don't say 'we'! Where were you during the campaign?"

The results were wonderful. Ran Harding got 45% of the votes - more than Herridge ever did in his 23 years as M.P. The vote was out there; all we had to do was go out and get it. It was marvellous.

However, the result was crushing to Herridge's ego, and he endorsed the Liberal candidate in the next election (although he was getting senile by then, and the Liberals took advantage of his condition). But it had no impact on the 1972 result as Ran hit 55% of the vote. Herridge had had an illustrious career and was an excellent constituency Member of Parliament.

FIRST PROVINCIAL ELECTION

We had demonstrated that it was possible and the doubters had begun to believe. It was now much easier to organize and I continued to do so.

In September, 1968, Lyle had started working at Pacific Logging, an IWA certified mill in Slocan City, a small town about 45 miles from Nelson. He commuted every day – in winter leaving home at 5 a.m. and arriving back about 5 p.m. But he was finally in the IWA union, complete with benefits and, most importantly, job security.

Now it was time to plan the provincial election that would be held within a year. Many people expected

Lyle to be the candidate, but he wouldn't. We still had to demonstrate that people work in elections for other than personal interest and, we desperately wanted to run a strong and potentially victorious campaign. The search was on for a candidate. We persuaded a very popular city councillor, Mickey McEwen, to run but, within weeks of agreeing, he died suddenly of a heart attack.

The search continued. I was elected to Nelson School Board at that time, and the Board was in contract negotiations with district teachers. One day I came home from a meeting and called out to Lyle, "I found us a candidate."

We invited Lorne Nicolson (the chairman of the teachers' negotiating committee) and his wife, Frances, to our home for dinner and sounded them out. Lorne was 36, had voted CCF and NDP – most of the time - and was interested. He was articulate and ruggedly handsome. He was well respected amongst the teachers and those who knew him.

Lorne agreed to stand for nomination. Four others also ran: John Hecker, Bob Cunningham, Bill (from Creston), and John Fletcher. Lyle recruited all the candidates with an eye to balancing both socio-economic interests and geography. While we quietly supported Lorne, Lyle wrote press releases and gave his best advice to all of them. No more flipping a coin. Now people were fighting for the nomination. All-candidates meetings were held and more people signed up. Lorne won.

The election was called in late July, just weeks after I gave birth to Colin (on the 9th). Lyle quit his job at Slocan Forest Products, became campaign manager, and started putting the campaign together.

Electa Bunce and I started silk screening lawn signs. I kept Colin in the car alongside Mike and Polly Makasoff garage in Taghum. Every couple of hours I would stop, change a diaper, nurse the baby, then back to the signs. It was hard, dirty work. But in this election there were people who would put them up.

We lost, but everyone was amazed at the results. We increased our vote from 30% to 40%, while elsewhere in B.C. the NDP lost both votes and seats.

We spent $6,000, of which $3,000 was still owing after the election. We spent the next 3 years trying to pay off that debt with garage sales, bake sales, dances, and raffles. Then, a year before the next election, the Bluebell Mine in Riondel closed and the Steelworkers Union helped us pay off the debt because they were closing their accounts.

When the provincial election was called in 1972, we ran another effective campaign. Lorne was the candidate again, and the whole province went NDP with Dave Barrett the first NDP premier of B.C. Nelson-Creston became and remained one of the strongest NDP ridings in the province.

There was jubilation at the victory party. Toward the end of the evening, Ron Nelson, editor of the Nelson News arrived at our hall, (we knew he had spent the first part of the evening at the Socred campaign headquarters lamenting what fate awaited B.C. under the NDP). As soon as he came in, he announced, "Drinks for everybody." He congratulated us and expressed great hope for the future. Then he asked me how he could join the NDP. Without thinking, I said "Ron, get off your knees. It's unbecoming." He was grovelling, so obviously. He phoned a few days later, insisting he wanted to join the NDP. I stalled until he forgot the question.

A panoramic view of the Valhala mountains from the peak of Idaho lookout above Silverton.

SCHOOLBOARD - 1968-70

When we bought a house in Nelson in 1967, I was at loose ends. I didn't want to leave my children to go to work, yet I couldn't just sit at home. I loved my children dearly but resented being trapped at home. We could seldom afford a babysitter to go out in the evening. I felt like the world was turning, while I sat outside it, watching.

Lyle suggested I get involved in something in the community. I couldn't get involved in anything that would cost us money because there was none. We had three mortgages on the house.

Local school board elections were coming up, and I decided to run. I took the two children with me when I filed nomination papers, and with a reporter present, announced I had two good reasons for running for school board, they were Eric and Haida. That was about all I did to campaign. I won with 89 votes. Very soon thereafter I found I was pregnant!

Heading for my first meeting, I contemplated how much I had to learn. I had a grade 10 education. At the meeting I listened to a report on negotiations with the teachers. It was recommended the Board should reach agreement on wages and sign a contract covering only that. All working conditions in previous contracts would be cancelled and it would be up to the Board to make all future decisions. I kept saying to myself, "This is union busting." However, it was my first meeting and I made no comment.

When I got home I phoned the chairman of the teachers' negotiating committee, Lorne Nicolson. I was astonished to hear his version of the negotiations. They were not as unreasonable as made out by the secretary-treasurer. Although I supported the concept of unions, I had never been a member, and here I was sitting on the other side.

There appeared to be only one avenue open. I had to get the trustees to hear the teachers' side directly. At the next meeting, after hearing from the negotiating committee, I moved that we meet with the teachers' committee. The secretary-treasurer went through the roof. "No way!" When he saw other trustees agreeing with me, he then wanted a quick decision in principle that night, in advance of any joint meeting. I kept asking, "What's the hurry? What will the teachers think if they see the meeting as a farce, with the decision already made. It isn't fair to those of us who are new to this Board. You are asking us to make a major break with previous practice. We have to have all the facts if we must make this change." The majority of Board members agreed with me. It was agreed to hold such a meeting.

When we met, I sat back and smiled and smiled. The other trustees were as amazed as I was at the teachers' reasonableness. We retired to another room, discussed the proposals for ten minutes, went back into full session, and an agreement was signed then and there, similar to the last contract.

I felt good about this. However, the full force of what I had done didn't come home to me until weeks later. At a Kootenay regional meeting, a trustee from Trail came up to me, introduced himself, and asked how the experiment was going with our teachers. He said the rest of the region was holding up finalizing their contract until they found out how we made out. I asked, "What experiment?" "You know," he said, "Cancelling the teachers' contract and signing an agreement covering wages only." I smiled and said it didn't work out. I suddenly realized I had done more than bring about an agreement; I had thwarted a region-wide, perhaps a province-wide, strike.

I learned that one person could make a difference. I was surprised how many "like minded" people get elected. The business community gets its representatives elected, and they work harmoniously together. Get a different person on, and some clichés get challenged. Replying to someone on one occasion, I said, "In this society, a person doesn't get paid what he's worth. He gets paid what he can get his hands on." Later I heard it repeated by someone who had scoffed at me at the time.

The next negotiations were with outside workers: janitors, bus drivers, and secretaries. At one point, a long-time trustee, a prominent local pharmacist, asked, "Why does nobody ever think of anything but their own selfish wants? Why can't they think of the good of the community." I leaned over and asked, "And what have the pharmacists done for our country lately?" This was very timely as there were many news stories about increases in drug costs. The government was threatening to buy drugs for hospitals and welfare recipients wholesale because druggists had been increasing their prices so greatly.

A trustee raged on and on about the bus drivers wanting three weeks vacation. He wondered what in the world they would do with three weeks holidays. It sounded like he thought they wouldn't know what to do with free time.

When our auxiliary workers went on strike, our secretary-treasurer undertook to drive the school bus in the morning. We had an early committee meeting one morning, and arrived just as he returned from driving the school bus. He looked shell-shocked, breathing hard and sweating. He asked for a few minutes delay to collect his composure. I smiled and asked if it was hard work driving a bus full of children. He said, "Oh, yeah, it sure is." I then asked him to tell it to the trustees who wonder why bus drivers wanted three weeks vacation.

We couldn't reach an agreement, so had to bring in an outside arbitrator. The union agreed to our suggestion, a corporate man from Cominco, in Trail. We outlined our differences, and then retired to separate rooms to discuss and make new proposals.

The arbitrator came with the trustees, and joined in the discussion, giving us suggestions on what to do. After he did this a second time, I turned to him and asked him what he was doing? Wasn't he supposed to be an impartial arbitrator? What did it look like when he left the room with us? He turned many colours of red and left the room, never to join us again.

But my greatest contribution was with the integration of mentally handicapped children into the mainstream school system. All across the province, with the compliance of the provincial government, these children were being moved into schools from church basements or drafty, barren halls.

The Handicapped Society approached our Board. The issue was assigned to my committee for discussion and recommendation. I argued for integration, but was met with opposition. Reasons given, "There's only 8 of them and it's not worth the trouble." "It's not as if they would become productive citizens if we do this. Just not worth the time." We couldn't agree on a recommendation and this got delayed several months. I was finally told to bring in a recommendation for the Board to consider. The other members on the committee voted "Non concurrence." That meant we would not be integrating.

The day the issue was coming before the Board, I wondered what I could do. I kept thinking, if only the parents of these children could hear the excuses given against it. I had travelled a number of times with the bus driver that picked these kids up to take them to their current school in a local church, so I knew how much love there was between the parents and children – the hugging and kissing.

Then I realized, that's it! Get the parents to the meeting. Let them hear it. Would those trustees have the guts to state their reasons for opposing integration with the parents present? I phoned every parent I knew. I phoned the Handicapped Society and urged some of their members to attend.

I arrived at the meeting a few minutes late and was met by a glare from the chairman who informed me that my 'friends' were there. He then asked the chairman of the Handicapped Society if he had a statement to make. He did and he made it, urging integration, then sat down. The chairman thanked him and said, "You may leave now." Everybody stood up dutifully to leave. I jumped up and said, "No, they don't have to leave. This is an open public meeting. They can stay. No doubt they will be interested in the outcome." They sat down.

With a little bit of muttering under his breath, the chairman put the issue before the Board immediately. After the committee recommendation was read, I made an impassioned plea to reject the recommendation and move to integrate. Trustee Dr. Bitnun agreed with me. Nobody else spoke. The vote was taken and it was unanimous to integrate. Everybody in the public gallery was jubilant.

The next day the newspaper gave all the credit for this decision to Dr. Bitnun. The kids were integrated and into my children's school. Haida came home one day and told me her class had a field trip, and how she held "Lucy's" hand because "She's handicapped. But she sure enjoyed the trip. She laughed and laughed." Good, I thought. Why not learn early we are not all alike.

I was the Board's rep on the local Health Board. The chairperson of that Board was known as "Mrs. Social Credit", in the same way as I was known as "Mrs. NDP". We would be at loggerheads from the minute I walked in the door. However often we disagreed, I thought business would be conducted in a rational manner. No way. Any letter she disagreed with, she would say, "I won't read it. It sounds like some NDP junk." She didn't even pretend to be civil.

At one meeting we spent an hour discussing some hippie's toilet being located a few feet too close to a creek with a couple of homes below. We discussed every possibility, ad nauseum.

Finally I said, "For heaven's sake. Let's get this into perspective. We are discussing the possibility of flies and perhaps seepage of one person affecting two others. While here in Nelson we have 10,000 toilets dumping raw sewage into the same Kootenay River that some 5,000 Castlegar residents are using as the source of their drinking water." The chairman replied, "That's different. We have permission!" With that logic, I just walked out.

In 1970 the provincial government made major cuts in transfer payments to School Boards. We called the principals in and asked them to help decide where to cut. They were annoyed but agreed, asking that we cut expenses everywhere, including trustees'.

The trustees attended a provincial convention in Victoria. I attended, taking my two younger children (Eric being in school) along. With a babysitter in tow, we found a motel on the outskirts of town with a kitchen and children's playgrounds. Everybody else stayed at the very expensive Empress Hotel.

At the next Board meeting, I looked at the cost of attending that convention and compared it to previous years. I found it to be considerably higher than the previous year, and double the year before. For the first time, we undertook to pay the expenses of the travelling spouses. I found this incredible since this was the year we told the principals we would cut trustees' expenses.

I informed the Board members I was unhappy and that, at least, the spouses' expenses should be paid back. They were furious with me. They insulted me. They berated me. I faced them down and said that, if the expenses were not paid back, I would go public with my complaint. After more bluster, they agreed to repay the spouses' expenses. I didn't go public.

Two weeks later, in the election, I was defeated by 60 votes. A thorn had been removed from the exclusive club!

I learned a lot from that experience. For one thing, there is no democracy unless people participate, in more ways than just voting. As the wife of a blue collar worker, with three children and three mortgages, I couldn't afford any kind of campaign. I expected members of some of the organization I helped to undertake at least to phone their members. Nothing was forthcoming. Nobody made any donation.

It is amazing how fast one loses one's fame. When elected, people spoke to me on the street, in stores, invited me to functions. The minute I was defeated, thunk! No phone calls. No speaking engagements. No one asked my opinion on anything. Nothing!

But for a few years Lyle went around introducing himself as "Mr. Vera Kristiansen". Later I was proud to be called "Mrs. Lyle Kristiansen."

RECYCLING

The 1970s were "environmental" years in West Kootenay. There were many organizations and think tanks. Lyle joined the West Kootenay Pollution Control Society and became a director. Under the chairmanship of Ron Sawyer, Lyle and the Board worked hard to successfully oppose the establishment of a pulp mill on Kootenay Lake.

At that time the federal Liberal government set up the Local Initiative Program (LIP grants), funding local make-work projects. While many worthwhile projects were funded, many others were not well supervised, leading to a strong public backlash.

I suggested to Lyle that the Pollution Control Society apply for a grant to set up a recycling depot. We drew up an application, and they submitted it for approval. We got the grant.

I was appointed, along with Mike Jessen and Audrey Rothkop, to oversee the program. The other two were theorists, and I was the practical person.

Our objectives were twofold: to sell the public on recycling and to set up a depot. We rented the old jam factory building and made some primitive machinery for crushing glass and baling paper. Bins were set up around town for people to drop off glass, paper, and tin. Some people delivered their material directly to us.

We undertook to call on every house in Nelson to explain why recycling was necessary, to promote composting, and generally answer questions. If the city had taken over where we left off, we could have been leaders in this field. Years later it caught on.

These were the days of the hippie movement. During our interviewing of prospective employees, I stated that anyone doing door-to-door canvassing would have to be clean-shaven, neatly dressed, and very polite. No way! How dare I stifle their individuality? I had no right to tell them what to wear or how to look. Mike and Audrey disagreed with me. I capitulated. But I had done enough canvassing to know what to expect.

Within a few days, "the worst of the lot" came back to the depot saying he couldn't do door-to-door canvassing. He was tired of having the door slammed in his face before he opened his mouth. I smiled.

But this guy wouldn't do anything else either. He didn't like something else I said, and proceeded to show me how he could avoid work. He would pick up a piece of cardboard, walk slowly and deliberately down the long hall, place it down very carefully, and then walk slowly back. Oh, yes, we would get no work out of him. Mike and Audrey still argued that he had to be given a chance. Within a week, he insulted Mike, and then it was decided he had to go.

Other employees weren't much better. Many times we had to drag our drivers out of the beer parlour. One 60-year old man worked all day. Toward the end of the LIP grant, we hired a young fellow who had arrived from Vancouver and was seen riding a bike around Nelson. He wore a trench coat, a beret, had a short haircut, and was full of energy. He worked like a Trojan. His name was Gerald Rotering. Later he would become a Nelson Daily News reporter, Lyle's constituency executive assistant and mayor of Nelson.

At this time Nelson had just built its sewage disposal system. Audrey and I called on them and were shown through. We asked them how they were going to dispose of the sludge after it remained in the bins the appropriate length of time. They said they would probably dig holes and bury it.

We knew other cities were using theirs' as fertilizer for parks and roadsides. Checking Nelson's park maintenance shop, we found that they were using sludge from Milwaukee. We were able to inform the sewage people how to dispose of their sludge, and the parks people how to save money.

It was obvious from the beginning that the freight costs to move the recycled material was prohibitive. If we couldn't get subsidies from some government, we could not continue to exist. The plants that took our recycled stuff were located in Vancouver and Seattle. We did our best to find some long term financing, but to no avail. We could not sell city aldermen on recycling. We folded.

I continued to sort my garbage. Wet vegetation went into the compost. We used very few tin cans. We seldom had one full garbage can a week for the garbage collectors. Looking across the back alley, I saw a retired couple fill three cans every week. It would have been so easy to cut the city's garbage disposal budget in half, and be leaders in the field, which finally took hold in the 2lst century, with some finances and encouragement from the NDP government. Communities were required to cut their garbage by 25% by certain dates, and surprisingly, they met the demand. In Madeira Park, where we were living, we surpassed that requirement. I was on the Board of Directors at the time. However, until the government got involved, nothing happened.

My organic garden was a good producer!

LEADING UP TO 1980 ELECTION

When Bert Herridge retired as Member of Parliament for Kootenay West in 1968, Ran Harding ran for the seat, and won. He ran again in 1972, getting 55% of the vote.

Ran Harding was the hardest working, most selfless politician I have ever known. Whenever he achieved something worthwhile for the riding, we asked him to put out a press release. He would refuse, saying: "I can't. I'm only doing my job. It would sound like bragging." It was so frustrating. Provincially he had represented Kaslo-Slocan, a small riding with no local newspaper or radio, the only communication being by word of mouth. Kootenay West was a much bigger pond.

In 1972 a minority Liberal government was elected, with the NDP holding the balance of power. In this campaign the NDP leader, David Lewis, concentrated on the "corporate welfare bums" issue, detailing subsidies given large corporations by taxpayers, if not in direct payment, then in tax breaks. We made gains across the country but did not become the Official Opposition. However, the issue of the "corporate welfare bums" became understood by the electorate, and the government had to address it.

The NDP agreed to support the Liberal minority government in exchange for certain pieces of legislation, including improving MPs working conditions with office space and staff. For the first time they got an office in the constituency with staff. Increased travel by air made it fairer for those representing constituencies thousands of miles away from Ottawa.

Changes in the Election Act let people make donations to the political party of their choice and write 75% off their income tax up to $100, with lesser deduction for larger donations. Corporations had always been able to deduct all political donations as a "promotional expense". Now ordinary people could participate in the democratic process. Spending budgets were limited for parties and candidates, and per capita vote subsidies were introduced for local candidates receiving over 15% of the vote. It breathed new life into the NDP.

But the NDP caucus was soon faced with supporting a less than desirable Liberal budget or bringing the government down. Ran argued against bringing the government down. However, he was in the minority, and they withdrew their support. The government fell, and we were into another election. It was the last thing we needed. We still had election debts; the provincial NDP government was doing some very good but controversial things and it was low in the polls. We were into the third election in five years.

This was one of the hardest elections I ever worked. Nobody wanted to talk about Ran or federal politics. Everyone was talking about provincial issues. Lyle was campaign manager. Janice D'Arcy (whose husband was the MLA in Rossland-Trail) was in charge of the campaign in that part of the riding. A month into the campaign we found she had done nothing, and then left her husband and children to move east. Others had to be found to head that campaign. We couldn't find the material sent to Janice. We couldn't even find the keys to the committee rooms.

Ran came to us in tears, a month into the campaign, as he was yet to talk about anything federal. The Socreds were filibustering in the provincial legislature, keeping our elected people in Victoria instead of in the ridings defending their legislation. NDP members were not used to defending government policies and were having difficulty facing the public. Although our members supported what the provincial government was doing, we couldn't get people to conduct our usual door-to-door canvassing. We organized a number of select, well prepared, and fortified canvass teams and transported them from town to town. We did everything we could, but we lost the election. For the first time in some 30 years Kootenay West went Tory to Bob Brisco.

A provincial election was held in 1975 and the NDP lost the government. In 1977, Ran Harding announced he would not be running again. He had been in elected office for some 30 years and he really had had enough. The federal election was coming up and the NDP in Kootenay West did not have a candidate. It should have been the No. 1 (in terms of winning it back) riding in BC, but no prominent person came forth. Phone calls started coming in asking Lyle to run. Lyle changed his mind daily: Yes, he would. No, he wouldn't. I, too, couldn't decide whether to encourage or discourage him.

Lyle was happy working at KFP for good wages, enjoying children and home life, attending meetings or conventions almost monthly. He was off the job on union (or Party) business so often his bosses called him their "permanent temporary". He used to say he had the best of both worlds, and was so happy he felt guilty. But the pressure was on. Finally he told everyone he would attend the federal leadership convention in Winnipeg and make up his mind.

We drove our station wagon with our children, now 12, 10 and 8, to Winnipeg and participated, unenthusiastically, in electing Ed Broadbent federal leader, replacing David Lewis - the last of our giant politicians. Ed was not an exciting choice. One of the candidates was Rosemary Brown, a black woman MLA from BC. She immigrated to Canada from Jamaica about 5 years before. She did not know Canadian politics, but came a close second in the race. The NDP practices reverse discrimination at times.

Someone at the convention pointed out to Lyle that there were only five members of parliament that could be considered blue-collar workers. Even our own party was loaded with lawyers, ministers of the church, and professors. While there was a hue and cry about women being under-represented in Parliament, it was not nearly as bad as the under-representation of blue-collar workers.

On the way home Lyle appeared to be favouring running for the nomination. Finally I said to him "I don't want you waking up on your sixtieth birthday saying, 'I wish I had'." That did it! He decided to run. We discussed the situation with the children and they agreed, "Dad should."

Before Lyle announced his intentions, he had to phone one of the other candidates and advise him of his decision. Len Embree was a trade unionist, active in the PPWC and a supporter of breakaway Canadian Unions. Lyle neither agreed with nor liked him, but he had previously agreed to support him as the only "labour candidate". It was an awkward moment, but Lyle had to apologize and advise before going public.

We set up a nominating committee with representatives from the different parts of the riding. They undertook to raise funds and help with contacting members. Lyle's friend, Maurice Eggie, couldn't make a donation so he undertook to deliver the 200 letters to Nelson members. Besides Lyle, others running for nomination were: Gordon Titsworth, Len Embree, Chuck Kenny, Doug Joiner, and Martin Vanderpol. Lyle won on the first ballot.

The federal election was called for June, 1979. There was a swing toward the Conservative Party in the West. With their usual trickery, the Socreds called a provincial election to fall ten days before the federal election date. This was confusing for people, as they could not sort out provincial and federal issues, nor candidates.

Our full-time paid organizers were re-assigned to work in the provincial election. Even Lyle and I canvassed more toward the provincial election than the federal. There was such fervor to defeat the Social Credit government. Chris D'Arcy, MLA, promised faithfully to work full-time in our campaign as soon as his was over, if we agreed to release our paid personnel to work in his election. He broke that promise, and left on vacation immediately after his campaign.

We won Rossland-Trail and Nelson-Creston, but failed to win back B.C. People were demoralized and it was impossible to get a federal campaign going again. All we could do on Election Day was attempt to bring out the vote identified during the provincial election. Despite increasing our vote over 1974, we lost Kootenay West and incumbent Bob Brisco was re-elected to the minority Conservative government with Joe Clark as Prime Minister. The Conservatives immediately announced they would govern as if they had majority.

Nine months later the finance minister, John Crosby, brought in a disastrous budget. Because Pierre Trudeau had just resigned as Liberal leader, the Tories thought the Liberals would not defeat the minority government. They were wrong. Both opposition parties voted against the budget and the handful of Social Credit MPs abstained. The government fell in December, 1979, precipitating a new election.

There should have been no question who the NDP candidate was in Kootenay West. However, Gordon Titsworth decided to run again for nomination, and then Glen Suggitt, Martin Vanderpol, Marty Horswill and Len Embree joined the race. There was a full-fledged fight for the nomination. This was counter productive because energy went into the nomination fight, but it also provided enthusiasm for members and garnered publicity.

Lyle won the nomination on the third ballot. Remembering

what happened in the first campaign, Lyle challenged Brisco to attend community open-to-the-public all-candidates meetings in the riding. In 1979 Brisco refused to attend all-candidates meetings, thus saying one thing in one part of the riding and the opposite in another. Lyle wanted to tie him to some public statements and give the public a chance to compare candidates on an equal footing.

With the press present at the nominating convention, Lyle posed the challenge to Brisco, stating that in a winter campaign, and the issues of such importance, the candidates had to give voters a chance to make an informed decision. The press presented this challenge to Brisco, and he replied he would attend all public meetings. That was what we wanted. Invitations immediately started coming in from every part of the riding.

The first meeting hardly qualified as "open". The Labour Council contacted the Nelson Chamber of Commerce and appeared to be working together toward a joint public meeting. But the Chamber took over and informed the candidates this meeting would be held after the Chambers' annual meeting. The Labour Council was left out of the planning. It was, in fact, a dinner meeting, and Chamber members were seated on the floor of the hall. After dinner, the meeting was opened to the public, who were relegated to the far edge of the room, roped off so that there was little chance of participating in questioning candidates. It was so blatantly a "loaded" meeting favouring the Tory candidate, it was insulting.

What happened was exactly what was intended: Brisco got a standing ovation almost every time he spoke, while the other candidates were laughed at, booed, ridiculed, derided. Lyle was hardly able to finish an answer to a question. It didn't bother him too much, except for the scorn he felt for the organizers. A proper public meeting was held in Nelson much later in the campaign, sponsored by the Labour Council and the University Women.

The next meeting was held in Riondel, a small, isolated community. The meeting was well attended by young and old. The audience was polite, each candidate receiving the same applause. It was impossible to gauge the reaction to what was being said. The candidates, as well, seemed to be sparring with each other, watching the others' move; careful, polite, and considerate.

But the meeting in Kaslo was worthy of an Oscar. The NDP never won this town, provincially or federally. However, it was obviously turning against the Conservatives. Brisco ended his remarks by saying he felt like the messenger who brought unpleasant news and got his head chopped off. He could feel he was losing support in the safest part of his riding.

Lyle, on the other hand, was at his best. His knowledge, quick wit, and ability came to the fore. I was so proud of him. I heard one elderly woman leaving the meeting say, "That was the best NDP speaker I ever heard." Another lady came up to Lyle and said, "My, you are very literate." He smiled, gritting his teeth, knowing she meant "for a woodworker".

The meeting was packed with people sporting "Brisco" buttons, and pieces of paper from which they read their questions, probably supplied by Brisco's organizer. "Mr. Brisco, if the Prime Minister was to interfere with the Bank of Canada and try to lower interest rates, wouldn't there be chaos in Canada?" To which Brisco answered, "Why, yes, of course. The governor of the Bank of Canada would resign and there would be chaos." To this Lyle replied, "I seem to remember, a few years ago, another Conservative prime minister, a western prime minister, a Mr. Diefenbacher, who did in fact demand lower interest rates, saying that if the Bank of Canada refused

Diefenbacher would DEMAND the governor's resignation. Interest rates were lowered; there was no chaos, and there was no resignation." Brisco sank into his seat; a hush fell over the crowd.

Another questioner: "Mr. Kristiansen, do you support Canada having an army?" Lyle: "Yes, I do. But I don't think the army should be sitting around waiting for a war. We have just had an accident off the coast of BC and it took four hours for a rescue team to reach it. This is shameful for a nation surrounded by oceans on three sides. There are things an army could be doing like patrolling our coastlines, cleaning up after tornadoes, or fighting forest fires."

To another question Lyle reached for his briefcase to pull out a newspaper with huge headlines (which I had just torn off the Vancouver Sun on the way to the meeting), and disproved whatever Brisco was saying. Brisco answered a questioner by saying, "It's time to bite the bullet; tell it like it is." Lyle retorted: "This isn't a John Wayne movie, Bob. This is a real life situation."

It was like that all night. The Liberal candidate was hardly even speaking. Time after time, when called upon to answer, he would say: "I'll defer this one to Lyle." He was, however, laughing and enjoying the exchanges. Besides being very new to politics, he had stopped at Ainsworth Hot Springs for a swim on the way to this meeting, and had the misfortune of diving into the shallow end of the pool and scraping the side of his face. I guess it was gutsy of him to show up at all. Perhaps he was after the sympathy vote. Lyle and I? Well, we thoroughly enjoyed ourselves.

The following meetings went well at Nakusp and Winlaw. Castlegar was another memorable meeting. It started with each candidate getting the same amount of applause. As it progressed, Lyle's applause got louder and longer. Kendall took a hawkish stand, which was inappropriate because many pacifist Doukhobors lived here. The hall was filled to capacity; the meeting was carried live on radio, and repeated next day.

Conservatives at each meeting kept searching for an issue to stump Lyle. No question was ever repeated. There was nothing they could latch on to as an issue. And so many things tripped them up. The biggest issue was selling off Petro Canada which the Conservatives were proposing to do. It was very unpopular. The Conservative government was to do it anyway, in 1990.

A question was asked about the disastrous Columbia River Treaty (which was costing B.C. millions and power was shipped to the U.S. at subsidized prices), and the Murphy Dam. Brisco pulled out a paper and quoted something about the Saskatchewan CCF government, decades earlier, being advised by David Cass-Beggs to divert one river into another, and then damming it. He had used that trick in the 1979 campaign, and Lyle was not given time to answer. This time Lyle was ready for him.

Lyle started out by saying, "First, I want to comment on the Murphy Dam, since that is what the question was about." He outlined the different options facing local citizens in choices of dams. He went on to say, "If I had to make a choice, I suppose I'd say Murphy Dam was preferable. Ten years hence I suppose someone could say 'Kristiansen supported building Murphy Dam'. That would not be true. It is not what I am saying. I don't know what Brisco is talking about in Saskatchewan. And quite frankly, I don't care. I know who supported the Columbia River Treaty: the Conservative and Socred parties. I know who opposed it, fought tooth and nail against it: the NDP and our MP, Bert Herridge. Bob knows it, and you know it." That question never surfaced again.

Salmo's meeting was wonderful. Trail's was sparsely attended and poorly run. Chris D'Arcy, MLA, canvassed several polls. Bill King (former MLA for Revelstoke-Slocan) attended meetings in Nakusp, Fauquier and Burton. Dave Barrett came to Castlegar and Trail. MLA Lorne Nicolson raised some campaign funds.

Brisco tried running ads saying, "A Vote for the NDP is a Vote for Nuclear Power", but the NDP campaign threatened to sue and it backfired on him. On Election Day there were ads on Trail radio suggesting the NDP was promoting abortion; killing babies before they saw the light of day. That didn't hurt us.

Election Day: February 18th, 1980. We voted in Nelson. I went to work in Thrums, Glade, and Shoreacres. Lyle worked in Winlaw. It was winter, but the weather was good. Because I spoke Russian a little, I always worked the "Valley". Many Doukhobors who lived there didn't speak much English. Some couldn't read or write and for this and other reasons many still wouldn't vote. It was an uphill battle getting them to vote. The last election before we moved to West Kootenay had only 10% of the Doukhobour population voting.

In the 1968 federal election, we hired Ernie Boulet, a retired IWA rep, to work full time to get the Doukhobors, many of whom were IWA members, to vote. He travelled extensively among them. The Union of Spiritual Christian Community charter states that because the federal government took the vote away from them in 1931 because they were pacifists and refused to swear allegiance to the king, they would never vote. If they did vote, there was a better than 90% chance they would vote NDP.

Boulet worked on Election Day in Crescent Valley - Krestova area. He went back to people he thought he had convinced to vote and offered to drive them to the polling station. He was met with stonewalling. Finally one family went. When he brought them back, their neighbours went. By the time he brought them back, several others stopped him on the road and asked to be taken. By late afternoon he said they were lined up on the road waiting for him. That day 104% voted in that poll, because those not registered could swear in in rural polls.

In 1980, I worked all day, running constantly into people who would not vote. They would tell me how much they wanted Lyle and the NDP to win. They offered donations, which I refused, saying what we needed that day was votes. One old man insisted that, if he voted, the government would have the right to order him to do military duty. I asked him why that would give the government that right any more than the fact he used government roads, or accepted government pensions? Well, he didn't know. "Anyway," I asked him, "what army accepted 70-year-old recruits?"

It was like that all day. I just kept returning to people asking if they had been out to vote yet. I was thoroughly tired before the polls closed. I got back in the car to head for home, thinking I now had to face three children who didn't want to attend the victory party that evening, although Lyle wanted them. I didn't know how to talk them into coming.

I was still thinking of arguments when I walked into the house and found three kids with their best clothes on. I said, "What's wrong?" They replied, "We're ready like you asked us." I asked why they changed their mind, and Haida replied, "Eric said that Dad would probably like us to be there." I was so relieved. I changed quickly and we all drove back to Castlegar, to the victory party.

Victory parties are always fun. Canvassers and other election workers gather. In B.C. the minute the polls close, the results from the rest of Canada start coming in, so within minutes we know who will be the government. Very seldom do B.C. results make a difference. When we reached the party everyone was watching television for results. The children found it exciting. The local radio station was flashing results from within our riding. Canvassers were anxious to see what happened in their own polls. Lyle took an early lead and never fell behind. It was victory all the way.

Lyle was at the Trail headquarters until there was no doubt as to the local results. He didn't accept victory just because CBC and other stations declared him elected. He remembered what happened in the last election when the early polls showed him winning handily at first when rural polls were in, but losing when larger centres reported. The Nelson newspaper reporter stayed with Lyle the whole time. At 11 p.m. he finally arrived in the hall. When he entered, everybody stood up and cheered. Lyle spoke briefly and humbly. I was so glad the children were there. Eric said later that it felt like one big family.

A reporter from the Nelson News, Gerald Rotering, told me he wanted to apply to be Lyle's constituency assistant and why he would be right for the job, including his research and writing abilities. I considered what he said, and decided he was right. Lyle agreed it made sense. It was the smartest thing we did. He was the best. He could solve problems and find information no one else could.

After much singing, dancing, drinking, talking, laughing, and speech making, we piled into our car and headed back to Nelson. The enormity of it all was settling down on all of us.

On the way home Eric announced that he would not move to Ottawa with us. He would stay behind in Nelson. We didn't argue but realized something had to be done. How do you order your 15- year-old son, who towers over you by 6 inches to pack up and move? Next day started at 7 a.m. with phone calls of congratulations. Telegrams arrived from friends across the country. Flowers from Lyle's Mom and Dad.

That day Lyle went back to KFP to thank the guys for their help and support. At 3 pm he went to Trail's Cominco plant to meet the guys going off and coming on shift. They appreciated it; saying nobody had ever come back after the election was over. The next day he visited the Building Trades at the 7-mile dam. He phoned all zone managers to thank them. And held a meeting with MLAs Chris D'Arcy and Lorne Nicolson to discuss office plans and staff.

On Saturday we flew to Vancouver for five days rest. Mom and Dad were happy to see us. Dad kept saying, "Me, an immigrant, with a Member of Parliament son." I know my father would have said the same.

Eric's first experience in canvassing at Sam and Inez Piro's door.

Gerald Rotering (Lyle's assistant and mayor of
Nelson) and NDP leader, Ed Broadbent, join Lyle in
opening campaign headquarters.

BLIND DATE AT THE G.G.s

In May, I attended an orientation session, informing new Members of rituals in swearing-in ceremonies, opening of Parliament, and the formal Governor-General's ball. I kept an eye open for something to take one or all the children to, but there was nothing. I mean, not a thing! In desperation, I wrote a letter to Mrs. Schreyer, wife of the Governor-General (Ed Schreyer had been the NDP premier of Manitoba a few years before, and I had met them at conventions), outlining our dilemma. I said there must be other families in the same predicament.

About a week later, the phone rang and a woman said, "Please hold the line for Her Excellency, Mrs. Shreyer." Hold the line? For who? Me? Vera Sharko from Coolidge, hold the line for Her Excellency? I was flustered. And there she was; Her Excellency in person, on the phone, saying, "Mrs. Kristiansen, I was just in the office and read your letter. I think perhaps there is something we could do. Why don't you bring your oldest son ... I see he is 15 ... to our Ball? I have a daughter who is 16, who could escort him around. Carmelle is very tall with long blond hair. How tall is your son?" I stuttered, "Oh, he's tall. He's over six feet, Your Worshi, I mean Your Highne.. ah.. Mrs.Schreyer."

"Terrific. Then it's settled. My children will take him under their wing and tell him how they resisted moving to Ottawa. We went through exactly what you described in your letter, no one wanting to move. Once they got here it has been very interesting for them. I am sure by the time we get finished, your children will be happy to move." We exchanged some further niceties, with me continuing to stutter, unsure what I was supposed to call her. Later we were informed she was to be addressed as "Your

77

Excellency" at all times. With Ed Schreyer, after the first "Your Excellency", one could call him "Sir".

And then we were off the phone, and I was in shock. Did I really just get off the phone from the Queen's representative? And did she just invite my son to escort her daughter to the Governor General's Ball? I had to talk to someone. I phoned Mother in Vancouver and told her the story. She replied, "Hmph. Eric's first blind date and he goes straight to the top." We laughed.

Eric was happy to accompany us to Ottawa for the formalities. To find him a tuxedo we phoned every rental company in Vancouver, Ottawa and Toronto. Nobody could outfit him. After all, he had shoulders yeah wide, and a tiny waist. He was 6`2", with size 13 shoes. We finally rented a jacket from one company, pants and shirt from another and shoes elsewhere. The pants were too short, so he had to wear his cummerbund low down over his waist to give the pants more length. But he looked gorgeous.

When we arrived at the Governor-General's residence on the night of the ball, it was so exciting. The glitter, the jewels, the furs, the gowns mesmerized me; the long halls covered with red carpet, and the paintings of royalty on the wall.

We stood in the receiving line soaking in the atmosphere, when a bedecked officer in a red uniform walked up to us, I cringed, thinking, "He knows we don't belong here!" Instead, he said, "Would you, by chance, be Eric Kristiansen?" Eric answered, as nervously as I felt, "Yyyes." The officer replied, "Good. Come with me. They are waiting for you in another room. I was told to watch out for you." He led Eric off through another door.

The next time we saw him he looked like he was part of the receiving line with the Schreyers, chatting away with Carmelle.

The Schreyers did exactly what Mrs. S. said they would. Eric was taken to their living quarters later and chatted with all the members of the family, of which there was an older sister Heather, a younger brother Kevin, and a baby brother (about five years old) Toban. Eric was told the story about the first time the Schreyers invited Prime Minister Trudeau to dinner, and there was a lot of political discussion. At the end of the meal young Toban got off his chair and announced very loudly, "Well, don't blame me. I voted NDP". There was also an elderly aunt. They all told Eric how they hated moving from Winnipeg, but how much they were enjoying Ottawa.

On the way home, Eric said he would move to Ottawa. He said, "I guess I will be moving away from Nelson sooner or later. I guess this is sooner." I was always so grateful to Mrs. Schreyer and her family.

The Schreyers were so good to children. Every January they held Winter Parties for MPs' and ambassadors' children. They would be invited for six o'clock, take toboggan rides, horse and sleigh rides, skate on their rink, do some curling. Marshmallows were roasted on a bon fire. Around 10 o'clock everyone went inside, had a big meal and danced until midnight. Colin was too young to go the first year. Haida said Mrs. Shreyer went from table to table; introducing people, making sure everyone was involved. Their children were great hosts as well.

I must also note that the first Halloween we were in Ottawa Colin was 11, his last "Trick or Treat" year. Hilary Duignan and I packed up her three children and Colin and headed for the Governor General's house. We were invited in and given a friendly reception. We then went across the street to the Prime Minister's home. We were stopped at the gate and questioned. They said the mothers couldn't go in, but one of the officers walked the children up the long driveway to the house. The children said a witch came down the staircase and handed them treats. We always wondered if it was Margaret Trudeau. The children really enjoyed Ottawa and it was good for them. It was a good time for our young fish to be thrown into a larger pond.

I am standing with 15 year-old Eric all decked out in his tux for the Governor-General's Ball.

SPORTS IN OTTAWA

When I went house hunting in Ottawa, I asked about schools with the best sports record. The school most often mentioned was Sir Robert Borden, in Nepean, so we bought a townhouse in the area.

Borden had a good program in many sports, but especially in basketball and football. They could beat all the surrounding schools except the Catholic high school, St. Pius. While all the schools accepted students only from within certain boundaries, Pius brought students in from all over Ottawa, Nepean and even Hull (Quebec), because they were the only Catholic high school around. Their sports program was kept at a high level on purpose to attract new students, some attending only because of it. For the school, this was financially desirable. This made them formidable in almost every sport.

Some months into the school year (1980) the basketball coach, Mr. Hakim, told me this story: "I was walking down the corridor on the first day of school, thinking about last year's basketball season and how we beat every school except Pius. I wanted so badly to beat Pius, and we had come so close. I was trying to remember which of my players graduated, and which of Pius'. I realized we still had the makings of a very good team, but oh, god, we desperately needed one tall, strong forward.

"All I ask, god, is for one new tall student." No sooner had I thought that when I see coming toward me a tall kid, with a swagger that made him a natural basketball player. I couldn't believe my eyes! With my eyes bulging, my mouth salivating, I start half-running toward him, when I glance to my left and see the football coach, eyes glazed over, heading straight for the answer to my prayers. We reach this new student at the same time, and each knowing the other's interest in him, try to jostle each other out of the way as we introduce ourselves and proceed to query him on his sports interests. I was so happy to hear he played basketball, never football."

Eric came home from school that day saying it was such a friendly school. Everyone made him feel so welcome. I didn't think Eric would want to play football, as he never entered any contact sports. I had tried to get him to play hockey, but I watched as he quietly followed the mob chasing the puck back and forth on the ice, but was never in the huddle fighting for it. After a few weeks I asked if he wanted to quit and he said, "Yes". He chose, instead, individual, no-contact sports, such as ski racing, baseball, volleyball, and basketball.

However, he agreed to go on the football team. It started first, and basketball followed as soon as football season was over. Surprisingly, he enjoyed football. They won, and won, and then beat the dreaded Pius team for the first time ever, and were (representing Nepean) in the play-offs against Ottawa's best.

These playoffs were held in Lansdown Park, and I was proud to pay $2.00 to see my son play. The last time I was at Lansdown was during our honeymoon in 1961 at the NDP founding convention.

Let me set the scene: Nepean fans were seated in one section, and Ottawa's in another. School was closed to give fans the opportunity to cheer the team on. Team pride and spirit reverberated throughout the arena. Cheerleaders were at their best; school colours were flying. Mothers of the teams were out in force, prepared to do their share of the cheering; me among them.

I cheered on cue with others on our side. We were up and down like yo-yos. When the ball was passed to Eric, a voice rose amongst us: "Drop the ball, Eric."

We grew silent. There was a traitor amongst us! We glanced questioningly at each other.

And then it happened again: "Let them have the ball, Eric. If they want it so badly, give it to them." This time there was no mistaking the intent of the comments. We turn, in unison, to look at the dark little man. I am new so I don't know who he is, but am assured by others that he works at our school.

Then our team made another successful pass, and Paul caught the ball, and we go crazy cheering. Again we hear: "Throw it away, Paul. Drop the ball." I couldn't stand it. I walked over to this man and asked him whose side he was on, anyway? He laughed and introduced himself as the basketball coach at Borden. Basketball started next week, and he was there to see that none of his players got hurt.

We didn't win that football game, but nobody got hurt. Basketball season went well, and they beat Pius for the first time ever as well. It was a good year for Borden. It was after a victory with Pius that this coach told me the story about the time his prayers were answered.

It was always thrilling to hear a whole auditorium chant "Er-ic, Er-ic, Er-ic." He was their star player, and a born leader. Other players told me how he encouraged them, and was always a team player. He never tried to go it alone and hog all the glory.

IS THE WHOLE WORLD CRAZY?

One day when we first moved to Ottawa, I took Haida to a beauty salon to get her first perm. I left her there and went to Lyle's office on the Hill. I no sooner got there, when I received a frantic phone call from the hairdresser, asking me to pick up my daughter, as she seemed very ill.

I ran back to the car and drove as fast as I could, with terrible visions flashing in my mind. Haida was never ill, so this had to be serious. As I pulled up, I saw two white-clad women walk my little girl to my car. She was draped over the shoulders of the women. She fell into the car and started moaning and groaning: "I'm in such pain. I'm going to die." She clutched at her stomach and continued to moan.

I had to get directions to the nearest hospital, but being unfamiliar with the city, had difficulty following them. It was a hot sultry day. I was frantic. I was trying to keep one hand on Haida, comforting her, trying to remember the directions to the hospital, trying to drive safely. Sweat was pouring down over me. I had to ask for directions several times, all the time feeling that every minute counted in the life of my only daughter.

Finally, I saw a sign: "Hospital Zone". Thank goodness. Another sign: "Quiet, please. Hospital". Good. Further on, "Emergency Only Entrance". That's us! I pulled in, flung open the door; ran around the car and half carried my daughter into the building. Relief was washing over me.

Inside the building there was not a soul in sight. We could not hear a sound anywhere. We walked down a hallway until we found an empty room with a bed in it. I laid Haida down and told her I would go look for a doctor. Further down the corridor I heard voices, so I rushed in that direction.

I walked into a room with 6 people in it. They stood there staring at me; nobody asked me what I wanted. I told them my daughter was very ill; would somebody please look at her. There was silence. Then someone asked me what year my daughter was born. I answered "1967". There was silence. My mind was whirling with questions, "Was that a bad year for girls?" After a long pause a woman said, "I'm a doctor. I'll look at her".

I led the way, and all six people followed. I walked into the room where Haida was lying, and told her a doctor will see her. The doctor picked Haida's hand up, and said, "What seems to be the matter?" Haida replied, "I'm not feeling well." By now I know the whole world has gone mad, including my daughter. I started jumping up and down, "What do you mean you're not feeling well? You're dying, remember?" Six pairs of eyes turn to look at me, and I could see they think I am crazy. I started to mumble, "Well, she ... I thought ... well." Oh, what's the use!

The doctor continued talking to Haida, and then she walked over to me and told me Haida was fine. She was probably experiencing her first menstrual pains, and the fumes at the beauty salon had probably agitated her and made her ill. "Take her home, put her to bed and give her some hot tea. She'll be fine."

She then added, "And, by the way, this is a military hospital. We haven't see anyone under 80 years of age for ages." "Oh," I mumble, "Why didn't someone... I didn't know..." Oh, forget it, I thought. Let me out of here.

I walked out to the car. Haida walked behind with a young intern assisting her. He tucked her gently into the car, patting her arm sympathetically, purring reassurances. I can see the pity in his eyes! He walked over to my side of the car, and I can almost hear his thoughts: This crazy woman shouldn't be in charge of this delightful little girl! He tries to say something reassuring to me, but I just want to yell at him, "Get away from me, kid." How can I explain the trauma I just went through. I pulled away from the curb as calmly as possible.

Haida, as a teenager.

CONSTITUENCY WORK

In the 1970s, long before Lyle considered running federally, Lyle and I got the reputation of being do-gooders, of being able to help when all else failed. We got calls from senior citizens, immigrants and people on welfare who didn't know where to turn for help. One day I saw a young woman on the street, crying. On asking what the matter was, she said she was new in town, had no money, had two little children, and was out of food. She had just been turned down by the Welfare Office for a food voucher. I turned her around, marched back to the Welfare Office, asked to see the manager and went in with her. With a witness present, he gave her a food voucher.

I did many advocacy jobs. Later a Welfare Advocacy Committee was formed because there seemed to be no consistency in how this department treat different people. I did income taxes for senior citizens and new Canadians. I always went out of my way to help new Canadians, in memory of my parents who couldn't speak English and were treated like idiots.

Lyle worked on many people's behalf through his union, the IWA. The longest case we worked on involved a fellow worker at the sawmill, Bob Podevilnikoff. He was on his way to work one afternoon. He wasn't late, so he wasn't speeding. He was on a main thoroughfare, Gordon Road. It was shift change so there were vehicles on that street as well as on the side streets. His car was hit by Bob Allen, a reserve policeman and owner of the A & W, as Allen's car darted in from a side street. There were witnesses on three sides saying Allen did not stop at the stop sign before entering Gordon Road. Police viewed the situation, and then charged Podevilnikoff with dangerous driving.

Bob P. wanted to pay the ticket and forget it, but the fine was not the only expense involved. It also meant a considerable increase in his insurance rate. He was encouraged to fight the case. I filed a defense for him.

On the trial date, we arrived at the courthouse with witnesses. We were kept waiting for a couple of hours, and then told the case was dismissed. I asked why, and was told, "Because of lack of evidence." Everyone was furious. Bob and the witnesses had taken a day off work. We talked Bob into continuing the fight. He and Lyle went to see a prosecutor and demanded that Allen be charged with dangerous driving. After a lot of convincing, the prosecutor agreed to do it. A list of witnesses was left with him.

Again the trial date arrived, and we went to the courthouse. None of our witnesses were present. I ran to a public telephone, got Joe Diotte off the job at the plywood plant and asked if he had been contacted to appear in court as a witness. He said, "No." I begged him to get time off and appear as a witness, because no other witnesses were there. Joe arrived in his work clothes, covered in sawdust.

The prosecutor called Joe as a witness. A clear case was made. Judge Evans dismissed the case, saying it looked like a gang-up because everyone mentioned was a member of the same union. We were furious. This was not an unusual judgment for this judge who was a layman. When the NDP formed the government in 1972, I wrote a letter to the Attorney General outlining this case and asked that this judge's rulings be reviewed. He was in his eighties. They retired him.

By the time Lyle got elected, we were both seasoned workers in the field of advocacy. With the words "Member of Parliament" it became much easier and the results were quicker.

One night, around 2 am, Lyle returned to Nelson after travelling around his riding for a few days. He met a friend in Nelson and said, "Hi, how are things?" The guy replied, "No complaints." Lyle stopped dead in his tracks and said, "You must be the only one in the whole riding."

Lyle and Noel were in Ottawa from May onward. Noel's wife Hilary and their three children moved in with me in Nelson. Thus, with a built-in babysitter, I could work with Gerald in Lyle's office in Castlegar. It was most enjoyable. It was similar to what I had been doing for years: advocacy for people in need. People in business, and those with a good education, could always get help when they needed it, but ordinary people - the workers, the poor - seldom asked for help from anyone and too often were not given any when they did ask. We knew this and were determined to help these people first.

The first case I handled, a hunchbacked, wrinkled little old man arrived at our office on his bike. He sat dejected in a corner until I coaxed him into telling me his problem. He told me he was at his wits end. He didn't know where to turn. Everybody he approached told him there was nothing they could do for him. He didn't really think we could help, because it wasn't a federal matter.

His problem was this: he bought a piece of property in the outback (Pass Creek), miles off a secondary road, for the quiet and peace of mind. He was a refugee from Austria, who had lived through the war. His nerves were shot, and he looked it. He grew a garden, did some pottery and some painting. He had lived on this property for 3-4 years. Recently someone bought a piece of forestland next to his (about 30 acres), and set up a small sawmill next to his house, working only on weekends.

Now, every weekend he was faced with the most piercing, whining, buzzing noise, until his teeth rattled and his eyes felt like they would pop out. The picture he described was vivid, and I had no doubt this man was in a desperate state.

What to do! I knew I could dismiss him and say that if local government agencies couldn't help, there was probably nothing I could do. A few phone calls determined that was exactly the situation. There were no zoning laws or noise level laws in the area.

However, I didn't give up. I got the owner of the sawmill on the phone and informed him what he was doing to this man. He was very callous and said it was too bad but he bought the property for its lumber value, what was he to do? Give it up?

We went round and round. He knew his rights; he didn't care. But I kept at him, pointing out he had thirty acres, lots of room to relocate the sawmill. He wasn't buying that. I then described the condition of this pathetic old man, and suggested he might be moved to take desperate action if this agitation continued – to himself or to someone else. I asked if he might regret not doing something before that happened. Lo and behold, he agreed to move his sawmill. And he did.

Next election I ran into the old man, and with a toothless grin, he told me he would be voting for the first time in Canada, and would vote for Lyle.

During the first term in office, we worked like Trojans on behalf of our constituents. The staff was informed that nobody got turned away, regardless where the problem fell - provincial, municipal or federal jurisdiction, we tried to help.

A woman wrote to Ottawa complaining that her retaining wall in Trail was falling in and nobody would do anything. Lyle picked up the phone, talked to the only city alderman he knew, and within a month the wall was fixed.

A Nelson resident visited China, met and married a woman, and returned to Nelson. For six months he tried to get his wife's visa so she could join him. Finally he came to our office asking for help. One phone call found the Canadian Embassy was waiting for a medical certificate from her. When her husband contacted her, she said, "They keep telling me to get a Medical Certificate. So I did - twice." But she didn't take it in to the Embassy. Within a couple of weeks she was reunited with her husband.

Just before Christmas one year we got an urgent call from a woman in Genelle, saying she wanted to accompany her young grandson to Iran to spend Christmas with his father (her son). Could we speed up the visa? I took the documents to the Iranian Embassy personally, and returned for three days, waiting to be seen and explain. It was an intimidating feeling, sitting in the line-up, being glared at by officials, and during the interview being "interrogated". But I got it and the woman was able to go. She later identified herself and thanked me, saying, "You didn't even ask me how I voted."

But the most annoying incident involved a teacher in Fruitvale. I went to the office on a Monday morning to find a message on our machine: "I need to get my passport immediately as my wife's mother in Sweden is dying." He left a phone number. We called, and called. Gerald took the number home and called all evening. No response. Finally we wrote a letter telling him we could not reach him at that number. About a month later a letter appeared in the local paper saying this guy needed help getting a passport and our office couldn't help. He had to contact the defeated Tory M.P. to get help. We were furious!

During the 1988 election I met this bastard in the Fruitvale bar. I remembered the name and asked him what happened: why was there no answer at his phone; why the letter to the editor? He tried to avoid a discussion. Finally he said, "By Monday morning I was flying over Canada, heading for Sweden." I asked how could we have helped him? He admitted it was unreasonable.

Lyle and I spent our summers travelling to every part of the riding, sometimes camping. It was interesting, and we made it as enjoyable as possible.

One day we were in Burton, the hinterland of the riding. As usual, Lyle phoned his office, and Gerald told him he had just solved a problem for someone in that area, and would Lyle like to deliver the results in person. The guy lived on a remote back road, and we had difficulty finding him. But it was worth it. The look on his face when he saw Lyle at his door was priceless. Lyle told him the results Gerald gave him, and he just kept staring with open mouth. He had just called in his problem that morning.

When we got back to Nelson we would unload the problems collected along the way and, together with staff, try to solve them.

One day we arrived late at the office to find a note from Gerald: "Enough! Enough! I don't mind the thousands of little requests, but this is too much! How do you expect me to solve this problem?" We had left him a case about wild geese eating the alfalfa intended to be used as feed for a small farmer's cattle. The farmer wanted the federal government to compensate him for the loss of feed. We did find out that the government would have provided him with a permit to shoot the geese, or help him get a loud noisemaker to scare them. This would not do, but we could do no more.

The only other time Gerald complained was when a Doukhobour from Crescent Valley contacted the office and asked if Lyle would please come and shoot the beavers on his property because they were building dams and flooding his pastureland. Gerald asked him, "Can't you shoot them yourself?" "No," he replied. "I am a pacifist." Gerald then asked, "Don't you have some family in the area?" He replied, "Yes, I have a son." "Then can't you get him to shoot the beaver?" "No, I can't ask him to do that for me." "Well" Gerald said, "I can't ask your MP to fly here from Ottawa to shoot your beavers. Sorry."

Gerald went far beyond what most constituency staff would do. There was a request from Trout Lake, located in the uppermost part of the riding, asking for federal help building a wharf. Gerald searched for days, and found a department with money set aside for this purpose in remote areas.

After he got the financing for Trout Lake, we circulated this information amongst our MPs in case they had similar situations. Nobody applied. This department went back to Gerald and told him there was some more money available if he could use it. Gerald found several other places in the riding that needed wharves. We used up the entire budget.

We worked hard in Ottawa as well. I went to the office almost daily, as a volunteer. I concentrated on reading Kootenay West newspapers (two dailies, three weeklies) clipping what I thought Lyle needed to know. It would simply not be prudent for him to arrive in an area and not be aware that a sawmill got closed, or a school burned down. We also needed information for the Ottawa Report we prepared and sent out to every household in the riding, four times a year.

We were not so fortunate with our staff in Ottawa as in the constituency. Noel Duignan, who came with us from the riding, was Executive Assistant. He was a good political practitioner, but ill suited to the administration demands of an MP's office. Anne Jean-Baptiste, who was hired to be executive secretary, wanted Noel's job, which she had done before, and would not help Noel in his position.

Before I moved to Ottawa, Lyle came back from Ottawa saying he was drowning under the paper that arrived every day at the office. There was no way he could handle that amount of paper and do anything else. When the mail arrived every bit of it went to his desk for handling. There was some obviously useless material, but nothing was thrown away.

Later, with better staff and procedure, Lyle got to see very little mail. Most of the letters had an answer or solution already attached to them for him to approve or change. It was much easier.

When I arrived at the office, I saw what he meant. A stack of mail a foot high came in every day. I had a huge backlog of mail to go through. Simple letters asking for a copy of a certain bill sat on Lyle's desk waiting for him. It took a couple of weeks to get through the papers and assign letters to one of the staff to handle. The third person, Anne Burgess, part-time office worker, did most of the work. Anne Jean-Baptiste, or J.B. as she was called, would come in at 9:15, drop her purse and announce "Going for breakfast." She'd return an hour later and pick up the morning paper. Then it was time for a long lunch. Noel was not able to demand anything of her.

Nobody could get any work out of her. If I assigned a letter to her, she passed it to Anne Burgess. If I gave her a document to print, she did it, but wouldn't correct any spelling errors or make any changes; just copied as it was. We knew she was capable, but she would not put out.

Finally the day arrived when there was urgent work. Lyle and Noel left for the Maritimes for several days; Anne Burgess was on holidays, and I had to finish putting out the Ottawa Report - the last for the year with a deadline at the end of the week.

J.B. would not assist but put obstacles in my way. She was opposed to having a wife come into the office. I can't remember what she finally did that went too far. I phoned Lyle and we decided to fire her. I told her next morning not to bother coming to work until Lyle got back. My friend, Alma Said, who worked for NDP MP Arnold Peters for years, came in to help me.

Lyle and I then spent the next two months trying to fire J.B. She knew every trick in the book and used them all. In the end we had to re-hire her. Two months later she quit. It was most stressful.

Noel was not much better. He tried but there was so much he simply couldn't do: he couldn't type, he couldn't spell, and he didn't know office procedure or his way around the House of Commons. I did all I could to cover for him but there was no keeping up with the work.

Finally Lyle told Noel he couldn't carry him any longer. Lyle offered to help him get another job or move him back to Trail. Noel got a job with another MP in his constituency office in Ontario. A few years later he was elected an MPP in Ontario.

During all of this time, the constituency office and staff had to take up the slack. They did, but it was tough and unfair. We found ways of rewarding them accordingly.

Lyle was flying back to the riding 2 or 3 times a month. He would take a flight out of Ottawa Friday evening, arriving in Vancouver at 9, stay overnight, and fly to the riding Saturday morning. He would put in two full days of meetings, speaking engagements, and socializing in the riding. Late Sunday afternoon he flew back to Vancouver, and then to Ottawa via Toronto, on the 'red-eye' midnight flight. He would arrive in Ottawa about 7:30 a.m. Monday and sometimes go directly to the office.

One weekend afternoon, while on the platform of a Nelson university public meeting, his whole body started shaking and he felt faint. He had logged over 60 hours in the air in a two week period. He stayed put for a month and started slowing down.

HOBNOBBING WITH THE ELITE!

We had dinner with Queen Beatrix of Denmark, attended Queen Elizabeth`s reception on the Royal Yacht Britannia, met the king and queen of Spain. But for all that, I think my most humbling experience was at the Italian Embassy in Ottawa.

We were invited to the Italian Embassy in 1983, shortly after we attended an Italian Film Festival in Ottawa featuring actress Gina Lolabrigida in person, which thrilled Lyle immensely.

It was a bitterly cold night when we drove to Aylmer to the Ambassador's home. Lyle let me out at the door, and drove off to park the car. As I entered and started up the front staircase, a beautiful woman appeared at the top of the stairs, in the most colourful, fluttering dress. I stopped, turned; wanting to go back to the car and home. I remembered Lyle had driven off. My escape route was blocked. Reduced to being Vera Sharko from Coolidge, I continued up the stairs to shake hands with the ambassador's wife.

Actually, it was an enjoyable evening. There were several hostesses, and nobody was left sitting by themselves. People were introduced and included in conversations. We went downstairs to dinner. I was seated by a senator and across the table from Jeanne Sauve, the then Speaker of the House of Commons (later to be the first woman Governor General).

This was a time when the Liberals were trying to get a bill through the House of Commons called The National Energy Program, and the Conservatives were determined to stop it. The Tories walked out of the House before the vote was called, and refused to go back. This forced the House to continue ringing the bells, calling the MPs to vote, for weeks. It was deafening, especially in offices like ours that had bells just outside their doors. Procedure was changed after that.

Sauve kept asking me what people in our riding were saying, how we assessed the situation as to who was losing support over it. I said it was my opinion that the Tories were not winning any kudos with their shenanigans, and Ms. Sauve thought so too.

When Lyle and I attended a NATO conference in Copenhagen, Denmark, we attended a dinner with Queen Beatrix. In the receiving line the Queen shook hands with everyone. We were advised not to bow or curtsy and not to say anything. Everybody just smiled a lot. Her husband stood slightly behind her, and did not shake hands. This was quite different from procedure with Queen Elizabeth.

Lyle shaking hands with Queen Beatrix of Denmark.

During the opening of Expo in Vancouver, Lyle and I were invited to meet Queen Elizabeth at an evening reception aboard the royal yacht Brittania. Walking through a long, roped-off area, where thousands of people lined up for a glimpse of the Queen and other dignitaries, I remembered how often I stood on the other side of the rope.

Standing just behind Chunky Woodward (owner of Woodwards) and his wife, I kept gawking at Mrs. Woodward's fur coat: it was an ankle-length, grey-black, probably wolf, so thick it rippled gracefully. I blurted out, "That's the most beautiful coat I ever saw." Then added, "But I could never wear it in Kootenay West with all the environmentalists there." Dave Barrett, standing just behind us, burst out laughing. He agreed, I probably couldn't.

As we moved along in the line, uniformed guards stepped up, five times, to inform us of protocol: the man goes first and bows, the wife follows and curtsies. We were allowed to say a few words.

I was a little concerned because I read the story in Margaret Trudeau's book, *"Beyond Reason"* about her first meeting with Queen Elizabeth, whom she wanted to impress. She said, "I went down into a deep curtsy, and then realized I went too far and couldn't stand back up. The Queen, realizing my dilemma, gave my hand a little tug, and helped me back up." I did not go into a deep curtsy.

The Queen was wearing flat shoes, no make-up, and looked about five feet tall. Prince Philip wasn't tall either. She had arrived early that morning, attended to some functions, flew to Prince George for an event, had dinner with about one hundred people, and at 10 p.m. was welcoming another couple hundred. Oh, well, that was her job. We enjoyed roaming around the Royal Yacht, looking at trinkets.

Being elected meant a lot of special privileges. In the riding, many restaurants wouldn't let us pay for meals. It got embarrassing. It was easy to get the feeling of being very special. Wherever we went, into a small store, a new establishment, or attending anniversary parties, the owners and participants treated us like royalty, thanking us for coming. One day Lyle and I went for a swim at Nelson's aquatic centre. I went in first, and when Lyle came out of the change room, I heard two teenage girls go, "Aaah. Look, there's Lyle Kristiansen." I rolled my eyes.

DENMARK AND OTHER PLACES

During a 1983 NATO meeting in Denmark, we arranged to have Haida and Colin (Eric refused to go) to fly to Lahr, Germany, on the military flight. Actually, Colin had not wanted to go either, as he was dating Paula Copeland, the daughter of the family that started Mitel. He had just spent a weekend with the family at their "river home", which was different from the "summer cottage". He was learning to windsurf and didn't want to leave. However, Haida persuaded him to follow his parents' orders, and he came back to Ottawa, just in time to catch the plane.

After landing, they had to spend a night in Lahr. We were sure everybody spoke English because the Canadian army was based there. However, they didn't, so the kids went out to find an English-German dictionary. It took quite a while for them to realize that "Deutsche" meant "German" and not "Dutch". The next morning they had to get up at 5 a.m., and walk to the railway station. En route to Copenhagen they changed trains twice.

As I stood waiting for them in the Copenhagen railway station, I realized we hadn't made any contingency plan in case they missed a train. We had moved out of the hotel to a cheaper one once the conference was over, and thus nobody knew where we were staying.

If they missed even one connection, they would have been lost somewhere in Europe for days. I could hardly breathe until the train arrived and they got off safe and sound.

All together again in Copenhagen, we toured the city and its waterfront, saw H. C. Anderson's Little Mermaid, and spent hours at the famous Tivoli Gardens amusement park. Before leaving Copenhagen, we rented a car that had a tent attached to the top. The tent dropped to the side of the car and we entered it through the car doors. Most convenient.

We drove west across Sealand, to Esbjeg, where we visited the Frichs, Danish friends who had lived in Vancouver for several years. Spending a few days with the Frichs, we cooked and ate eel, the kids went swimming in the North Sea, and we all attended a Mid Summer Festival witch-burning ceremony (to scare away witches coming over from Britain) with dozens of huge bonfires of driftwood along the beach.

While I remained in Esbjerg, Lyle and the children drove to Lemvig, where Lyle's father lived as a child and teenager. For an address all they had was one word that turned out to be the name of the old house he had lived. They stopped at a downtown store to ask for help and were given an explanation and directions. In thanks, Lyle left a Canadian desk flag with the storekeeper, who set it on the counter.

Shortly after they left, an old lady (in her 80s) pulled up on her bicycle. Entering the store, she asked about the flag, and was told that people from Canada were looking for her house. Amazed, she hurried home, just in time to catch Lyle and the kids.

They stayed for tea and a long conversation in a combination of English, Danish, a little German and French, with some sign language thrown in. Turned out, she was the same age as Lyle's father, and remembered him. She even remembered the day Dad lost his eye chopping wood.

Re-united in Esbjerg, we then headed for Belgium to attend an anniversary of the battle of Waterloo. There were so many small roads, we simply chanced upon arriving at the right town.

The next morning we arrived in time for the re-enactment of the battle of Waterloo. We saw the fields, farm homes, barns, and hills, described in the books we read. We walked the whole scene, picturing where the British were; where Napoleon stood, in pain, watching the battle; where the Prussian army entered the war arena. We watched horses feeding in the field where the French cavalry charges broke upon the British squares, and wondered if they knew that 12,000 horses were buried beneath them.

It was a moving experience. After that we headed for Paris. We parked the car in a campsite and took the bus downtown. When we neared it we cried, "Look, children, there's the Eiffel Tower!" They both looked, and calmly said, "That's nice." We could not transfer our excitement to them. They trudged through all the museums with us. The only excitement shown was when we went shopping.

The last day, Lyle was left to pack up the tent and car, while the children and I took the bus to see the Louvre Art Museum one more time. As luck would have it, it was closed that day. As we walked across the courtyard, we were besieged by a group of eight motley young girls that looked like they hadn't eaten in days, in rags, hair uncombed. They spoke French, so we couldn't understand what they were saying. Finally Haida said, "I think they are saying their mother died and they want us to give them some money." I said OK, and dug all the change out of my purse, which was slung over my head and shoulder. Haida gave whatever money she had.

They then seemed to rush at me, pressing a piece of cardboard against my chest, all speaking very loudly. I couldn't understand what they were saying or doing. Finally Haida hit the cardboard out of their hands, and found a hand in my purse. Haida was so mad she grabbed the money back that she had given them. We were so upset. They just smiled, shrugged their shoulders and walked away. It felt like a re-enactment of Fagan and the orphans in the play "Oliver". The girls seemed in training to be thieves and this practice just wasn't successful.

In the meantime, Lyle packed the car and headed out to meet us. The traffic was heavy, and he had difficulty getting on the right street. Finally he thought he found it, completely empty. As he headed along the wide street, he suddenly saw five lines of cars coming straight at him. Oh-oh: he was on a one-way street, going the wrong way. A quick U-turn and he headed into a tunnel, ending up on the wrong side of the river Seine.   Three tries later, he finally picked us up, an hour late.

We had to go past the circle of traffic at the Opera House, with about eight lines of traffic, cars pulling in and leaving the circle at top speed. Lyle had been told the trick to driving in Paris was never to make eye contact with other drivers. Just push forward. Oh, he did that, all right. But at one point he made more than eye contact. His bumper connected, losing a piece of it. He and the other driver kind of looked at the situation, neither being able to open his door the traffic was so tight, shrugged their shoulders, and moved on.

It was so good to get out of Paris. We visited Versailles, toured the palace, and walked the gardens and woods. I had been here as a young woman. We then headed for England, leaving the car at Calais, before catching the Hovercraft ferry to Dover.

When we got to London the children complained about all the museums they had to tour, so we offered to do whatever they wanted. They wanted to look at postcards. We withdrew the offer.

We walked to the London Bridge, Tower of London, and Buckingham Palace. The children went to see a sound and light show with the Beatles. That made their whole trip worthwhile. Later they were happy they had gone and Eric wished he had.

CPR'S ROGERS PASS TUNNEL

The most posh occasion we attended had to be the opening of the CPR's new Rogers Pass tunnel between Golden and Revelstoke. We were given a room in the Lake Louise Inn.

The evening started with hors d'eouvres of the most

fancy seafood imaginable. There were heaping platters of smoked salmon, arctic char, piles of shrimp on ice. When dinner was announced I looked around and saw that the 200 people milling around had hardly put a dent in this food. I didn't want to leave; my favourite food was right there!

Dinner was ever so fancy. Vegetables were all cut to represent different railroad symbols. There must have been eight courses, topped off with a chocolate railway stationhouse to take home. We sat with eight others, mainly from the company. One guy sitting next to me was determined to talk politics.

The conversation turned to whether women should stay at home after they have children. I asked, "Should women get an education?" Yes. "Should they have a career?" Yes. "Then how can they keep their career if they have to stay at home for 20 years? Isn't it a waste of education?" He didn't know. I suggested perhaps men and women should take turns staying home with the children. He said, "You mean, I should stay home for a year while my wife works?" He said this with such incredulity in his voice. He then asked his friend what he thought of the idea. The friend replied, "You mean, I give up my $100,000 job so my wife can work as a secretary to keep her occupation?" I agreed it was a stupid idea.

I thought about the difference between his wife's life and mine. We could hardly afford a babysitter. With $100,000 one could hire a nurse, a nanny, a tutor. There was no comparison. We lived in entirely different worlds. How could we discuss anything when our worlds were so different?

The next day we rode the train through the tunnel. Every half-hour someone would walk in and hand out gifts: CPR hats, books, key chains, a commemorative plate. And we got to see the tunnel.

TRAVEL ARRANGEMENTS

When travelling overseas, there is a special booth at the customs counter for 'diplomats'. No waiting in line-ups. And even nicer, on diplomatic trips, a civil servant took care of luggage, assigned hotel room numbers, paid all bills.

After one such trip, Lyle and I left the official group and stayed in Paris for a few days. We had to make all our own arrangements and felt a heavy burden descend upon us.

During our first term in office, MPs' wives and family travelled free by train only. Until 1969, MPs, too, could only travel by train - families not at all. Someone representing Kootenay West had to travel 4 or 5 days to get home. Now MPs were younger with young children. Changes provided some fairness to Members who lived 3,000 miles away. We appreciated being able to travel home, even by train. Then someone told us there was a military flight going west which we could take at Christmas. We were overjoyed. It was faster.

The first Christmas we were booked on a military flight, the regular plane was grounded, and we were transferred to a "Hercules"; a plane that was used to deliver tanks and trucks to remote areas. The whole back end of the plane would open to load and unload. The temperature was very high while in flight, but plunged to below zero when we stopped and the doors opened. We sat sideways in canvass mesh seats, lighting was so bad you couldn't read, the noise so loud you couldn't talk. Lunches were served by passing cardboard boxes up and down the aisle.

By the time we reached Edmonton Haida said, "Let's get out and walk, mother." It took us 11 hours to reach Vancouver. It was most uncomfortable.

Whenever possible we took the regular military flight. We were treated as dignitaries. After the plane was loaded, an officer escorted us to the foot of the plane and saluted until we embarked. We were always seated at the front of the plane. To disembark, an officer would stop all other passengers until we were off the plane. A uniformed person would meet us at the foot of the plane, salute, and escorted us to a waiting room.

One day when we were embarking, Eric walked ahead of us. When he got to the foot of the plane, a military man walked up to him and berated him severely for wearing jeans, "even if you are on leave." Very sheepishly Eric informed him he was an MP's son. Well, were they embarrassed! There were apologies: then, and at the next stop, and the next.

Quite often I had to fly with the children alone, Lyle coming on a regular flight. Once we stopped at Trenton and were informed that the Prime Minister needed our plane. They would get another one for us as soon as possible. That was 8 hours later.

The children and I were immediately taken to the officers' lounge, fed, watered, and even taken for a tour of the city by a padre in the army. He was an older man, a Liberal he informed me immediately after asking what party we represented. He then laughingly told me about the first time he encountered one of 'your' people, back in the 1930s, in Nanaimo, at a public meeting. All candidates were asked if they would give the Chinese the vote. Only the CCF candidate said, "Yes". He said "And he lost every possible vote." I replied, "And after all that has happened, are you telling me you still don't admire the fact that the candidate did the right thing? Are you still giggling about it?" He changed the subject.

When we got back from our tour, we walked through the public waiting room. It was like a torture chamber: children were crying, the noise was deafening, it was stifling hot and dusty. We were so grateful for the officers' lounge. In 1990, under the Conservatives, even our children could fly first class.

We were invited to many embassy functions. We could attend such parties three or four times a week. All we had to do was choose which ones we wanted.

We were invited to the Soviet Union ambassador's home for dinner with about 15 other people. I sat next to the ambassador from Switzerland, who was practising his recently-learned Russian. I said I could speak some Russian, so we exchanged some comments. Finally he said, "I think you speak Russian with an Alberta accent."

At one such party we met Anna Amaluk, high commissioner from Uganda. She was a big woman with a hearty laugh. We met for lunch once a week and discussed world politics. She was informed and interested in everything. At one such luncheon, she asked me, "Why are Canadians so stupid as to keep electing millionaires?" She went on to tell me about her first experience with "democracy".

Her parents lived in a rural area. After Idi Amin was ousted, and the first elections held, an American-educated Ugandan announced he would run in their area. He made it known he knew exactly how to win elections. He held meetings in every village in the area. At each such meeting he had a calf butchered and barbecued, and provided food and drinks for everyone. "Now, remember," she said. "This is an area where people eat meat once a month, partly because of shortage, partly because of lack of refrigeration." Everybody, from grandparents to kids, attended; ate, drank, and listened to him. But nobody was fooled.

She said, they would turn to each other and ask, "Do you think we would be welcomed in his home?" The man got less than 15% of the vote. "Your people are so educated, have so much information from newspapers and T.V. How is it they can be bribed so easily?" I had no answer.

I remained friends with Anna for years. We enjoyed dinner at her house, meeting her children and sisters. They came to our house. Idi Amin had killed her husband, and she was left with three little children to bring up. The new government gave her a diplomatic post. She was the first woman from that rural area to get an education. Haida visited her sisters and father in 1991.

Shortly after Lyle was defeated in 1984, Anna was transferred to Belgium. When we got back to Ottawa, I wrote her, and was informed she had died from cancer. Her three children were sent back to Uganda to live with a sister, whose husband was a Member of Parliament from the rural area Anna grew up in. We met them during our visit to Africa.

During the second term, we were not invited to the G.G.s once and seldom went to embassy parties. Generally, it was not as exciting as the first term.

While most people respect whoever wins, regardless of party, the Conservative element in Nelson was always trying to belittle us. One July 1st parade Bob Brisco, who was just the Conservative candidate, was at the front of the parade, where elected people are usually placed. Lyle and Lorne Nicolson, MLA, were third from the last car. Members of the Chamber of Commerce felt no embarrassment at abusing their power this way. What they didn't know was that it did not go unnoticed by many people, and we were to benefit from it.

FOUR YEARS OFF FOR GOOD BEHAVIOUR

We faced our first re-election in 1984. It was an easy election, as Lyle had made a good impression. Everybody admitted he had worked hard and got results for his constituents. We had lots of volunteers, loads of money, and Lyle and I were received very warmly throughout the riding. But there was a swing to the Conservatives across the western provinces and a real desire to get rid of the Liberals who had been in power for so long.

Lyle got 3,000 votes more than when he won. However, the Liberal vote collapsed, Conservatives taking the majority. For the sake of 700 votes, we were faced with moving back to Nelson. For the next four years Lyle went around saying he got four years off for good behaviour.

By now, Eric was enrolled at Simon Fraser University. Haida would be in grade 12. But Colin didn't want to leave Ottawa. He said we ruined his life when moving to Ottawa, as he expected to be recruited by the Crazy Canucks national ski team and compete at world competitions.

Now, he wanted one full season of playing on his high school football team. There would be no football in B.C. We agreed to stay in Ottawa until the Christmas break. We travelled the Maritime provinces for 10 days. And we had all the time in the world to attend Colin's football games.

At one game the other star player wasn't there, so Colin had to play both offence and defence. When he came off the field after the game, I was shocked. "Colin," I screamed. "You look like you're coming home from a war. Shirt torn. Mud and sweat on your hair and face, blood on your clothes." "Oh, don't worry, Mom," he said. "This isn't all my blood. See this and this? That's not my blood. That's somebody else's." Well, that was good to know!

When the season was over, Colin finished half a term of Grade 10, and we put him on the plane for Vancouver. The movers came for our furniture and canoe. It cost over $10,000 to move us back to Nelson. That was an expensive defeat for the government because they then had to move Brisco to Ottawa. We packed our plants into the back of our station wagon and headed home.

It was warm when we left Ottawa, and we enjoyed travelling the northern route. We stopped for the night at Sudbury. During the night the weather turned cold, and sleet covered our car with a sheet of ice. In the morning we couldn't get into our car. Lyle pulled the handle right off his door. When we finally got in, we found the plants all died.

The highway was closed for a few hours. When it opened we headed out again, not stopping when night moved in, thinking we could travel late into the night like we did driving to Ottawa. Near the Manitoba border we hit black ice, spun around a couple of times and slid into the ditch. We stopped for the night in the next town we came to.

After Winnipeg the new snow started to blow. It blew so hard we could not see the highway. A large truck passed us, and we moved into its wake, just in the whirlwind. We drove that way across Manitoba and into Saskatchewan.

As we neared Alberta, the radio reported warnings that a major storm was moving down from the north, closing the highway in its wake. We had to push it before the roads closed. We stopped for a day in Nelson, unloaded some things, loaded others, picked up Haida and drove to Vancouver for Christmas.

We had sold the townhouse in Nepean with a $40,000 profit, taking a personal mortgage from the buyer. We lived on these mortgage payments for the next 4 years. After all the years we paid interest on our loans, it was nice to receive some back.

My garden provided us with vegetables all year round. Lyle offered to provide the meat by killing a deer. He wasn't exactly sure he could do it, because of his childhood fascination with Bambi, but he was going to try. His friend, Maurice Eggie, and he went hunting many times, but the opportunity never presented itself. I think Lyle was happy it didn't.

During this time, Gerald Rotering, our former assistant, was elected mayor of Nelson. This might have been bleak times for Nelson. The three main industries closed - Kootenay Forest Products sawmill, Kootenay Plywood, and David Thompson University. This meant hundreds of families were left without a good income, and many moved to other places.

Fortunately, Gerald was a full-time mayor, and attacked the situation with all his energy and perseverance. He said, "All I wanted for Nelson was complete equality in terms of profile. I wanted Nelson to be known on par with Vancouver, Toronto and Montreal." Years later, Eric asked me how come when I tell people I grew up in Nelson, everyone knows where it is and has a very high regard for it. Gerald nearly achieved his objective.

His first promotional effort was with CKNW, where Rafe Mair, former Socred cabinet minister, was a talk show host. They knew each other from Gerald's news reporting days. Gerald had nearly a full hour on this syndicated program, which was heard on many stations throughout B.C.

Shortly after he won the mayoralty, Gerald was the

lead speaker, interviewed by Peter Mansbridge, on CBC TV's first "National Town Hall Forum". He appeared on Peter Gzowsky's show with volunteers starting up the Nelson University Centre. He made national news by appearing at a hearing in Spokane by the U.S. Energy Department regarding the Hanford nuclear compound (which he was very familiar with through Lyle's office).

Gerald went to Victoria and met every cabinet minister he could tackle. He was not able to get an appointment with the Premier.

When Lorne Nicolson, MLA for Nelson-Creston, was unable to attend, Gerald used his ticket to the opening ceremonies of the Skytrain, and got into the VIP area. As Premier Bill Bennett and Deputy Premier Grace McCarthy left the podium to board the first car, he fell in behind them. He looked back and heard Vancouver mayor, Mike Harcourt, call to him, as Mike was not able to get in that car. The train pulled away, and after five minutes of everyone aboard complimenting the Skytrain, he introduced himself to the province's premier and deputy, and told them about the situation in Nelson. He said that Nelson wanted to work with the Province to rebuild its economy.

Nelson stopped paving roads and laying sidewalks. Instead, they concentrated on economic development initiatives to create employment. It worked. After determining that it was not possible to establish a university or satellite, Nelson bought the David Thompson University buildings from the province for $1.00. Gerald twinned Nelson with a Japanese sister city, Shuzenji-cho, which led to many homestay exchanges. This also laid the foundation for bringing in the Canadian International College to these buildings. CIC brought up to 700 students per year to

Nelson, employed 70 locals full time and ran for 10 years. When the Japanese economy slowed down, the project ended.

Gerald encouraged all downtown restaurants to apply for permission to put tables and chairs out on sidewalks. Con Diamond from the Main Street Diner was the only one interested. The Council responded by setting out by-laws on how this could be done. Soon after, every restaurant wanted tables and chairs outside. Nelson may now be the sidewalk-dining- capital of B.C. Even a pub has a licensed terrace.

About this time, the Capital Theatre project was completed and performances began.

Before Lyle was defeated, he and Gerald arranged funding for the first stage of restoration of Streetcar 23, which still toodles along the waterfront (although they wanted it on Baker St.)

Nelson, together with provincial and federal monies, built a tidal-quality city wharf to accommodate pleasure craft and tour boats. In the face of much opposition, Gerald arranged for re-zoning waterfront land and funding a pathway construction around the site to facilitate a lakeside hotel - the Prestige Inn was built there.

In the end, Nelson's population did not drop, and it continues to be a vibrant and thriving city. Without the full-time effort from Gerald, and his ability to get information and put it to good use, this may well have been a very different situation.

Colin enrolled at the high school. While he failed French in Ottawa, in Nelson he was at the top of his class. He didn't like being back. He said the kids' main entertainment was bullying someone. He befriended one boy who was the victim of such harassment, and helped him with homework, assignments, and studying. The kid went from failing to passing with honours.

Haida played on the basketball team, but was not happy with the coach or with the other players. Colin also played basketball and didn't like his coach. He took up wrestling. WRESTLING! Now we had lots of time to attend games, and he picks wrestling!

We drove his team to Vancouver to a tournament. While there his coach told me Colin's nickname was "Slime". I was amazed: "Slime? What kind of a nickname is that? And how can you tell a mother such a thing?" Suddenly the coach realized how it sounded. "Oh, you don't understand," he said. "That's a very good nickname for a wrestler. Just watch and you'll see what I mean."

Within minutes the referee stopped Colin's bout and had someone wipe him down with a towel. His opponent complained Colin was so slick he could not grab hold of him. The bout had to be stopped several times for Colin to be wiped down.

Another of Colin's nicknames was Colin "Podborski" Kristiansen when he was a skier because he fit the description of a Crazy Canuck. He knew no fear. Bruce Cargill told me he and Eric watched Colin bash the moguls under the chair lift at Whitewater, and said to each other, "He's a better skier than we are." But agreed never to tell him.

At UBC (he was in engineering) he was referred to in a newspaper as the "Aryan Barbarian" and "Steroid Monster". I always called him "Punkin".

Colin was good at wrestling. He was always in Eric's shadow in basketball, being 5'10", while Eric was 6'5". He didn't have the height but he sure had the strength. Simon Fraser U scouted him at the wrestling tournament and hounded him for months to enrol at that university and be on their wrestling team. He went to UBC.

Haida worked hard in her last year in high school. In Ottawa she had received the award for Best All Round Student two years running. This had never happened before in that school. She was always volunteering for extra curricular activities. Haida lived at home and attended Selkirk College in Castlegar. She found college much more to her liking because she was treated like an adult.

Colin had two more years of high school in Nelson. He was not happy. The first summer he talked us into letting him go back to Ottawa. He said he wanted to see his friends once more. He was going to stay with a friend whose father was a doctor. I phoned and confirmed it was fine with them.

Two weeks after he left there was no word from him. I phoned that family and the mother told me Colin had moved out and was living with a group of guys near our old home. I was annoyed that she let him move without informing us. I got him at his new place, and everything seemed fine. Years later, he told us this frightening story.

Colin got a job flagging with a road construction crew. He came home late one afternoon, tired and hungry, and started to make his dinner. There was a knock at the door, and when he answered, there was a great, big biker-type guy standing there. He had chains on his belt and a kerchief round his head. He asked for Kevin, and Colin pointed him to the back of the house, and went on with his dinner.

Suddenly he looked up and this guy was back with a gun in his hand, saying, "Sit down." Panicking a little,

he sat down, thinking, "This is it! I'm a dead man."
The guy said, "I'm police. This is a drug raid." Colin
said, "Oh, thank god" and started back to the stove.
The guy said, "Sit down. You live here. You are
involved too." Colin said he was hungry and could he
please eat his dinner. No. He said. "Can I at least
turn it off before it burns?" He could do that.

Their house was surrounded with police, roped off,
and all the neighbours were standing around watching
as they were led to the police car.

At the police station with the other guys, he was
fingerprinted, and stuck in a cell. Around 3:00 in the
morning, after they searched the rooms and found his
room clean of drugs, he was allowed to go home. One
would think police would notify parents.

During his last year in high school, he dated a lot of
girls. One Saturday he was invited to a girl's house
to a party, her parents being out of town. Before he
left, he said, "I wonder if she knows what to expect."
He had lots of experience holding parties, inviting a
few people, and having a hundred show up.

This was no different: A hundred kids showed up. One
drunken kid kept punching Colin, trying to pick a fight.
Other kids were urging Colin to hit back, but he
wouldn't because it would have wrecked the house.
He took several punches from the kid, and slowly got
him out of the house. He started to refuse entry to
other people arriving, and slowly they cleared the
house. The next day he went back and helped the girl
clean up.

Apparently there were many such parties at our house
in Ottawa. Every time we went away we made the
children promise not to let anyone know we were out
of town. Oh, yes, they promised. They crossed their
hearts! I would give Eric money for pizzas and other

treats. We were to find out later the parties started before we got to the airport. The money was used to buy the booze.

First time, we came home to a very clean the house. It was dusted, vacuumed, kitchen cleaned. I said, "What happened? How come everything's so clean?" The reply came, "We thought you would like to come home to a clean house."

One day I was poking around the potted plants and found a beer cap: "Aha! You had a party!" "Oh, no. My friend brought a beer over. That's all." It took many such occasions before I realized THEY WERE LYING TO ME! When Lyle and I attended a sports award ceremony, we heard a coach conclude the event with, "And now, I hear the Kristiansens are out of town, so everyone knows where the party will be tonight." Oh, Really? Even the coaches knew?

One Friday Lyle and I were scheduled to take the plane back to the riding to attend something very important, when I got a phone call at the office from Colin. "Mom, I got into a fight in school and my nose is broken." What to do. Lyle said I absolutely had to go to the riding with him.

I drove home, took Colin to the hospital, left instructions with the doctor, and headed home again. As I was driving a police car pulled me over. He asked, "Do you know how fast you were driving?" I shook my head. "Do you know the speed limit here?" I shook my head. "Didn't you see me at the curb?" I shook my head. I then burst into tears, and told him to do whatever he had to do, but do it quickly because... and I poured out my troubles to him. He grimaced and told me to get along home. However, the next time I tried that, it didn't work.

My other bout with the law was not so pleasant. Eric got his license at 16 and loved driving. One night when Lyle was in the riding, Eric called out to me that he was driving his girlfriend home. Around 3 am, the phone rang. It was a policeman from Ottawa telling me Eric was picked up for drunk driving. Apparently after dropping her off, he decided to go for a further ride. He'd had a few beers, and could not be considered drunk – but the breathalizer said he was over the limit.

I took a cab downtown and the cop sat me down for a minute. He told me he had Eric in a cell. He didn't have to do it but thought it might scare him enough that he would never want to get picked up again. He said Eric resisted going into the cell, holding back and asking over and over if he had to.

When they brought Eric out I thought he was going to burst into tears. He looked so downhearted I couldn't even yell at him. The policeman drove us back to the car.

All the way home he kept saying, "What will Dad say?" When Lyle got home, Eric, head hung low, told him about the incident. "That was pretty dumb," Lyle said. "But it's your tough luck. All it means to me is less competition for the car. It's you that will have to pay the price." Well, that upset Eric more than being yelled at. He lost his license for two years automatically. He does not drink and drive to this day - I think - but what do I know!

Haida had no bouts with the law.

NELSON'S CAPITOL THEATRE

During the years 1984-88, we spent our time involved in the community, working at enjoyable projects. Lyle was involved in theatre and politics. He acted in 3 plays. First was a local musical: "I Always Wanted to Ride a Streetcar". In the second play, "Arsenic and Old Lace", he played an Irish cop. The third was called "Cinder Fella", two roles with no speaking parts: an Egyptian eunuch and a hockey player.

As an MP Lyle had played a part in reviving and preserving an old opera house in Nelson. The federal government provided money (some $300,000 to $500,000 annually per riding) for work projects to municipalities or community groups who applied for whatever they thought was needed in their locale. Members of Parliament considered and recommended to the government which projects should be funded and to what degree. His first year in office, Lyle and Gerald worked hard to see that the money was distributed fairly to eligible applicants throughout the riding. Dissatisfied with the worth and long term impacts of this method, Lyle and Gerald decided that, in the second and future years, they would insure that there were at least two significant applications of lasting socio-economic value to the area, with the balance to be disbursed amongst applications.

One interesting possibility of significance, was a proposal for the restoration of Nelson's turn-of-the-century opera house – come vaudeville theatre – come movie house, which more recently served as a downtown warehouse or simply stood vacant. People had talked about it for years, but did nothing.

So, Lyle and Gerald, quietly dangling the prospect of funding, found some local people to form a society, flesh out the idea, and develop an initial and substantial application for restoration. The idea was to sink enough into the project that it would have to be completed. And it worked!

As each year passed the theatre started to take shape, and the beauty of it showed through. Even most of the nay-sayers became boosters, albeit some of them grudgingly. As it progressed, other government programs, and later the province of B.C., came through with more money. By the time Lyle was defeated in 1984, the project had progressed so far, there was no turning back. The business community started to support it, the community rallied around it, and much of the work was proceeding with voluntary help. There was debate about its viability, but by then over a million dollars was spent. It was obvious it could be a valuable asset to the city.

When it was finished, it was beautiful! The seats (there were over 400) were beautifully refurbished. Original décor and paintings were restored. The stage was a masterpiece. But it was the acoustics that made the theatre. Microphones were not needed. You could hear the players to the back of the hall. An expert from the coast said the acoustics were, along with Vancouver's restored Orpheum Theatre, the best in B.C.

When the formal opening took place, we attended with great pride because of the part we played. However, by then it was our Conservative MP Bob Brisco, who took the bows. But we got even; after he lost to us again, Lyle presided over the opening of the new RCMP building for which Bob had worked so hard to get funded and completed. Gerald Rotering, as mayor of Nelson, in his speech, remembered the part Lyle played in the Capitol Theatre rebuilding.

KOOTENAY COUNTRY CO-OP

During this time I was involved in other things. I learned to do ceramics, and then entered a partnership in a ceramic shop, making greenware, selling it, and selling the finished product. It was not profitable, but it was enjoyable.

I was also on the Library Board. Of course, one goes on this board because of one's interest in reading. But, on the Board, all we ever did was talk about the building that housed our library, how to improve it, and how to get the rural areas to share in the costs.

Nelson had some 9,000 people within its city limits and another 9,000 in the surrounding areas. Many people buy homes outside city limits because the taxes are lower. These people use the civic centre for hockey for their children, the library, and other facilities paid for by Nelson residents.

They would demand Nelson's fire department respond to fires in their area. When they were billed for the cost, it was a matter of "sue me". When the firemen stopped responding to calls, Nelson was called selfish and unfeeling. When a referendum was placed before the North shore residence to share in the cost of the fire department, it was voted down.

It was the same with the Library. Every referendum placed before them to make it a regional library was voted down. Although some residents worked very hard to pass the referendum, they were always in the minority. We hated placing a higher fee for outside residents because it discouraged reading. That was the last thing we wanted to do, but we had to. So - the Library Board was a very unsatisfactory involvement for me.

My most satisfying community involvement was working with the food co-op. I had first helped set this co-op up in 1973, when it was just a bulk-buying club. It was all voluntary and no profits were involved. It then moved to Blewett, and later to South Slocan.

When we moved back to Nelson in 1984, the only natural food store in town was closing. The co-op, which was still located in South Slocan, was also considering closing its operation, or moving back to Nelson and taking over the building and stock of the natural food store. They decided on the latter. I renewed my membership and volunteered to work.

When the annual meeting came up, I got on the Board of Directors, and at their first meeting, I was named secretary. Harry Berlow was president. We met in people's homes, and business was conducted very haphazardly: no agenda, no motions, and no votes taken. At 10 o'clock everybody went home.

Three members and the bookkeeper that had been running the co-op in South Slocan, continued to run it. New members were not given any explanation of what was being discussed. The few times I spoke I felt nobody was listening. A young woman from Fruitvale travelled 40 km. on her bike to attend, spending the night at the local campgrounds. She never participated in discussions. She stopped coming, as did others. In fact, the general complaint was that, although people ran for Board positions, most of them would quit before their year was up.

We hired a part time manager who was supposed to use volunteer members to do some of the work. If a member worked two hours a month, he/she was allowed 10% discount on purchases. If a member was in town and had nothing to do for an hour, he would drop in to the co-op and ask to be put to work. The manager had to drop whatever he was doing, find a job for the volunteer, and then teach him how to do it. This was time consuming and inefficient.

I suggested we phone all members and ask them to undertake a specific time each month to do a specific job. That way the manager knew who was coming in and that member was familiar with what he was doing. I offered to do this, although I was already putting in my two hours by doing Board work. I cut and wrapped the various cheeses. However, we could not get other members to do it. Nobody. At that time we were losing about $1,000 every month, almost exactly the amount of the discounts.

Something had to be done. Our manager was very unhappy with the Board. He asked for certain decisions to be made. We kept putting it off from month to month. He stopped coming to board meetings. We couldn't carry on business without him. Finally he quit and nobody was unhappy.

But that didn't solve our problems. I knew our bookkeeper, Dee Lerch, was not taking any wages because there was no money. At times I put up personal funds to meet certain cheques. Finally we proposed to go the route of regular co-ops: no immediate discounts would be given. If there were a profit at the end of year, it would be distributed amongst the members.

There was opposition. Some members said they would stop shopping at the co-op. I told them, quite frankly, they would stop shopping because there would soon be no co-op. We would close our doors if something didn't change. We took this to the annual meeting and the members approved the change. I was nominated as president, beating Berlow narrowly. I had threatened to quit earlier if we didn't conduct our meetings more business-like. Now the directors gave me that chance. This was the first time I was president of anything. I was anxious to see if I could make a difference.

We started meeting in an office, sitting at a table. I consulted the new manager about an agenda, and each member got a copy. Whenever there was something controversial, I would stop the monopoly of debate by a few and go around the table for every member's view. Surprisingly, those who seldom spoke up were listening very intently and would make good input into the debate, but they would have to be asked for their views every time. That year nobody quit the Board before their term ended.

Things started to run smoother. We had a new manager, Bonnie Carlson, who was bright, friendly, and competent. We were paying off our debts and doubling our sales. We hired staff to do the work, and the store was run in a more business-like manner. The previous year we were averaging $300-$400 a day. Now we were reaching $1,000. We opened a fruit stand. Bonnie's husband, Gary Canon, was making improvements around the building. We had volunteers for events like bake sales, seed exchange, cooking and selling soup, membership drives, and a booth at the Castlegar Trade Fair. Tom McKenzie (Board member) and I picked cherries or apples or blueberries whenever the opportunity arose. Our membership kept growing. By the end of the year we had paid off the debts and were showing a profit.

Then Bonnie Carlson quit and asked that her husband replace her. We wanted to, but he came to us with ultimatums. He wanted to be paid for every hour he had put in previously, as well as all extra past hours that Bonnie had clocked. There were other demands. I was alone in opposing his demands. I was overruled. Gary Canon was hired, and his every demand met.

This was a big mistake. He ran the co-op like it was his own corner grocery store, answering to no one. He stopped buying local eggs although there was a demand for them. "Too much trouble buying in small lots; better one delivery from Creston." Organic fruits and vegetables were at times mixed with commercial ones. Those wanting only organic stopped trusting us. We carried groceries that were cheaper in the supermarkets. It was complete chaos again.

Finally we called Gary to a meeting with the Board of Directors. He appeared at the meeting, made a statement and walked out, refusing to hear our side. Next day Tom McKenzie and I went to the co-op to talk, but Gary was not in. We phoned and asked him to come in and he refused. We fired him.

The next four or five months were hell. Gary threw every roadblock possible in our way. He rallied a few members to protest his firing and to attend meetings demanding his re-instatement. He cancelled our telephone because he had signed for it. No amount of begging or pleading would give us back our number. We heard from the income tax department, consumer affairs, the Co-operative Society, and the Health Department. One day the RCMP phoned to say they wanted to see me. With the bookkeeper and vice-president Tom McKenzie present, we answered all questions. Everybody went away satisfied with our conduct. Nothing was found wanting.

At the annual meeting we were vindicated and were finally rid of Gary Canon. Some members wanted to expel him from the co-op, but I vetoed that idea. My experience with expelling members in the Youth movement told me that this effort would not be worth the trouble.

Our bookkeeper, Dee Lerch, acted as manager in the interim period. We advertised for a full-time manager, and got many replies. My first experience interviewing and hiring. We just about agreed on a person, when a late entry caught my eye. I asked the

Board to bend the rules and consider the late applicant. Some tried to refuse, but I convinced them to read it.

Lyn Cayo was our perfect candidate. She had previous experience with co-ops and every qualification we were looking for. We struck the perfect compromise. Lyn would share the job with Dee Lerch. Each would work two days a week alone, and together Wednesday. This provided them with an opportunity to consult with each other and make plans for the future.

By the time we left for Ottawa in 1988, the co-op was selling close to one million dollars of merchandise a year. It was time to loosen our reins on spending. The two women wanted to attend a trade show in Vancouver, but I couldn't stop penny-pinching. I knew it was time to go.

As it happened, Lyle won the nomination again, with support from co-op members. He won the election and we prepared to leave for Ottawa. It was a good time for me to leave.

MOTHERS EVERYWHERE

"Good Bye." "Good Bye." "Love you, sweetie." "Love you, too, Mom." "Please write." "Nah. I'll probably phone. See ya."

With a few more hugs and kisses, my son, Colin, the last of my three children, jumped into his grandmother's car, gave us a casual wave, and pulled away from the curb, heading for Vancouver.

We watched until he was out of sight. As the car turned the corner, I turned to Lyle, and collapsed against him, letting my sobs engulf me. Slowly, with arms around each other, we walked back to the house. The house, the big old empty house. The house that had seen us through so much, so many changes, now standing there, looking abandoned, empty, sad. As sad as I was feeling. I felt deserted, abandoned.

We sat on the veranda at the back of the house, overlooking Kootenay Lake, as we had so many times before. But never so desolate. My sobs continued unabated. The pain in my heart was excruciating. Oh, god, how could I go on living when the centre of my universe was yanked away from me!

A neighbour, who had been watching our son load the car all morning, called out: "Last one gone, eh? Never mind. He'll be back, with grandchildren for you." "Grandchildren? What are you talking about? He's just a child. He doesn't even know where babies come from." I call back.

Lyle continued to sit in his favourite chair, looking sad, but not sharing in my grief. Finally he said, "Look, he's just gone off to university. He'll be back. He's a fine young man and will be fine wherever he goes. You don't have to cry for him."

"I'm not crying for him!" I sob, "I am crying for myself. How can I live without him? Without any of my children at home?" Lyle continued to try to put things in perspective. "He'll be visiting soon. He's not dead, you know."

I think about that for a minute. It's true. He isn't dead. I looked over into the yard of another neighbour who did, a few years ago, lose a son in a traffic accident. I try to share the pain she would have felt, but can't. If my pain is this great when the last one leaves, how does a mother live through a death?

But I do feel a stirring of kinship with other mothers, with all mothers, throughout the world. A picture comes to me of a scene in an airport in Azerbaijan. I was touring the Soviet Union in 1985, and standing in a queue waiting to board a plane, two women with arms around each other, hugging, kissing, laughing, and crying. I understood the language enough to hear them say: "You'll eat well. Promise me, you'll eat well." "Yes, of course. I promise. And you won't cry, will you? Promise me, you won't cry, Mother." "No, no, I won't cry." She replied, but the tears continued to stream down her cheeks. I smiled as I watched them. I knew that was me in a few years, and there was nothing I could do to stop it. I could only wait my turn. I felt a kinship with that mother, with mothers everywhere. And I was feeling it again today.

Throughout the whole morning as I watched my son pack his belongings - waterbed, stereo, speakers - how could anyone get so much into such a small car? - I had a nagging feeling that this was a replay of an earlier experience in my life. But I could not think of where, when, who?

It wasn't when my other two children left home to attend university. They were both 19 years of age;

mature and ready, I felt, to face life on their own. Eric had had Grade 13 in Ottawa. The way he matured between the ages of 18 and 19 was phenomenal. At 18 he was a big overgrown kid. At 19 he was a young man. I knew he was ready to live on his own. He had always been a careful, considerate boy, and I knew he would be fine as a young man, wherever he was.

Our daughter, Haida, attended a local college for a year after graduating from high school in Nelson. At 19 she was ready to live on her own. Actually, she was mature and able to take care of herself from the age of 12. She was the middle child, with characteristics as outlined in a book on middle children.

When she was two, she was faced with having to wait for me to dress a newborn. Her older brother (age 4) was used to being waited on by six adults: parents, grandparents and great grandparents. He had no desire to dress himself. She developed an ability and determination to dress herself. Soon she was also dressing her big brother.

Her 'know-it-all' attitude would drive me up the wall at times, but her grandmother made me refer to her 'attitude' as 'determination' instead of 'stubbornness', and in that way I could cope. After all, determination, especially in a woman, was a good characteristic. In fact, I was anxious for her to leave for Vancouver, for two reasons. Firstly, I wanted her to attend a university because I never did, and I could live through her vicariously.

Secondly, because she was in love with a young man, and I was so afraid she would give up higher education for him. When she finally packed and left, I felt relieved. I knew she was hurting because she was leaving her first love. If it was as great a love as she thought, it would sustain through this separation. It didn't last through a few months.

But here was my little boy, Colin, my unplanned baby, leaving home at 18. He was the comedian in the family, the artist, the musician. His teachers said he was something of a fluke: not only was he a straight 'A' student, and a muscle-bound jock involved in every sport, but a sensitive musician and artist. A teacher said to me "If I have six 'Colins' in my lifetime of teaching, I can die happy." Is it any wonder that I felt such a loss?

But, I asked myself, if the replay that haunted me was not the memory of my older children leaving, then what was it? I flip back through my memory; and then it comes to me. The scene starts to form in my mind. It was me leaving home for the first time. It was my mother's eyes that I saw in the same way I felt today; haunting, pleading, fearful, willing me to stop packing; words saying "good-bye", but her eyes saying "don't go". It was my mother today.

I was 15 when I left home to work as a waitress in Edmonton. But oh, god, how I wanted to go! I wanted to start living. I wanted to see the outside world!

In the same way, my dear son was eagerly packing, avoiding my eyes, as though he was afraid I might stop him. As I was afraid my mother would stop me. I was burning with desire; I could hardly breathe I was so anxious to go. After 35 years I could still feel the panic. In my case, I was leaving a very lonely, isolated homestead.

My only contact with the outside world was through books. I read everything in the school library, any book I could beg, steal or borrow. My eyes were always glued to a book. I would bring the cows in from pasture and read as I walked. While milking, I would have a book in one hand. It infuriated my parents. There was so much to learn about the outside world. When it was agreed I could quit high school after Grade 10, I was overjoyed. It meant I could go to the big city of Edmonton and start living.

But what of my mother's mother? What did she feel when she watched her daughter, together with husband and child, packing up to leave her family and community in the Ukraine to emigrate to a country half way round the world? What pain did she feel? She had to know she would never see them again, nor other grandchildren. I reached out to her, to share her grief, to feel her pain. I could see her standing, smiling, but the wringing of her hands would have betrayed her pain. I never saw a photograph of her, but in my minds' eye I could see her with a long, dark dress on, a babushka tucked round her forehead and over her ears. Her pain would have been great. Women. Mothers. It is a sisterhood that cannot be penetrated by the other sex, no matter how they try to empathize. Yes, hers would have been a great pain.

And what about my mother? Was she as anxious to leave as I? As my son was today? When asked why she came to live in Canada, my mother would always reply that she wanted to live and raise her children in a country that had no wars. She knew my father's intention was to move to Canada. She hinted that was the reason she married him.

She would describe her childhood as one lived in constant fear. Soldiers were always stopping in her village to spend the night and gather whatever food was available, on their way to war, or returning. One side or the other. As a child she didn't know who they were, nor did she care. She was always afraid. She watched their chickens, geese, ducks, pigs, cattle and sheep get slaughtered. Sometimes their horses would be commandeered; sometimes her father would be drafted on the spot to drive the horses.

After he left, the family lived in desperate fear for months, not knowing if he was dead or alive. Because he wasn't in the regular army, there would be less effort - if any - to notify his next of kin in case of death. So her greatest desire was to find a place to live where there was no war.

My sobs subside as I share my pain with past generations, with mothers everywhere. Lyle leaned over and said, "There, now, have you got it out of your system?" I nod, feeling easier. I look at my husband of 26 years and for the first time wonder how he feels. I asked him, "How do you feel about all this, Lyle?" He laughs. Standing up, he lifts his hands in the air in a dance position like Tygvey in "Fiddler on the Roof". He sings, "Free at last! Free at last! Great God Almighty, I'm free at last!"

I burst into tears again. How could he? How could he! Even in a joke! I see he is only trying to cheer me up. He reminds me of what Bill Cosby said in his book 'Fatherhood', which we read together out loud recently: "Only the human animal holds on to its young when they are ready to go. Every other animal loves its babies, teaches them to fend for themselves, and then shoves them out of the nest and onto their own, never to return." At this moment I find this to be profound. It is true. We, the superior animal, the human, cling to our children, unable to let go.

As I ponder the wisdom of the animal kingdom, I remember walking along the Rideau River in Ottawa one spring day. I noticed a small waterfall and wondered how ducks swam over it. Further along I saw a mother duck swimming with six baby ducklings. The ducklings were scurrying about, tumbling over each other, flitting back and forth, while mother duck swam quietly behind with an obvious pride.

Suddenly she felt the water current quicken. She swam toward the middle of the river where she got confirmation that the current was in fact growing stronger. They were nearing the waterfall. Mother duck swam back to her brood and herded them gently but firmly toward shore.

After a short stay she swam back in the direction they came and without the playful frolic displayed earlier, the ducklings followed, all in a row. I marvelled at this display of obedience. I tried to picture a human trying to get this kind of obedience from six little children. Never in a hundred years!

Lyle broke into my thoughts again, reminding me that our lives weren't so bad before we had children. In fact, all through the past 23 child-rearing years, we would fondly refer to our "BC Years" meaning "Before Children". He said we now go back to those years.

He's right, of course. There is life after children. Perhaps we can't go back to our first years of marriage exactly, but there are still some pleasures we can rekindle. We had four glorious years of married life before the children were born. We were newlyweds, both working, spending every cent we made on travel, books, cultural events, eating out whenever we wanted.

I remember buying the book "Never Cry Wolf" by Farley Mowat. We found it so titillating we read the whole book out loud to each other. Lyle read while I prepared dinner. I continued while he washed the dishes. We read through the night, howling at the funny parts, finishing just as dawn broke. We then had a hearty breakfast and slept through the day.

"Look, enough of this." Lyle says. "I'll miss him too. I miss all three of them. They were such a joy to have around. But you can't hang on. The time has

come and they are gone. We did our job, and we did it
well. No, you did it well. You should feel good about
it. All three of them are wonderful young people. But
the time has come to let go. So let's get on with our
lives."   He's right. I know he's right. I'll do it – soon!

AND THEN IT'S BACK TO OTTAWA

The federal election was called in September 1988. This election was fought on free trade with the U.S. The Liberals and the NDP opposed it, and in fact got the majority votes. However, the Conservatives got a majority government.

It was an interesting election because people were talking about the free trade agreement. Strong Liberal voters told me they would vote for Lyle to keep the Tories out, in order to defeat the Agreement. Liberal leader John Turner took a very strong stand against the Agreement, and Liberal voters were very much against it. Sadly, when the Liberals won in 1993, they had six months in which to make some major changes, but chose to do nothing.

Lyle was re-elected. This time we were without children. We bought a penthouse in Vanier, which is a city within Ottawa. This time we didn't have a car. We could walk to the House of Commons or take the bus. If we had visitors for a few days we rented a car. This time I could travel with Lyle to conferences all over the world.

In the summer we spent our time travelling to the different parts of the riding. We participated in all parades and celebrations. We became proficient at taking in two parades in one day. The Canada Day parade in New Denver was at 10 a.m. As soon as it ended, Lyle and I would quickly strip the decorations and hit the road for Kaslo. This was a winding, country road, but Lyle could really move. We knew the RCMP were involved in parades. We would reach Kaslo just as the last few floats were about to cross the highway. We would jump out, plaster Lyle's magnetic signs to the hood and doors, and quickly manoeuvre our car into their parade.

We participated in everything. We joined in two-man log-bucking contests with a crosscut saw at Slocan Park. This was so difficult I nearly passed out in the hot sun. There were nail-hammering contests, frog jumping races, and bull-chip (cow turd) throwing. At Lardeau Lew Days there was a contest of crossing a log over water pulling a choker chain which had to be set around a huge log.

Then there were the dunk tanks. And more dunk tanks. Whenever the weather was half decent, every community seemed to have them. But the worst was the one at Meadow Creek. Lyle was the only celebrity target in the dunk tank. Kids and adults would throw balls at a target attached to Lyle's seat which was suspended over a tank of cold water. If the ball hit the mark, he would be dumped into 'the tank'. This tank was too shallow and every time he dropped, he would hit his tailbone on the bottom.

To make matters worse, the Socred overseer would trip the lever himself if he thought the target was not hit often enough. After what seemed like hours with no relief, Lyle finally called it quits. Most dunk tanks were fun, but this one was way past a joke. Boy, did his backside hurt!

Lyle usually enjoyed the celebrity grape stomp at Trail's Silver City Days. However, one year the grapes were still half frozen. His feet were soon numb and every step felt as if they were being sliced by razor blades. But - he kept on stomping. The 'contest' was to see which two-person team (one stomping and the other one adding the grapes and draining the juice) could get the most juice out of several crates of grapes in 20 minutes. He never won this contest but he never placed last, either.

And then there were the ski races at Whitewater. I was never a great skier - and Lyle even less so. One year someone talked Lyle into entering the obstacle race. This involved walking across tires in skis, over logs, and ended up doing the limbo under a pole. Lyle bent backwards under the limbo pole and landed with his rear end on the skis. He then had to muster every bit of will power and strength to stand up again. He said that the muscles in his legs felt like jelly and that it was only his political ego that forced him to stand up in front of all those people – and the press.

Later that day as we were skiing down a cut behind the bunny trail, Lyle veered off under the trees. The snow gave way beneath him and he hung, suspended by branches, over a small creek below. His one leg lost its ski and went straight down, while the other was hung up above the snow with the ski still on – doing a form of the splits. The more we laughed, the farther down his leg went. He could never have gotten out alone. I finally got his other ski off and he was able to crawl out of the hole.

But the funniest of all the contests had to be canoe jousting in Silverton. Colin and his future wife, Cindy, joined us there. Colin and Lyle dressed in Nordic costume and wearing horned helmets, took on all challengers. They won easily.

A couple of guys would not accept defeat and kept challenging them over and over. The last time up, as the two canoes headed for each other, Colin and Lyle gave out a horrendous roar and the challenging canoe tipped over without even being touched. The people on the shore were in stitches laughing. The challengers were a little drunk. Then Lyle and I challenged Colin and Cindy, and … well, suffice it to say, youngsters have no respect for their elders!

The victorious Viking canoe-jousters.

Colin and
Eric
"Huppty-
Huppty!"

OUR FIRST "JUNKET"

During Lyle's terms in office we had several trips to Europe; NATO conferences held in Denmark, Germany, France and Turkey. He also attended European Parliament sessions at Strasbourg, France. These were working trips. Lyle attended sessions all day, all week. I got to travel free, but paid for my share of hotel rooms and meals.

At one particular cocktail party after a long and bitter dispute in a NATO conference, I heard that the U.S. delegation had, for the first time, lost a crucial vote at the meeting. I listened to the issue being debated, at a party, between the U.S. and a Portuguese delegate. The American was very tall, very big, and very loud. He leaned over to shout at the short, dark Portuguese: "Just you wait. When you need help, you'll come to us." The Portuguese shrugged his shoulders and said, "Heh, who's going to attack us? Iceland?" And he walked away.

The NATO conference in Antalia, Turkey, in 1990, was the best trip of all. We visited so many old ruins that were in such good shape; you could almost hear the chariots rolling and people cheering. It took one right back to ancient times.

Some of the coliseums we visited still held outdoor concerts, and the acoustics were fantastic. We sat in the last row of an Alexandrian amphitheatre that held a crowd of 18,000, but could hear the string quartet excellently. The aqueducts were still in place and the cobblestone roads showing the grooves from carriage wheels, were very much intact.

What wasn't so pleasant was the security system. Every time we entered our hotel, we had to go through the scanner and have our purses searched. When we travelled with the MPs, our buses had an escort, police cars ahead and behind, with sirens blaring. Every street crossing had policemen holding back traffic so we didn't stop for anything. On the highway we travelled at break-neck speed, and traffic ahead of us was pulled over with sirens. Security men surrounded us everywhere.

The hotel was magnificent, located on the Mediterranean Sea. There were tennis courts available. I used them one day. Not finding anyone in our group who would face the 100-degree (F) sun, I had to coax one of the young men tending the courts to play with me. We had two games, and I lost both, with scores like 6-2 and 6-3. The young man came off the court saying, "Well, I win but you sure made me sweat." I don't play the usual game, hitting the ball from end to end. My "returns" are long, then short, then.... This made him run forward, back, and forward.

On the way home we stopped at Istanbul, a city with 12 million people, that straddles two continents: Asia and Europe. It's crowded, dirty and smelly! We were besieged by the most aggressive beggars, peddlers, and con men. It was most unpleasant.

Our only "junket" was to the islands of Barbados and Dominica. We were assigned to represent the NDP at a Commonwealth Parliamentary "seminar". We left Ottawa on a cold, stormy day in February, and arrived in Barbados in hot, sultry weather. Meetings were held with other parliamentarians, for no apparent purpose. It seemed to be an excuse for a holiday. Parliamentarians from these countries have come to Canada in the same fashion. Thus, the Barbados government picked up the tab for hotel and meals.

We stayed at the Paradise Resort, which was the most complete vacation spot I could imagine. The beaches were clean, swimming area roped off and the swimming was wonderful. Sailboats were provided, along with lessons from the men who cared for the boats. Every evening we were invited to an outdoor cocktail party by the beach.

Our best tour was in a submarine, made in Vancouver, which took us a 500 feet under the ocean. We watched a shark, a barracuda, and thousands of colourful fish. We took other tours around the island with the whole delegation.

When we flew to Dominica we had to pay for our own rooms and meals, because they couldn't afford them, quite rightly. This is a very poor country. Every three or four years, tornadoes strike the island, devastating it. Buildings are flattened, trees uprooted, crops lost, and parrots (national symbol) killed to near extinction.

On the first day we sat in the open, facing the sun with our lily-white skin, while they prayed, during the opening of an airstrip that Canada helped finance.

We also attended the opening of a senior citizens home. This was partly financed by Canada and opened about ten years earlier, but every few years Canada added a few new rooms and got another opening. The prayers were even longer and the white-faced Canadians again faced the noonday sun.

I refused to sit with the delegation. I felt it was a kind of revenge, a punishment. Instead, I sat with Michael Douglas, leader of the opposition Labour Party, and his brother Rosey, who was educated in Montreal (and of some notoriety arising from the burning of a McGill University computer department during 1960's sit-in) who was an MP. They were a riot.

Their Chamber of Commerce (called Hucksters' Association, very appropriately) opened an office, and we were invited to participate. This time we were under a roof but the prayers were very long. When everybody was asked to bow their heads and pray, I looked around and found every head dutifully bowed, except the woman prime minister's. She moved her eagle eyes over her flock throughout the whole prayer as though she was judging them.

In Barbados, we even went to church. There was a special service because of a celebration and their Governor General was present. What we heard amazed us. A whiter than white minister was speaking to a predominantly black congregation about the evils of overtaxing people with property (who are mostly white). It sounded political and racist. After the services I went over to the minister and told him I had not been in a church for 20 years, and after today, would not be for another 20.

When it was all over, Lyle said, "So that's what a junket is. And it's called a seminar." This trip was entirely different from the working trips he had taken before.

CHANNEL ISLANDS

Later that year we were on a Commonwealth delegation to the Channel Islands: Jersey, Guernsey and Sark. When we started out we hardly knew where they were, except that they were British. We found them in the North Sea, 14 km. off the coast of France. Everything about them is French, but Britain held them because of her naval superiority, and has kept them by giving all kinds of concessions. They are a tax dodge sanctuary for the British elite.

These are very affluent islands, with the strictest immigration laws anywhere. You cannot immigrate there except through marrying someone on the island or if you agree to build something they really need. Being as small as they are, and having strict building codes to preserve what agricultural lands they have, these laws make sense.

This was the most "safe" country we visited. After Turkey, this was heaven. The Governor General's home was wide open, no fences or security gates, no guards. Farmers leave their produce on the side of the road, and people stop to pick up what they want, leaving their money in the box beside the produce. I couldn't help thinking how much more desirable this was than seeing people sleeping in the streets, begging, stealing, armed guards protecting the rich.

When we were to fly to Guernsey, it was a cold, windy, rainy day. The plane was ancient. We had to be loaded according to weight to keep it balanced. There was no co-pilot. Among us was a Quebec senator who was deathly scared of flying. It didn't help when Lyle pointed out that there was a graveyard alongside the airport, and encouraged him to read the pamphlet on how to fly the plane, since there was no co-pilot. The poor man was green before he got out of the plane. Guernsey was not as memorable as Jersey. However, we did visit the island home of Victor Hugo, where he wrote Les Miserables. The island is about 40 miles long and 14 wide.

I visited Arthur Durrell's animal sanctuary where he breeds endangered species and returns them to their homeland. I saw many of Durrell's nature films on TV so was pleased to see his work. There was also the most beautiful orchid plantation. Lyle visited some farms and other agricultural projects.

On the way home we had a couple of days in London, England. We visited their parliament and Lyle sat in on some interesting discussions about world trade.

SPAIN

In 1991 we went to Madrid, Spain, to a NATO Assembly. We had to leave Canada one day before the BC election. We phoned back at 7 a.m. Spanish time, to get the results: an NDP majority government.

During these official trips, spouses avoid talking politics like the plague. However, Judy McCreath, a Tory from Newfoundland, persisted in making snide political comments. Someone at lunch congratulated me on the BC election results, and I gave a little cheer. She sneered, "Don't know what's to cheer. They've already ruined one province." I leaned over and said, "Oh, really? Tell us about the federal Tory government." (They were down in the polls to single digits.) Everybody else said, "No politics. No politics. We don't talk politics."

Later Judy was telling us how great it was to have Medicare; how she didn't mind paying taxes to have Medicare. I smiled and said, "Thank you very much." She nearly burst out of her skin and insisted Diefenbacher brought Medicare to Canada.

Sunday the whole delegation was bussed out to Escricial, an old Roman village where an historic royal palace and monastery sat on a hilltop. Many of Spain's kings and queens are entombed here. We were preceded and followed by a police escort and ambulance, and two helicopters hovered above us. Protection is always heavy at NATO conferences, but this seemed extreme. We were told later that they were practicing security measures in preparation for the coming Barcelona Olympics. It was strange for Lyle to be at a NATO conference with people from Soviet republics and the Baltic. Wasn't this the reason for forming NATO - to protect the west from these countries?

**Lyle and a Senator at a North Atlantic Assembly
in Munich, Germany**

Monday was the last day of the conference. At noon we were invited to meet the king and queen. The castle was across the street from the Senate (where the conference was), but they insisted on driving us over there in a bus. We left at 12 noon for a meeting scheduled for 1 o'clock. One hundred of us stood in a barren hall for an hour waiting for these royals.

The king and queen were 15 minutes late. The king stayed 15 minutes and left - I didn't even get a glimpse of him. The queen stayed 45 minutes and I saw her. And then drinks were served with little tidbits to eat. What a dumb experience!

FRANCE, FRENCH REVOLUTION, CORSICA

Whenever Lyle was on a European assignment, we always found some time to spend in Paris. It is such a beautiful city, filled with historic places, buildings, churches, fountains, monuments. We never ran out of new places to visit. One day we found a street named "Morland" (Lyle's grandparents' name). Later Lyle found a story about a General Morland who fought with Napolean. He was killed in battle in Austerlitz.

They stuck him in a barrel of cognac and shipped him back to Paris. Years later, someone opened that barrel, and out fell this general, in perfect condition. He had been pickled in cognac.

During our first visits, we were disgusted with the state of their streets. There were dog and human excrement, vomit, litter, broken glass, and puddles of urine. In fact, there were grooves in the cement made by men urinating. I knew the women of Paris could bring a stop to this: imagine a thousand dresses being flipped up, asses bared, and flows of steaming fluid let loose on the streets. This would bring such howls of protest and screams of indignation that it would not take long for proper laws to be drawn up, passed, and enforce!

In 1989, in preparation for their 200th anniversary of the French Revolution, the streets were cleaned up, more street lights were installed, and traffic was more controlled. We stayed in the 5th-floor, walk-up apartment of Yahia Hechehouche, a friend who would later immigrate to Canada and live with us.

Paris has some six million inhabitants, and that year another one million tourists came to join in the celebrations. The first evening's celebration was the opening of the new Opera House designed by a Canadian architect. We felt we had to attend. It was so crowded in the Place Bastille we could hardly breathe. We found a table at an outdoor café and could stay out of the way of the young and restless.

The next day we lined up to see the Bastille Day Bicentenary parade at 6 pm. At about 10:30 pm the parade started. By now there was a solid wall of people behind us. Then the pushing started. At first I thought it was accidental. But it happened again and again: a surge forward, crushing us against a structure. It was frightening, and we soon worked our way out of the crush of people, and watched the parade on TV sets situated all over the park.

Next morning MP Svend Robinson, who was part of the official delegation, phoned to tell us he had tickets for that evening's event, "Colours", which he could not attend. Did we want them? We did, indeed.

We got all decked out in our fineries and took the Metro downtown – an experience in itself. When we got on there was hardly breathing room. At every stop more people got on, with a lot of shoving. By the time we got off we felt like we'd been dragged through the streets. It reminded me of going to Athabasca on the back of the truck in my childhood.

When we got to the entrance gate, we found a solid wall of people between the barricades and us. In fact, tens of thousands lined the streets, on the bridge and the far bank of the Seine. No amount of "Excuse me" made any dent in this wall. Finally Lyle shoved forward, telling me to stick close behind, and with his tickets held high in the air, tried to catch the eye of the gendarme inside the barricades. At one point, somebody in the crowd, annoyed at Lyle's pushing, brought his elbow back, missed Lyle, and got me square in the chest, knocking the breath out of me. I didn't have time to think about it and kept on staying close behind Lyle. When Lyle finally reached a gate he waved his tickets at the policeman, who waved us to the other end of the barricade.

We went at it again, pushing and shoving our way, only to have the policeman look at them and point us back to where we were before. Back again, pushing and shoving. By this time everyone was furious with us. An older policeman behind the barricades saw our dilemma, opened the gate, moved through the crowd and, using his baton, broke a trail for us. We finally fell through the gate – into serenity.

We stopped for a few minutes to catch our breath. Somewhere in the crowd someone yelled, "Want to sell your tickets?" We didn't even consider it, but were told later that tickets were being scalped for $2,000.

When we regained our composure and calm settled in, we walked the six blocks along the Seine to the show, which was held in the plaza and gardens of the Trocadero Palace. We were shown to our second row seats, just behind the mayor of Paris. There were representatives from many parts of the world. The night air was fragrant, warm and sultry. A full moon was out. How different from the night before at the Place Bastille.

We were treated to the most spectacular display of music, lights, colour, and fireworks. It held us speechless. The huge fountains in front of the Trocadaro had coloured lights illuminating the water. Speakers blasted music and commentary about the French Revolution and events since. Extraordinary fireworks were exploding all about us, and when we turned around, the Eiffel Tower – across the Seine – was illuminated and outlined by the dazzling lights of the fireworks display. It was magic! Breathtaking! And all under a Paris moon!

When it was over, wine and cheese was served. We stayed as long as possible, walking around the fountain. We were one of the last to leave, walking slowly back to the gate (everyone else left in limousines). As we got closer to it we walked slower and slower, hating to go back into that melee, to join the mob that was still milling around.

Finally we had no choice but to hit the streets. I found myself thinking "Rabble. Now I know the meaning of rabble." I then remembered why we were in Paris: to commemorate the French Revolution. And what was the revolution about? The "rabble" being sick and tired of doing all the work and living on a pittance, while the rich and idle partook of all the good things: food, culture, wealth, possessions. The people wanted a share of the fruits of their labour. Liberty! Equality! Fraternity! As simple as that. Now, 200 years later, has anything changed?

Well, yes, there are many changes. In fact, France gave the world so much out of that revolution: laws that applied to all equally (supposedly); opportunity for people to get ahead in whatever they were doing according to their ability and merit, and not just according to their birth, rank, class and means to buy themselves promotions. The example that people could govern themselves without a monarch.

We toured much of southern France, and arrived in Fontainebleau on July 26th, our 28th wedding anniversary. We bought some food and a bottle of wine and had a romantic lunch at the man-made lake. Lyle walked into town and bought me a gift and one long-stemmed rose. He enjoyed carrying it back through the beautiful park grounds surrounding the palaces, as he said all the ladies smiled at him, and some even applauded.

CORSICA

In recent years Lyle developed an interest in Napoleon Bonaparte, and I shared some of it. He got this interest from a book he picked up at an airport. It was entitled "Who Murdered Napoleon – a 200 year old murder is solved." Because of this interest, we took a midnight ferry to the island of Corsica, where Napoleon was born. The voyage was such a pleasure, with warm, sultry air and the moon reflected on the water – a one-night Mediterranean cruise.

Arriving in Ajaccio at 6 am, we rented a Euro-car, and stopped to buy groceries. When we got back from shopping, I screamed, "Our luggage. It's gone." Our two bags in the back seat were gone. We went to the police station to report it.

One officer had a smattering of English. As we were listing the items in the luggage, the phone rang and he left the room. When he came back he was carrying our luggage. Two men found them in a back alley, contents spewed all over. They gathered them up and brought them in. We looked it over, and found everything there. We had stuffed our valuables, money and passports, in luggage in the trunk. The only thing missing was a musical tape, Serge Lama singing "Napoleon". The thieves were patriotic!

We spent the week circling the Island, swimming in the ocean on the beautiful white beaches, visiting monuments. We found the "Menhirs", which were life-size human statues carved out of stone which are purported to be man's first art work in the world.

While travelling through the middle of the island, through the mountainous forest, we ran into several large groups of pigs, running free. We had heard about them roving the countryside. We fed one such group, located high on a mountain pass, with the rotting remains of a box of peaches we bought. We were so intrigues doing this that night found us a long way from any city. We just pulled the car off the road and stayed the night.

The next morning we woke to the sound of bells tinkling. We then watched a couple of dogs herd a large herd of sheep up the mountain, by themselves. We walked to the top of a peak and could see for hundreds of miles. What a wonderful experience.

After touring the whole island, we went back to a beach near Ajaccio for a last day of swimming – topless. Late in the afternoon, Lyle said he would go into town and pick up our ferry tickets. He went into our luggage to get money and passports, and found both missing. We were robbed – again! This time the thieves broke into the car, removed the back seat, and got into the trunk. Our travellers cheques, passports, credit cards, and my purse were gone. Fortunately, Lyle had some cash and one credit card on him. We went back to the familiar police station.

As we entered, we were met with smiles and greetings: "Hello, Mr. Kristiansen. We are waiting for you." We couldn't understand. When we walked into the familiar room, there was our luggage!

They had already picked up the culprits, trying to buy men's clothing with our credit card, and had them in jail in a town nearby. The clerk at the store had looked at the credit card and decided neither of them looked like a "Kristiansen", so phoned the police, who, of course, knew what the real Mr. Kristiansen looked like. We were so impressed. We accompanied a policeman to the town of Portocello to pick up some other possessions. They could not find our passports at that time, but did later, and forwarded them to the Canadian embassy in Paris. Our travellers cheques were cashed and had to be reimbursed by the bank. When our Mastercard bill arrived, we noticed a charge of $300 for men's clothing in Portocello. I guess the clerk didn't want to be entirely out of pocket from that sale.

We still had a credit card, and were able to buy ferry tickets and pay for hotel rooms in France.

NAPOLEON

I have to add a little more about Napoleon and his times. If one was to rely entirely on English language school texts and much of the popular media, one is likely to view Napoleon as a warmonger and tyrant. When you read his memoirs, serious biographies, and contemporary memoirs of his associates, you get quite a different picture. He was, in fact, a raving democrat, liberal, and progressive when compared to the monarch that ruled at the end of the 18th and early 19th century.

The French revolution of 1789 was a classic. French citizens were living in miserable conditions. When people are pressed so hard, work so long, and given no share of the wealth they produce – and with no opportunity for advancement – sooner or later they turn on their monarchs.

To forestall this, it was established that the greatest crime in the world was the taking of a monarch's life. This was tantamount to killing a god. Punishment for an attempt on a monarch's life was horrendous: in France, such a person would be tied to four horses with an arm or leg to each horse. The horses were then galloped off in four directions.

What is even more horrifying is that the people observing would sometimes be so outraged at the victim that one reported incident had the crowd fall upon the remains of such torn-to-shreds remains and tear at them further until there was nothing left. My mother told me that, in 1917, when her village in the Ukraine heard that the Russian tsar had been killed, people wept and wrung their hands, saying "Oh, god, who will take care of us now?" What did they think he did for them? My father's reaction was "The tsar pisses on the peasants and they call it rain, and give thanks."

In England, the historian, Thomas Carlyle, was thoroughly disgusted that Queen Victoria had invited Louis Napoleon (he had been crowned Emperor Napoleon III) and his wife to England and entertained them royally. Carlyle writes:

He gathers great crowds about him but his reception from the hip-hip-hurrahing classes is not warm at all. Just before they arrived, I came down Piccadilly. Two thin rows of abject looking human wretches I had ever seen. Lame, crook-backed, dwarfish, dirty-shirted, with the air of city jackals, not a gent hardly among them, much less any vestige of a gentleman – were drawn up in St. James Street to Hyde Park Corner to receive the august pair. I looked at them with a shuddering thankfulness that they were not drawn up to receive me."

I quote this paragraph to show the kind of disgust these "gentry" felt when they looked upon the working people of their country. These "lame, crook-backed, dirty-shirted" people were slaving at their jobs to provide wealth and services to these ungrateful leeches; these scum-of-the-earth creatures that still inhabit the world and suck off the wealth.

During the French Revolution, people took control of the country and killed the king. An attempt was made to set up a government made up of ordinary people. This frightened every monarch in Europe. It was setting an example for their own people. This could not be tolerated. Every monarch's throne was threatened. They could not let it succeed.

England led the assault on France, subsidizing and assisting successive coalitions of Austria, Russia and Prussia in their wars. French trade and trade routes were cut off, colonies seized, and ports blockaded. Many early battles took place in France. Later, after the invading armies had been expelled, Napoleon would move their armies onto the attack, so that the fighting took place on others' soil.

It was no different when the Russian Revolution happened. Some 21 countries stationed their armed forces on the outskirts of Russia, waiting for the opportunity to "crush the monster growing within". Why? Because those who owned large tracts of land and power in these countries felt their control was threatened.

Throughout the world, people with money and power help others in the same situation in order to protect themselves. What amazes me is the extent to which they go, and the hypocrisy they spew to justify their actions, and the way their public swallow it.

To me, the Russian and French revolutions were very similar. Nor is it any different when the USA in recent years harassed and attacked countries like Cuba and Nicaragua, when they tried to set up governments that dealt with problems such as poverty, illiteracy, and deprivation. These countries set an example and could not be tolerated. On the other hand, the American revolution was quite different. In that situation, a foreign power was expelled, but the same people remained in power.

What is even more amazing is that ordinary people will actually join armies and go out and kill and die to protect this wealth for the few. As U.S. railway magnate, Jay Gould, said in 1886, "I can always hire one-half of the working class to kill the other half."

Nothing has changed over the years. Different words are used, and we no longer call them kings and queens, but the rich in today's society are far richer and more powerful than any monarchy in history.

In 1799 Napoleon assumed the powers of the government. He immediately set about bringing order out of chaos (before that for ten years the revolutionary government was talking itself to death.) People rose through their ability rather than by buying their way to the top, especially in the armed forces and the public service. This was one reason why his armies won so many battles.

Napoleon used the plebiscite repeatedly to get approval of the citizens for what he was doing. How could history then record him as a dictator?

The "Code Napoleon" (still in existence today as the basis of civil law in France, Italy, Quebec, Mexico, Belgium, Latin America, Japan and Louisiana) broke new ground in family law, property and commercial law, and the laws of inheritance. Public education was a priority, especially in technical training, and first public schools for women.

Napoleon was, perhaps, the world's first modern politician. Not a ruler by hereditary and divine right, he knew he had to constantly muster popularity and public opinion behind him in order to prevail. In the royally-governed world of his time, he knew that if he lost – he was dead. He was right.

BACK TO FRANCE

In 1992 we were back again in France, to attend the commemoration at Dieppe of the 50th anniversary of the disastrous Canadian raid of 1942. We heard the veterans discuss the doubts about the use of Canadian forces. Could the raid have been successful if heavy bombardment had been used? Was it a mistake to concentrate on a frontal assault instead of flanking attacks? Was the raid mounted to appease "second front" critics in Moscow?

The Canadian casualties at Dieppe had been enormous. There were some 5,000 Canadian soldiers, 1,000 British, and 50 U.S. in the attacking force. Out of these, 900 Canadians were killed outright on the beaches, and 2,000 wounded or taken prisoner. Another 50 British met with disaster.

We were moved by the warmth of feelings expressed in hundreds of ways by the people of Dieppe. Thousands turned out at the cemeteries and at the dramatic sound and light show on the main landing beach. When the veterans and their bands marched to City Hall, the throngs on the street greeted each group with tremendous applause. It was nice to know "They remember. They understand the price paid. "

As we stood in the rain listening to the speeches, we heard a German veteran talking to a Welsh couple. We introduced ourselves and joined the conversation. He told us he had recently been to Canada "to protest the slaughter of seals." He told us he was a young lad during the war, and was in charge of a machine gun battery. He said, "It was crazy. It was sheer madness. The Canadians kept coming. They were being killed by the hundreds, but they kept on coming. It was lunacy!" And it was lunacy!

On the beach Lyle and I approached a young French couple with two young children. We thanked them for the great performance. "No" they said, in halting English. "It is we who thank you for all that your young men sacrificed – for us."

THE YEAR 1991

The year 1991 was not a good one. This year my mother died. I was never close to my mother. In later years I understood her and tolerated our differences. However, she was a brave, determined woman.

The year started with the Canada-U.S. Free Trade Agreement coming into effect January 1st. I cannot see it being good for Canada. Our only hope is that the Tories will be defeated in the next election, and the Agreement changed enough to make it palatable. I doubt it can be cancelled all together. Hopefully the Liberals would have a minority government, relying on NDP support, and together they could change it considerably.

This Agreement states that Canada cannot charge more for any resources sold to the U.S. than it charges its own citizens. With that we gave away any advantage we could give our own industry. We are a cold country with great distances between communities and it costs us considerably more than the U.S. to produce and move products. Furthermore, if we should face shortages in any energy resource, we cannot cut our energy exports unless we cut our own consumption as well.

The end of June we were looking forward to going back to the riding for some peace and quiet. The night before we left, I had a phone call from my niece, Rosanna, telling me that my mother had died. It was so unexpected as she had been feeling better than in many years. I had had a visit with her in January and found her very lucid, her memory so good she gave me many insights into her childhood.

With that on our minds we left for the riding, attending several functions, with heavy heart. We went to Vancouver, collected the children, and flew to

Edmonton. The funeral was held in a United Church, and was much more satisfying than my father's in the Greek Orthodox Church.

During my father's funeral, the Greek Orthodox priest gave a long religious sermon, said not a word about my father's life, and then launched into a diatribe of political comment about the horrors of the Soviet Union. He also attacked "those people who left the church." Nena and I looked at each other and wondered whether to walk out. However, Nena said, for mother's sake, we couldn't.

Thinking of my mother's life, I kept getting one picture. It was of Nena and I walking home from school in a snowstorm. We had left our cousins, Melvin and Olga, and proceeded the last mile and a half alone. It was cold and the snow was blowing so hard we could hardly stay on the road. The snowdrifts were over our heads. We were bundled up in so many clothes, scarves wrapped around our faces, heavy boots on, that we could hardly walk. At the muskeg we faced the worst part of the trek. We huddled together, creeping forward. Then out of the mist, we saw an outline of something coming toward us. The form was nearly upon us before we realized it was Mother, leading a horse, coming to help us.

In her eulogy, Nena told the story of Mother and Aunty Calishka manning the still, making moonshine, in the back woods of our farm. They had to keep tasting the liquid to know if it was alcohol or water that was flowing through the pipes. When Mother had to head home, she tried to climb up on her horse, but found she could not stay on it. She kept falling off on the other side. She couldn't understand why. It never occurred to her that she had tasted the moonshine so often she was thoroughly inebriated.

MY MOTHER'S LAST STORY

When I visited Mother in January, she recalled some childhood memories. This is what she told me:

"Your father lived in the village of Vorchyn. During World War I people were evacuated and his family was sent to Katerneslava. That is where they were during the revolution.

While they were moving, they stopped in a village called Liski, and in the first house they came to they stopped to bake the bread his mother had started before they left home. It had risen and was ready for baking. The outdoor ovens were fired up and other people were also using them. She put the bread in and waited. When done, she removed it and set it down to cool before bagging it. During this time another woman approached her and said that was her bread. A struggle ensued and the other woman took her bread. His mother was so upset she got confused and took a wrong road to meet up with the rest of the family. By evening she was completely lost, chilled, very upset, and a fever set in. There was a plague in the area that was taking many lives. She caught the plague.

"Dad's father had waited for his wife to join them. Finally he went in search of her. He located her the next morning with some local people who had taken her in when they saw how sick she was. They left the convoy and took her to the hospital but, within three days, she died. Dad and his family stayed in Katerneslova for about 5 years.

"My family was evacuated to Shipiterka. My father and brother worked for a contora (I think a feudal landowner). This was in Korskaya Gobarnia.

"We rented an acreage from a `paan' (lord), and worked the land, which had a large orchard on it. The house was large and nice. We shared it with another

family, and stayed almost 3 years. It was very good as there was a lot of fruit and food. Dad wanted to remain there permanently, but mother wouldn't hear of it. She wanted to go back to her own people.

"When the end of the war was approaching, we packed up our belongings, tied two cows and a sow to the back of the wagon, and headed home. When we arrived in Volodimir we found that the Austrian guards were still in control. We had to get permission from them to cross the `front' to get to our village.

"After spending the night, my father said he would try to get this `permit'. I (at age 5 or 6) insisted on going with him. I latched on to his pant leg and wouldn't let go. He agreed to take me.

"We approached the municipal hall slowly and found a German guard outside. Dad approached very slowly and, while still quite a distance away, removed his cap and bowed very low. The guard jumped to attention and spoke to us very angrily in German. He even pointed his gun and bayonet at us. Dad picked me up, turned, and ran back. The next day, accompanied by his brother, he tried again. This time the guard let them enter the municipal hall and they were issued permits. We arrived at our farm that night.

"However, we found our fields were seeded and the house occupied by a Polish family. They would not let us in. After much arguing, we were convinced to stay in another house and use another barn until these Poles could reap their crop and leave. We took possession after that.

"My father was hired to mow hay for the Polish communal cattle holdings. When he went to the meadow where he was supposed to mow, he found the German army retreating in great droves. Several Germans wanted to take his `fresh' horses. He and my brother repelled them. But one German commander rushed them, cut the straps on the harnesses that held the horses to the wagon, and drove them off. Someone approached them and offered a couple of old, tired horses in exchange. They refused and demanded their own be returned to them.

"Dad and my brother, Fedor, followed the German battalion all day. When night fell, they watched which barn their horses were put into. Late that night they entered the barn, which was pitch black, and slowly felt around for their own horses. They found one but not the other. If they led one out alone it would neigh, so they tried to find the other. Then a guard positioned himself at the door for the rest of the night. They couldn't get out themselves.

"In the morning the guard moved but it was too late to take the horses. They bought a couple of horses in a village, and drove back to where they had lived ,and brought back enough grain, flour, peas, beans, and potatoes to last us through the winter.

"That was a hard winter on the local population. People complained to the government agent that there was no food. They also complained that the Smolar family (ours) was hoarding food. The government agent approached my father and, very politely, explaining the situation and the complaints, asked if father would part with enough food to give each needy family two pounds of grain. Reluctantly, my father gave them enough for this request.

"When the Germans and Austrians started retreating from this area, they loaded many boxcar loads of black fertile soil and hauled them by train out of the country. However, the Germans had to leave many of their pigs and cows behind. When they left local people went to the communal pasture and stole a pig or cow, hiding it in barns or behind stacks of straw.

When the Poles arrived, they insisted that the livestock belonged to the government of Poland and had to be returned. They demanded we turn over our cattle. We told them we brought these animals from Shipiterka, but they wouldn't believe us and tried to take them. My mother wrapped her hands around the ropes on the cows and told them they would have to cut her hands off before they could remove the animals. They finally left.

"When the Poles took over governing this part of the Ukraine, they closed all the schools and made it illegal to educate any Ukrainian. My older brother, Fedor, had had a couple of year's education before the war. My father approached the municipality and told them we needed a school for the younger children. There were many small children around and they must at least learn to read and write. Some people criticized him, saying he wanted to rise above the local peasantry. However, he insisted if children were going to go off to wars and fulfill other obligations, they should be able to communicate with parents.

"The clerk at the municipal hall sympathized with Dad but said there was nothing he could do. Then he gave Dad the name of a young woman who was educated and was willing to teach if Dad could find a way to pay her and find a school. Dad immediately told him he would undertake to pay her and would provide a room in his home in which to teach and live. This was immediately set up. Other parents who sent their kids shared in the cost of paying her. My brother Alex attended this school. I went for 3 days and was removed. My mother said that there was too much work to be done for girls to waste time in school.

"About three months later the governing Poles found out about the school and informed my father it was illegal to teach Ukrainians. The school was closed down. I never learned to read or write.

"We made our own linen. Flax was planted and when ripe was cut down by hand. It was laid out in the sunshine to dry. After a few days, my mother would decide if it was ready for threshing (to remove the seed). When it was ready we shook some seeds out and then used a flailing stick to beat the rest out.

"After that we hauled the flax straw down to the river, which was about two miles away, soaked it, and weighed it down with tree branches. About a week later mother would go down to test it and decide if it was ready for drying again. When ready, we would haul it back to our yard and lay it out on the ground or stack it against the house for drying. When it was thoroughly dry we would beat it with sticks until the outer straw fell away. We then combed it with a wooden comb, and then a finer comb. By now only the silky strands were left. We would dry it thoroughly and then twist it together. Mother bought dyes and we dyed the thread, mainly orange, green, blue and black. Then we spun it into fine thread.

"Word would be passed around that we needed a weaver. A woman would arrive with her looms and we would instruct her what to weave: dishtowels, sheets, and blankets. These would be different sizes, and different colours and designs. We paid her by the yard. I had a trunk full of home-made linen when I got married. However, on the advice of your father's brothers in Canada, I didn't bring them with me when we emigrated. I sold them to a rich woman.

"I also want to tell you about a wonderful drink my father made every spring. He would tap the local birch trees and we would haul pails and pails of this sap and pour it into a large barrel. Dad would then add dried prunes, apricots, apples, and pears - whatever was left over from winter. This would ferment for a *couple of weeks; then we drank it. It was the best drink I ever had. I wanted to drink this again one more time when I went home to the Ukraine in 1982, but didn't get a chance."*

And that is the last story my Mother told me!

I want to add something else. Mother's parents were killed sometime during World War II. She presumed the communists killed them. However, when she visited her home village in 1982, her relatives and old neighbours assured her that it was not communists, but roving bandits, who were razing the countryside, attacking and robbing citizens. Her parents were defending themselves during a robbery and were killed. She spent years blaming the communists.

I am standing behind my sister Nena, Lyle and my mother.

Later that summer Grace McInnis died and we attended her funeral in Vancouver. Grace was an old family friend and the daughter of J.S. Woodsworth, the founding leader of the CCF. She had been both an MLA and an MP, and the wife of long-time MP Angus McInnis. We visited her many times in Sechelt when we travelled to our cottage in Madeira Park. We had the pleasure of having her attend our joint wedding anniversary celebrations: Mom and Dad's (Kristiansen) 50th, and Lyle's and my 25th. Our children - and we – enjoyed the special treat of hearing her give her father's grace, Grace Before Meat, which said:

"We are thankful for these and all the good things of life. We recognize they are part of our common heritage and come to us through the efforts of our brothers and sisters the world over. What we desire for ourselves, we wish for all. To this end, may we take our part in the world's work and the world's struggles".

Grace McInnis and Lyle

SOVIET UNION

It is sad that after 75 years of trying to build a communist society, it has now fallen apart.

Its failure decreases the hope that humans can be motivated by something other than personal gain, greed and avarice. If the western world had not hounded and obstructed the Soviet Union's existence, it would have been interesting to see if they could have succeeded.

Communism, to me, simply means *"the common ownership of all wealth".* That, I felt, was similar to the Christian philosophy *"Love thy neighbor as thyself."* But the Western world panicked. Twenty-one countries (including Canada) placed their armies on the periphery of Russia immediately following the Revolution, and assisted the White (tsarist) army to nearly capture all of Russia. Only two provinces held out and, from there, the Whites and foreign invaders were pushed out.

The Soviet people were trying to build a society on the premise "from each according to his/her ability, to each according to his/her need." The Russian Revolution took place in 1917, in a country that had changed from a feudal system only two decades earlier. It was one of the most backward in the world. People were uneducated, poor, agrarian, rife with religious mysticism and control. The priests were literally the tsar's informants.

There was a similar reaction during the French revolution. When the French king and queen were executed, it sent shock waves through almost every royal house in Europe. They feared their own people would realize kings were mere mortals, and not extensions of god as they had been led to believe.

So it was also in Russia. The capitalist powers saw a threat that, if allowed to succeed, could lead their peoples to question why the few who own the wealth could dictate the conditions everyone else had to live by: wages, prices, form of government. It must be remembered that, at the time of the Russian revolution, the idea of democracy (as in universal adult franchise) was still in its infancy and was being resisted almost everywhere in western society.

The western powers (including Japan), or rather the classes that dominated them, undertook a campaign to portray "communists" as evil-doers, cruel, ugly, out to control the world and take everyone's property away from them. They were so successful in this campaign that they could send ordinary people – soldiers – to fight and die in countries like Indo China, Malaya, Guatemala, Viet Nam, Cuba, Nicaragua, Grenada, and dozens of places in colonial Africa and elsewhere, to protect the wealth of the few. Taxpayers' money was used to fight in all these places – all to preserve the structure and control of society as it existed.

There never was a Soviet threat, other than the setting up of an example. Instead of improving their own societies, the "west" chose to discredit the USSR by fear, and impede the growth of progressive forces at home and in countries throughout the world.

Some of the capitalist powers went even further. Hitler's Germany, Mussolini's Italy, and Imperial Japan ruthlessly suppressed all progressive dissent within their own and neighboring countries and went on to aggressively expand their dominance in Spain, Central Europe, Asia and Africa in the same way as England, France, and other imperial powers had done so successfully in the previous century. Churchill called Hitler "the savior of Europe from Bolshevism". America and Canada branded those who volunteered to fight to save the Spanish democratic republic as "criminals". No western capitalist country among the so-called "liberal democracies" lifted a finger against fascism as long as the target was communism.

Is it any wonder that the USSR felt threatened, and began to recreate client buffer states, akin to the old Russian Empire, as they expelled the Fascists from their borders after WW 11, just as they had expelled the 21 foreign armies earlier.

Following the revolution, the leaders of the new USSR wanted to build a society where the means of production was owned by the community and profits would accrue to the benefit of the whole society.

Toward this end, they established full employment and, despite boycotts and economic blockade, built an industrialized state from a near feudal society. Through a policy of forced – and sometimes brutal – industrialization, they achieved their industrial revolution, arising from the ashes of civil war and large losses of European territory, in only 20 years.

The same industrial revolution in Western Europe and America had taken well over a hundred years, with millions of deaths, casualties, forced migration, revolts, starvation, and disease. But, of course, these deaths in the "West" were said to have happened due to the "invisible hand" of a "free market", and thus no person or party or state was said to be guilty of these crimes against humanity.

The first leader of the USSR, Vladimir Lenin, was a brilliant, well-educated man. He gave up a comfortable life to work toward a society where every person had an opportunity to succeed, and where everyone rose together toward a more equitable society, rather then constantly competing against each other. People made great sacrifices toward this goal. There were also people – and leaders - who misused their power or abused their positions to wreak vengeance. This can happen anywhere. And it has – left, right and centre.

However, the Soviets accomplished a great deal, and despite mistakes, blockades, and a devastating World War II that caused 25 million deaths, and destruction on a scale unmatched in this century, they went on to accomplish it all over again – after 1945. A great hindrance to world trade for the USSR was being kept out of the World Bank. Because their roubles were not listed with the World Bank, they had to pay for any purchases from other country with that country's money. When they bought wheat from Canada they had to pay for it in Canadian dollars (or sell us vodka in exchange). This made trade extremely limited and difficult.

Wages did not vary much from occupation to occupation. It was accepted that the state paid for the total education of a person, thus he/she owed it to the country to work for a reasonable wage. Wages were based on the number of people in the family. Thus, some janitors were paid more than some teachers. The reasoning was that the janitor worked and contributed to the teacher's education all the years he was in university.

Education has been a priority in every communist government in every country. It is free at every stage. In Cuba, not only was education made available to all young people, but a system was undertaken for students to work during the summer in cities, towns and rural areas, teaching every citizen to read, regardless of age.

I heard an American "anti communist" speaker say this was because the communists wanted the people to read their propaganda.

University students in the Soviet Union had free tuition, books, accommodation, and were paid a stipend of 80 rubles a month. Thousands of students from underdeveloped countries got their education in the Soviet Union with the same provisions.

When I toured the Soviet Union in 1985 I was surprised to learn that elementary students in every school were offered three hot meals a day. The rationale was a hungry child did not learn, and no child should be disadvantaged because his parents did not feed him. Although I was an avid reader about the Soviet Union, I never once read about this.

I lived all my life keenly tuned in to what was happening in the Soviet Union. But it was difficult to get facts. I would have to glean information through bits and scraps of news. We would hear ad nauseam how undemocratic that country was, and then get a news report giving the results of an election.

In time I learned that they based their electoral system on the U.S. example, because it was the newest "people's democracy". They also had two Houses; the House of Representatives represented the population. The House of Nations had an equal number of elected people from each of the republics: Russia with 100 million people had the same number as a republic with less than one million.

The major difference between the two countries was that U.S. has two capitalist parties (they outlawed the communist party), while the USSR had one Communist Party. Their campaigning took place before a general election when candidates were selected, similar to the U.S. electoral primary system. Trade unions, farm groups, and others placed names in nomination for potential candidates, and campaigned for their nominee's election.

Whoever won this nomination had their name placed on the official ballot in the general election. Not all candidates were members of the Communist Party (the year I was in the USSR, only 40% of elected people were members). In the general election, people voted "Yes" or "No" opposite each name. More importantly, people went out to vote! They had 80%-90% turnout.

The last time I heard the percentage of participation in the U.S. was in the 1990s, which had 50% of the adult population registered to vote. Of those, 50% voted. That brought it down to 25% participation. Since then, I understand the figures have increased, but it has been impossible to get any official figures. In Canada we get these figures immediately after each election, and there is concern if participation drops.

The USSR held elections for city councils, cultural centres, children's cultural centres, water boards, education boards, etc. In industry, they elected board members, managers, and foremen. They voted far more often than we did, but they were called undemocratic because it was a different process.

In the Soviet Union there was little crime, very little drug problems, prostitution was not visible, no begging or sleeping in the streets. Pornography was not legally allowed. Morality was high. We asked our guide (during my tour) if she lived with her boyfriend, and she looked startled. "Of course not," she said. "That is just not done!" Religion was tolerated, but door-to-door soliciting was not allowed. By the 1980s the vast majority of doctors, dentists, and architects were women. Day care was available to everyone. Thus women were able to participate fully in every aspect of life. There was no welfare system. The rule that no rich person should live off the avails of others, applied also to lazy people.

There was misinformation within that country: I met a young woman on a plane who told me if you didn't work in the Soviet Union the authorities would throw you in jail. I asked our tour guide about it and she said this was not true. " However," she added, "if you aren't working and have lots of money to spend, you may find yourself watched."

In 1985, the Soviet government announced, with pride, that they could finally say, "Everyone had a home." The buildings were uninteresting box frames, but everybody had a home. Now they could start on more individualistic designed buildings.

Their wages weren't high; the top was about 600 rubles a month, but rent was a maximum of 10% of wages (a family we visited lived in an old building and they paid 5%); bread had not increased in price since the 1930s; food was subsidized; fares on the metro remained at five kopeks (cents). Cars were expensive, but the metro and bus system was very convenient.

We took a ride on the metro in Moscow and got off at every station just to see the decor. Every station was beautiful, with paintings and interesting architecture. This was so different from what I saw in the New York subway. There, it was filth, garbage-strewn, graffiti on every inch of wall, and bag ladies lined the walls where they lived and slept.

Anyone with an aptitude in gymnastics, music, dancing, or sports got all the training they needed. That is why they shone in world competitions. But these star performers did not get huge wages. The reasoning was that the people paid for their training and expenses, and now they did the work they were best suited for.

Trechiak, generally accepted as the world's best hockey goalie, was paid his regular army wage (when he left to play hockey). I heard he was asked to defect. He said he wouldn't defect, but was planning to retire (1982), and was willing to teach potential goalies. He could only come to Canada if he defected and denounced his government. He chose not to.

I have to state again what agony I went through from childhood onward, being Russian, and hearing such horrendous things about that country. I was fortunate in having a father who could give me another side to whatever I was hearing.

One day I came running home from school, crying. I told Dad our teacher said all the churches were burned down in Russia (I was very religious then). My father explained the role that the church played in tsarist Russia. He said the priests had great powers over people, and would threaten eternal hell fire if anyone disobeyed the priests or the tsar. The priests literally assisted in tax collection, and informed the tsar of the names and ages of young men in every village, for conscription into the army.

When I was working in Vancouver, and after hearing something really bad, I finally said to myself: It's no use. I can't continue believing my father and disregard all this information coming from everywhere. It has to be the most horrendous government on the face of the earth. I have to start accepting it. Perhaps things are different from what my father remembered.

Shortly after this, I met a Canadian fisherman who told me this story. He and five others worked on a small fishing boat. They would go to sea for two or three weeks at a time. It rained a lot and they got soaked. In the evening they would warm some food over a small stove. They spent the evening drying their clothes, and trying to get warm and stay warm.

One day they ran into a Soviet trawler. They were invited to share a meal and an evening with them. The Soviet fishermen pulled up to their mother ship and someone else unloaded their catch. The fishermen had a hot bath, changed into dry clothes, sat down to a big dinner served them in a dining room, and then retired to another room to play snooker or cards or just read. It was like a luxurious hotel.

I was struck senseless! Why would such a horrendous government treat its lowly fishermen so well? What was the explanation? Who was lying to me? I was to repeat these questions over the years.

In 1957, my Mother's brother came to visit from Poland, where he took up residence after the war. In every letter he begged us to send him a ticket to visit his dear sister. My father was not fond of him.

My sisters and I, together with our parents, raised $1,000, and sent him a ticket to visit for six months.

Mother was overjoyed, as she had no relatives in Canada. When Alex saw the farm our parents lived on, with no electricity or running water, he wouldn't stay there. He returned to Edmonton with us sisters. We explained how our universities worked, and what it cost; how our medical services worked, and the cost (this was before Medicare). We visited used car lots (this being his business in Poland) and he was impressed that there were no restrictions on their profit. He could only make 5% on cars he sold.

I asked him what he wanted in a society? He replied he wanted all the social services Poland had and the freedom to do whatever he wanted in business that we enjoyed. I told him maybe he couldn't have both.

After he saw beggars in the street, he visited mother one more time, and then returned to Poland, only three weeks after arriving. He had spent many years going to his basement with friends to listening to Radio Free Europe. His visions of what life was like in America was not what he witnessed.

So my ears always perked up whenever I heard Radio Free Europe mentioned. In the fall of 1991, when it looked like the Soviet Union would break up, I was talking to a reporter from Tass, a Russian newspaper, about it. He told me what amazed the people in power in the Soviet Union was the extent to which their citizens thought life in the U.S. was ideal. They knew some thought it, but the numbers were far greater than anyone suspected. Radio Free Europe paid off!

President Mikhail Gorbachev was right in wanting to loosen restrictions. The time had long since passed for this. People needed to travel freely within their own country and the world. In the past, they had reasons for restrictions. People could not just pick up their things move to Moscow. They had to apply for permission, prove there was a job in their line of work, and that they had somewhere to live. They did not want overcrowding and homelessness in big cities. The authorities had to plan ahead and know what was needed. In time this lead to a bloated bureaucracy, and increased impatience and frustration.

For all the shortcomings, and I know there were many, was it necessary to completely dismantle everything that their forefathers put into place with so much sacrifice? Could they not build toward a better society from where they were?

Needless to say, the United States was working long and hard to undermine that society. Besides Radio Free Europe, there were many clandestine covert operations. And there was the arms race which was bankrupting the USSR and starving them of the resources needed to satisfy the legitimate aspirations of their people for a better life.

The final straw was in the 1980s when the U.S. announced they were building a satellite system that could intercept and shoot down any missile from outer space, at a cost of trillions of dollars. Gorbechev discouraged this undertaking by cutting military spending unilaterally, withdrawing troops from Afghanistan, and dismantling certain military bases.

The U.S. praised him, did some dismantling themselves, but refused to stop the "Star Wars", as it was known. While to the rest of the world Gorbachev looked like a diplomat, to his countrymen he must have looked weak and vulnerable. The Soviet "hard liners" and some leaders arrested Gorbachev in an attempted coup, which backfired, but the damage was done. Boris Yeltsin took over and, with his connivance, the nation tore itself apart.

My friend, Nina Perepolkin, in front of a mural of Engels, Marx and Lenin in Moscow.

HITCHHIKING THROUGH EUROPE - 1956

In 1956, after turning 21, and after I broke off my relationship with Danny Lys, I had some money saved. Through a co-worker I met two young women in Edmonton planning a 3-month trip to Europe. I had wanted to go to Europe since childhood, and decided this was the time to do it. When I told my boss, Mr. Davies, about going to Europe, he laughed, saying, "You've hardly been across the street. Now you are going to Europe?"

I met with Lydia Bellan and Eva Strachen, and they agreed to let me join them. In May we headed for Montreal by bus. I have many relatives in Montreal. Some, as children, spent summers holidays on our farm. In Montreal they treated us to several family parties and a night out on the town at nightclubs. This was a "first" for us as Alberta only had beer parlours as drinking outlets.

Travelling on the ship, Ascania, was wonderful. I had never even stayed in a hotel before, so this was fantastic! Lydia and I were seated at the captain's table, which was exciting. We, and the other four people at our table, were invited for cocktails in the captain's quarters. Our waiter, Dave, was the cutest guy, who kept whispering teasing things in my ear. I would want to burst out laughing, but had to demurely stifle the laugh, nearly choking on it. I fell madly in love with him and would meet him late at night when he got off work for some heavy petting. Lydia and I had a grand time. We danced all evening. I was proposed to twice, but never by my gorgeous waiter. Ten glorious days of holiday.

I met Dave in London, and he took me to Hyde Park, by Buckingham Palace. I thought it was the most beautiful park in the world. My heart broke when I had to say goodbye. I received letters from him throughout Europe, and we planned to meet, but I never saw him again.

I had a second cousin, Mark Sharko (stage name Sheldon) to look up. He was an actor in London. Lydia and I went to his beautiful home. Servants served tea. He took us around London. We saw a couple of movies he was in, including "*The Baby and the Battleship*". I shall quote directly from my diary during our trip through England:

May 9: After a few days in London, we were anxious to get going. Fully equipped, our rucksacks packed to the brim, we left our luggage at Alberta House. We caught the Greenline bus at Hyde Park corner and got a ticket to Slough (pronounced Slow). The driver showed us where to go to find the Bath road.

My first experience at hitchhiking. I haven't the nerve to stick my thumb out, so Lydia and Eva do that and I watch for cars that stop. It was raining pretty hard by the time we got out of the city and we were hoping people would have pity on us. It was only three minutes before we got a ride with a "lorry" (truck). However, he wasn't going very far - about 10 miles. We got out on the A4 highway again. It was still raining, but within a few minutes we got a ride in a panel truck with three men who were working on telephone wires. They asked us all about Canada. They took us as far as Reading, nearly halfway to Bath.

This time we didn't bother walking out of the town as it was still raining and we were looking like drowned ducks. I slipped up on my job, not seeing a panel stop and wait for us. It was a man that distributed blood plasma to the town of Reading, going back to Bristol. It was a very small panel so Lydia and I sat in the back on the bottles of blood. We were cramped. We pulled out the cheese and crackers and ate, sang songs, told jokes. Finally we stopped for a cup of tea, which we appreciated very much.

After the tea I was given the seat in front and Eva went in back. The driver sounded like a guide as he kept pointing

179

out places of importance. I saw the home and grounds of Sir Gordon Thomas, a famous jockey who was made a knight recently. He now has a farm and trains horses for people. Further on I saw a white horse carved on the side of a hill - dug out to the chalky lime under the black soil.

This is the first time I saw English countryside and I was impressed. Four or five acre plots surrounded by hedges. The trees are so picturesque. Quaint little villages, close together, with thatched-roof houses. I think people try hard to make their country beautiful. No wasteland here.

We got a ride to Chippenham - 12 miles from Bath. After a handshake and sad adieus we walked a little ways and stuck out our thumbs again. In a few minutes we got a ride in a car! With our rucksacks we filled the little English car. Entering Bath was beautiful; 5 miles of high stonewalls. When there was an opening we could see a big stone castle with lots of trees and grass.

Our first Youth Hostel, and such a lovely one, built in about 1832. Must have been some Lord's home as it has French windows and so much land full of trees and flowers around. Later we went down to the Common Room where people were playing table tennis and sitting around a fireplace. Struck up a conversation with 2 Australians, 2 New Zealanders and a Czechoslovakian girl. Also a boy from India (with blond hair). Lights out at 11. Breakfast at 8:15, with porridge, bacon and beans. For our daily duty Lydia and I peeled potatoes and Eva washed the dishes.

We headed downtown to see the Baths. Romans built this town in the 1st century.It has high stonewalls with flowers and vines hanging. Many churches with spires. Cobblestone streets. The Baths have very hot water flowing. There was the Common Bath, the Circular Bath, and the King's Bath with a large crown in the middle. We stopped at the Abbey and the Guide Hall. A man was showing students around, so we followed to hear the history.

Next day at 2 p.m we were off to Salsbury and Andover. Our first ride was to Trowbridge in a little car through very lovely country. We walked through town to the

Salsbury highway. Had some difficulty getting a ride. An army truck finally stopped and we were quite glad to jump in the back. They said they were going to Westbury and we thought it was on our way. When we got in, we looked at our maps and it was not. We found they had gone out of their way to take us there, only to find it was not where we wanted to go. So they went their way and we walked through this sleepy little town to the Andover highway. We saw a lovely little farm; pigs lying under the apple and cherry trees. Coming from northern Alberta, this was impressive! The trees are in full bloom. We got a ride in a little car with a Sun Life insurance man. He drove us straight to Andover to Eva's friend's house, where we had tea and buttered bread.

At 6:30 we headed out to Winchester highway. Got a ride part ways in a car, and then on the back of an open truck. Could see more country this way. Watched the pheasants eating in the fields. Jumped off at the end of town, walked through town, past an old watermill and found the hostel. After registering we walked back up town for a Guiness!

<u>May 11:</u> What a night! I knew this was The Old Mill, but I didn't realize what a spookie place it was with the lights out. Hardly slept at all because of the noise - and it was so cold, even with eight blankets. After breakfast we explored the bottom of this building and found what the noise was. Where we slept the water was running very swiftly. The old wheel wasn't turning, but it made a lot of noise. It is such a lovely little place, with a bridge and little garden. Went down to see the old cathedral which was made of white marble. Was more impressed with this than Westminster Abbey in London. Set out for Bexhill.

I got the first ride. We were walking up this awfully steep hill to get out of town, and I stuck my thumb out - my first time to hitchhike! We went through Midhurst where the Duke of Edinburgh plays polo. This was Eva's birthday so we had a drink and Eva got quite giddy. We treated her to a good hot dinner - our first since London.

Got a ride in a nice car and the driver took a side road to show us beautiful countryside, with yew trees among the chestnut. What I really like is the birch trees with the copper coloured leaves. He pointed out the castle of the Duke of Norfork and its hunting grounds which are surrounded by a high stone wall. Then we entered Aurendel where the duke's home is - at least 120 rooms. Another car picked us up and drove us to the Horse and Groom, and the owner drove us to Worthing, the first coastal city. He went a long way out of his way to put us on the right road to Brighton. We had a bit of difficulty getting a ride until an elegant looking man came along and drove us through Brighton. This is Dave's (my waiter) home town which he talked about lovingly. The streetlights had flowers around them. Saw the Palace of Fun on the harbour and the Pavilion which was really beautiful.

We caught a bus out of town and this time it really was hard to get a ride. We were cold and damp before a panel stopped. The man talked with us about Canada, and then said he would like to take us home with him, to Telescombe. He had a Canadian wife who would love to see us. She was so nice to us, gave us tea and buttered bread and cakes. Later Mr. Weston drove us about ten miles out of town toward Eastbourne. It made us feel so good to have someone take us into their home. Had another stroke of luck because just when we got out of Mr. Weston's car it was starting to rain hard, and before we got across the road a car stopped for us. This guy was going straight through to Bexhill. He drove us straight to the door of the Eva's friend, Elsie Kristenson, who welcomed us heartily, fed us, let us wash up, and gave us a lovely bed to sleep in.

May 12: What a wonderful bed to wake up in: soft, warm. Elsie brought us coffee in bed. We spent the day washing ourselves and our clothes. After dinner of roast chicken, we went to the beach to watch the waves splash and pick seashells. It is fascinating to watch the water roll in. Later we went with Elsie to Hastings to a dance held on the pier. Met some interesting characters - especially Eva's guy who was a lieutenant in the Army, and had a huge moustache. He wore a lime coloured vest, greenish jacket, *wine ascot - his name: Sir Jeffrey Hilliard-Millar! We took the bus home together.*

May 13: Sunday. It was 10 before we got out of bed, and had coffee brought up again. After a big breakfast, washing, ironing, sewing, packing, we were off again. Being Sunday, we had difficulty getting a ride. Families out for a drive, filled their little cars. Started the week off wrong by getting on the wrong road. We got a ride to Hastings, where we had to walk up a big hill to get on the highway, and we got a ride again in a stationwagon with a very nice couple and a baby. They showed us the hop fields near the beer factories in Kent. Also drove us through Wilshire and Rye, taking us into the church with a long pendulum hanging down the middle of the church.

These kind people dropped us off at the edge of Rye. We could not get a ride, nohow! Every car was full, and no lorries on the road. After walking 5 miles we decided to split up and meet at Dover. Lydia went ahead and I followed. I walked another two miles. I saw Eva pass and right after that a small sports convertible, with a sporty-looking guy in a funny hat stopped for me. He knew my cousin Mark Sheldon, the actor. We passed Eva on a motorcycle, and Lydia in a little car full of children. Eva and I met and found the hostel together. Lydia came half hour later. Next morning went down to the dock, changed our money into franks - getting 35 franks for $1.00. Wish they were dollars. Boarded the ferry. Had dinner on the ferry and then we docked at Calais, France. We had started a conversation with a Chinese student studying at Manchester University and he offered us a ride to Paris. Lucky for us.

To summarize, our trip through France was somewhat uneventful. While we enjoyed the historic monuments and museums, the language barrier precluded interaction with people. We went to see the Follies Berge, which to us Albertans, was quite pornographic. After a week, we headed for Spain.

We took the train to Spain, as we were told it was illegal to hitchhike there. There were no youth hostels in Barcelona, so we stayed at a pensione, which provided us with three meals. It was extremely reasonable. When we went to the beach, we were packed a lunch basket.

We enjoyed an evening of folk dancing at a local tavern, and then we dancing all the Spanish dances: samba and rumba – it was surprisingly easy with good partners. The bullfight, on the other hand, was not so enjoyable. After what I considered extreme cruelty, the bull was weaken by being bled with spears, and then the strutting peacock of a matador plunged the fatal spear through the heart. A man sitting beside me asked how I enjoyed the performance. I replied "Not at all. This is not a sport." He said, "Of course it is not a sport. It is an art." I didn't think it was an art, either.

We travelled back to France and, along the beautiful shores of the Riviera, to Monte Carlo. At the youth hostel at Cape d'Ail we met three fellows from New Zealand. Pairing off, we rented paddle boats and paddled around the palace and casinos. In the evening we went to a casino, where we played the slots and won some money. I walked through the rows of tables where people were playing cards. At one table I stood staring at the pile of money alongside a player. The pile looked enormous. I looked up to see him smiling at me, and beckoning me to come over. I turned and walked away quickly. I was such a coward.

Pisa, with its leaning tower, was interesting, and then on to Rome. Here, the usual tourist spots of the Vatican, and museums, the Colliseum, and Michaelangelo paintings and statue and churches. We travelled back to Florence and viewed some more churches. Then off to Venice. What a beautiful city, with its canals and bridges. The glass blowing factories were wonderful. And the gondola rides were romantic. I was falling in love and leaving friends in every city.

We stayed in Switzerland a few days. Eva had a friend to call on in a rural area, so we were able to experience living in a house that was attached to the barn. We slept in soft, down-filled mattresses. I was curious whether the smell of the barn would permeate the house. It was not an unpleasant smell.

We ate lots of chocolates. Toured the U.N. building in Geneva, and was impressed. And then headed for Austria. However, our ride suggested we do a quick detour through the small country of Liechtenstein. It was even smaller than Monte Carlo. We travelled through it in an hour. It was raining, so the impression I have is of mountains lost in clouds; with one small town built on the mountainside.

In Austria we spent a couple of nights in Salzburg, and attended a concert. Mozart lived there.

Germany next. This was different from any other country. Many waterways and castles built alongside. The hostels were brand new and very comfortable - probably the nicest in Europe.

Munich was the most fun. We went to the Haufbrau Haus, which was in the film "Student Prince", my favourite musical. We sat at a huge table with many Germans. Joined in the singing of "Ein, Zwei, Sopha", and other songs. One German leaned over to me and said, "We liked the Americans and Canadians during the war, but not the Russians." I asked him if American and Canadian population suffered what the Russians had. He didn't reply.

In Hamburg, Eva left us to go back to England. Lydia and I took an airplane to Berlin. Months earlier the

Soviet Union had placed an embargo on ground travel through the Soviet part of Germany, and all contact with Berlin had to be done by air.

On the plane we met two Saudi Arabian students studying in London. They talked us into staying at the hotel they were at. They were fun to be with and we did some sightseeing with them.

We phoned the girl we had met in Switzerland, who came by one evening and took us nightclubbing. One club was fascinating. As a floorshow, it had a coloured water fountain that moved to music. But that was not the best feature. At each table was a mail chute, where notes were sent from one table to another. One got asked to dance through this mail chute. We had our Canadian flag on our table, so got many notes and a general good time was had by all.

We had been warned, especially by American soldiers, not to go near the East Berlin border - that people were known to disappear just walking near it. We heard all kinds of horror stories. But our Berlin girlfriend told us another side.

She and her family had lived in East Berlin, and decided to move to the West. We were amazed! How? "What do you mean?" she asked. "We just packed our things took the underground train, and moved." She said her boyfriend was studying medicine in East Berlin because education was free. Every Sunday she visited him there, or he would visit her. This did not jive with our what we heard. We told her some of the things. She was amazed. She didn't know what they were talking about.

Lydia and I had to find out for ourselves. One morning we told our Arab friends we were going to East Berlin, and if we weren't back by evening to contact the Canadian embassy. We found the underground train, taking a seat in the first car where we could see the driver. We were told that drivers changed at the border, that we would be searched and asked for passports. The drivers didn't change. We didn't even know when we crossed the border. We got off in the centre of town, walked around, and took in a circus.

Later we stopped at an outdoor cafe for a coke, and at this point the waitress asked us for our "documentie". We showed her our passports and she served us. We asked why she wanted to see them. She told us that stores and cafes had to ask for papers because of the difference in money value - a West Berlin mark was exchanged for four East Berlin, although the prices for commodities were similar. This prevented West Berliners shopping there.

And that was it. We took a bus back to West Berlin. Noted there were many more ruins still in evidence in East Berlin, and that their buildings seemed very standardized with little relief from the boring box frames. But we were not searched, not stopped at the border, not followed.

For years after this, I heard news reports about people sneaking across the border to West Berlin and being shot. The horror stories continued until the Berlin wall came down. To me it remained a mystery. Rather than stealing across the wall, why didn't they take the bus? Why had those who wanted to live in West Berlin not move during the 13 years before the wall went up?

We flew back to Hamburg, spent a few days in The Hague, Holland, and took the all-night ferry back to England.

We spent some time with Eva's relatives in Scotland, on the Firth of Fourth, near Edinburgh. Then we headed home to Canada. I never felt so Canadian as during that trip home.

How do you keep them down on the farm after they've seen Paree? I couldn't go back to my old life, and would leave for Vancouver soon after.

Lydia and I in an outdoor café in Paris.

MY FAVOURITE CHILDREN MEMORIES

Like every mother, I have my favourite memories of bringing up my children. Or perhaps better said, children whipping their parents into shape. I wrote a series of columns for the Nelson Daily News entitled "Bringing up Parents". Mothers have so many preconceived ideas when babies are born, on how to raise them. It takes some bashing before children get parents to change.

When Eric was six months, we were spending an evening with friends. I went on and on as to when I thought I should start teaching him the alphabet and numbers, which was, I believe, soon after he turned one year old.

Finally, a teacher in the group snapped at me, "For heaven's sake, woman, you do your job and let the teachers do theirs. If you do yours right, the teachers will have no problem with theirs." I was shocked! "What do you mean? What is my job?" He said, "You just keep the child happy, healthy, interested, curious, and the teachers will have an easy time teaching him. Mothers always teach their children the alphabet in capital letters. Then the teachers have to un-teach them. 'A' can also be 'a'."

I kept his words in mind all through the formative years of my children, and worked hard at my "job". Whenever any doubts crept into whether I was doing the right thing with my children, I just asked myself, "Are they happy, healthy, curious, interested? Good. Then they're all right."

Many times I took one child out of school and let him or her accompany Lyle to Vancouver when he was attending a conference. Grandparents put a lot of effort into taking them to museums, the art gallery, the planetarium. I knew the children learned so much from these trips. It gave the father, as well as the grandparents, an opportunity to get to know them one-on-one.

When I was the distribution agent for the Vancouver Sun in the Nelson area, I delivered the paper to all the stores and paperboys at 5 a.m. Each of the children took turns accompanying me. It was my one opportunity to spend time individually. This was the time I could tell them a little of my childhood and parents. At least this was the time when each showed some interest. The early hours of the day changed with each season; the lake and the city looked so beautifully different. Eric actually said, "This is so beautiful." None complained. We were earning our own money for good ski equipment.

When we saved enough, we drove to Spokane and bought top of the line stuff, and on the way home, stopped at Sweitzer Mountain to ski.

I was determined that my children were not going to get a "sweet tooth" which they would have to live with the rest of their lives. On the farm there was no such thing as baby food in a can. Mothers made their own food, starting with cream of wheat, and progressing to soft scrambled eggs. All the food and water had sugar or honey added to it. This presumed babies liked sweet taste. In fact babies don't have a taste, and develop one by what is fed them. My children were not going to get a "sweet tooth".

One day I attended a Tupperware Party in the community. A woman came up to me and asked if I was Mrs. Kristiansen. On my affirmative reply, she started to laugh and tell this story, much to the amusement of everybody else: "One day I had a knock on the door, and found two cute little kids standing there, the boy with a mop of red hair. They said to me `Do you have any cookies? Our mommy doesn't make cookies.' I invited them in and fed them cookies." I was so embarrassed! Everybody in the room was laughing while I fumed. I could hardly wait to get my hands on those rascals.

Instead, when I got home I searched for recipes for healthy cookies, with lots of raisins, sunflower seeds, and oatmeal; I made cookies often. We picked apples from the many abandoned apple trees in the area every fall. All through winter I made apple bran muffins, and the smell filled the house. On cold days,

I enjoyed having a fire on when the kids came home from school and I served them muffins and cocoa.

I had always been a "liberated woman", and fought for the right for women to work. But when my children were born, I didn't want full-time employment. I wasn't happy staying at home all the time, but I couldn't leave the raising of my children to others.

I was grateful that I had the choice of staying at home as Lyle earned a good salary at Kootenay Forest Products sawmill. Not all mothers had that choice. But there were days when I felt trapped in the house. Being a mother and homemaker can be an isolated and lonely job. When Lyle got home I would want to talk, and would ask him what happened on his job. All he wanted to do was have some peace and quiet, and would get so annoyed with me because nothing interesting happened at the sawmill.

All I could see ahead of me was the same routine. The alarm would go off at 6 a.m. and my day would start. To get myself going in the morning, I would recite the poem 'The Walrus and The Carpenter', before going downstairs to turn up the thermostat and start preparing breakfasts and lunches.

I would swing my feet onto the floor and say, "The time has come, the Walrus said." Pulling my housecoat on, I'd head for the bathroom. "To speak of many things." Leaving the bathroom: "Of shoes and ships and sealing wax. Of cabbages and kings." A gentle tap on each door would get a grunt and I knew each child was awake. I headed for the staircase. "And why the sea is boiling hot. And whether pigs have wings." I knew they would be down shortly. Now all I had to worry about was getting Lyle out of bed. He always waited for my third visit to wake him. He would have 20 minutes to dress, grab a couple mouthfuls of porridge, pull his boots on without tying them, grab his lunchbox and coffee I handed him, bolt out the door, jump in the car, drive across town, and arrive at his job with a minute to spare.

My best friend, Marie Decaire (who had two children), and I would commiserate about our hard life; how the children kept us harried and worn out. It was such a tough life. One spring she and Maurice and Lyle and I were all delegates to an NDP provincial convention. The day before the convention started, there was a day-long Women's Conference which she and I attended. We left our motel that morning cheerfully, saying to our husbands, " Now you will see what it's like having to look after the kids all day!"

Our conference room was hot and humid, and the proceedings were upsetting as we seemed to disagree with everything going on. When we left we were hot, angry and frustrated. Heading back to the motel we said, "The only satisfying part of this whole day is knowing our husbands were stuck with those kids all day." Instead, we found Lyle and Maurice sitting in the swimming pool with a glass of wine in their hands, while all the kids played quietly nearby. NOT FAIR!

Eric loved desserts. He was forever asking me to make a cake. When he was about 8, I said to him, "Now that you can read, you can make the cake." I found a recipe for him, brought all the ingredients together, and told him to go for it. I kept busy nearby. The other two were hanging over him, watching eagerly.

Things were buzzing along. After a while everything was quiet for a long time. I asked if there was a problem, and Eric, holding the egg in his hand, answered, "How do I get the egg out?" Catching my laughter in midstream, I swallowed hard, and with a straight face showed him how to break the shell and get the egg out. It was precious moments like these that made me so happy to be home and not miss.

When Haida was about 8, I overheard her tell a friend, "Nobody ever bought me a gun." I was amazed. We tried hard to treat the children even handedly. Actually, I didn't want any guns bought for the kids but, I watched the boys play with neighbourhood children with guns: Eric's and Colin's were homemade. They played cops and robbers all the time. So we relented.

If Haida wanted a gun as well, so be it. I immediately bought a gun and kept it until a time when we were giving gifts. She opened it and said, "Oh, goodie, my own gun. Finally I got a gun." But she laid it down and never touched it again. So much for equality.

Eric decided to declare his independence when he was about 10. Every morning he took the garbage out. I would hand it to him as he left for school and, on his way through the back alley, he dropped it in the garbage pail. No big deal. But one morning, when I handed him the garbage, he said: "No. I'm not taking the garbage out any more. I don't want to. I don't have to. You can't make me." I was shocked. He was usually such an obedient child.

I decided to take the high road: When the kids came home after school, I was reading a book. They called out, "Can we have a snack?" I replied, "Sure. Help yourself." They came in again around 6 o'clock, and said, "We're hungry. When do we eat?" I replied, "I don't know. I don't feel like cooking. I don't want to cook today. I don't have to." I went on reading my book. Fortunately, Lyle was away that week.

There was a lot of murmuring in the kitchen. I could hear Eric getting the peanut butter jar down. Together they made something and ate it and nothing else was said all evening, by them or me. The next morning, I made their breakfast and, as they were leaving the house, I handed Eric the garbage. He took it without a word.

I took the time to teach each of them how to use the washing-machine and dryer, how to iron and vacuum. Not that they liked it. I impressed on them that mothers - women – were not servants.

When we moved to Ottawa, I went to Lyle's office as a volunteer. I enjoyed being involved. I was helpful, and Lyle wasn't faced each day with my asking, "What happened today." However, the work at home still had to be done. I prepared dinner before I left. Nobody missed us at dinner because each of them ate at different times: one had practice after school, the other at 6, another at 7. They ate whenever they could. But every night I was faced with dirty dishes.

I called a family conference and outlined the problem. I said I needed help keeping the dishes washed. "Aw, Mom. We hate doing dishes." "So," I said, "I hate doing them too. How are we going to solve this?" They retorted, "But you're the Mother!" I gasped, "So what does that mean? Am I to be punished because I am the mother?"

That got them thinking. We went round and round, but there was no avoiding the fact they would have to help. We drew up a schedule, and each undertook one day a week to be responsible for the dishes. Even Lyle took a day. That still left two days for me and, of course, I covered for whoever was out of town or unable to do their duty. But it was a great help to me and they took on some responsibility.

On Saturday morning, each took one hour to perform a duty: vacuum, clean the bathrooms (we had 3), dust, or do the laundry.

Haida was a feminist without even trying. She never backed down if she thought she was not treated equally. One year she and another girl in school decided to play baseball in the boys' league. They approached the league coaches who agreed, and nobody objected. They played the whole season.

One clear, sunny winter morning, I looked out the window and said: "This looks like a perfect day for skiing. There aren't many perfect days, so we have to take advantage of them when they come. Who wants to go skiing with me?" "Aw, Mom" came three replies. "This is a school day." "Come on. Doesn't anybody play hooky now and then? Who wants to go skiing." Not one. I wondered where I went wrong.

In later years, Eric came home for a week from university, and asked Colin to skip school and go skiing. Colin did. They always enjoyed skiing together, challenging each other. The next day Colin asked me to write a note to his teacher. I wrote: "Please excuse Colin's absence yesterday. He had to do some very serious skiing."

That night Colin came home and handed the note back to me; his teacher wouldn't accept it. I asked what that meant. Colin said, "I guess he wants you to lie." So I wrote another one: "Colin had some serious family business to attend to." The teacher accepted that one.

Eric had a hard time in elementary school. He was always a gentle child. One day he came home and said, "If I have to go back to school, I'll kill myself." I went to pieces. What do I do?

There was a kid in his class, Kevin, who would poke, or pinch or kick Eric every time he passed him. I knew Kevin since he was four years old. I watched him in the park one day. Wherever he was, a kid would walk away crying. I could see him hurting them. Once I caught up to him and asked why he did that? He turned his blue eyes on me and, ever so sincerely, asked, "Do what? I didn't do anything." Other mothers and I approached his mother, complaining. But she wouldn't accept the complaints; everybody was always picking on her Kevin.

Now the problem was too great to look the other way. Eric told me what happened in gym practice that day. Everybody was running. Kevin tripped him, jumped on his chest with his knees, and stayed there, smiling. Eric couldn't catch his breath and couldn't scream. When the teacher finally got Kevin off him, Kevin stood up and said, "Sorry, Eric." That was it, Eric decided. He wouldn't return to school.

Now it was my problem. I phoned Mother in Vancouver. She just said, "So don't send him to school. Let him stay at home. Let the school solve the problem."

That's what I did. Eric stayed at home the next day, while I went in and had a meeting with the principal and Eric's home teacher. I told them what happened and announced, "Eric won't be coming back to school." They said how sorry they were to hear it, but what school would I be sending him to? I said, "No school. He will stay at home." "Oh, you can't do that! It's against the law. You have to send him to school." I simply said, "So - sue me!"

Now it was their problem! They thought their problem would be solved - or shelved - by moving Eric to another school. But Eric wasn't the only one suffering from this Kevin. They admitted he was a real headache for everyone. They tried everything to control him, but failed. "Well, that's your problem. I'm keeping Eric at home," I said.

They solved it. They kept Kevin away from the playground, away from gym, at home through the whole lunch break. He would go straight to class and straight home. Eric agreed to return to school.

In grade school a teacher, Mr. Mowrey, noticed Eric's timidity, and realized that if he didn't become more assertive before he hit junior high, he would start developing other problems. He invited Eric to play on a baseball team he was coaching. Lyle and I were never sports minded, so hadn't encouraged our children in that direction. Lyle said the most energy he expended in school was vaulting a fence to escape gym class, and running down the block to buy a milkshake.

Eric agreed to play baseball, and enjoyed it immensely. The first year he received an award for being "the most improved". He was 6 feet tall at age 12. The heights of 12-year-old boys vary greatly. One day, sitting in the bleachers, I watched a little kid come barrelling down to first base where Eric was playing, and, upon arriving, look straight at Eric's knees. He looked up, and asked "Are you on stilts?"

After another baseball game, I drove to the ballpark to pick Eric up. Arriving there, I found the score was 45 to 2 for the other team. I thought, "Poor kid! He'll be devastated. Maybe I can cheer him up by taking him to the Dairy Queen and get him a sundae."

I watched him saunter over to the car. I asked, "How was the game?" He replied, "Not bad." "Not bad?" I exclaimed. "What do you mean, not bad? Do you know the score?" He said, "Oh, I know. That's because our good pitcher wasn't here, and the other team has the best pitcher in the league. Other than that, we didn't make any errors, and everybody got lots of good practice in their positions." I shook my head as I forgot the Dairy Queen and headed for home. "You're all right, kid".

In junior high Eric played basketball. The first game I watched, I noticed Eric threw the ball away as quickly as he could, every time he got possession. I mentioned this to the coach and he agreed. He said Eric needed aggressiveness. However, in a regional volleyball tournament in Salmo, a coach from another district approached me and told me that he never saw one kid dominate a tournament the way Eric did.

He loved basketball. That was his game. One day he asked us to send him to basketball camp at Pullman University in Washington State. We told him we couldn't afford it. He left it for a while, then came back again with the request, saying, "Call it an investment. I'll earn my way through university on basketball scholarships." That made sense, so we scraped up the money and sent him. And he did earn his way through university with scholarships.

He attended Pullman camp three years in a row, each year getting on the all-star team, and getting a Most Valuable Player award. The camp had 400 youngsters from western Canada and the U.S. They were split up into teams, and played against each other every day. Games were interspersed with practice and lectures.

Toward the end of the two-week camp they held playoffs. Two players from each team, a senior and a rookie, were chosen for the all-star games, which were played on the last day when parents were present. The last year he could attend he was again picked for the all-star team. Everybody was pulling for a certain rookie, who worked very hard, and deserved to be the second all-star. But, this year they changed the rules and only one player from each team was chosen. The rookie was so disappointed.

When Eric's name was called to join the all-stars, he stood up, and with tears in his eyes, he refused to accept the nomination. They then picked the rookie. But the gesture was not lost on the coaches. At the end of the games when trophies were handed out, Eric Kristiansen's name was called. This surprised us, as he was not playing. He was given a new award, never before given, called "Outstanding Sportsmanship Award". Thatsa my boy!

Colin always wanted to be, if not as tall as his brother, at least 6 feet. Perhaps, as a result, one could never accuse him of being timid or non-assertive. Not mean - but he went for the jugular! One day in Ottawa he had to guard a country kid who was 6'10". In fact this kid went on to play professionally for an American team. Colin worked so hard guarding, the kid only made four baskets. The kid was billeted at our house, and he told us, "I was afraid Colin was going to bite my knee caps."

As I watched Colin, I remembered my horse, Judy. I told the kids that my horse taught me everything I needed to know about life. Judy was a short, fat, mean-spirited mare. Nena's horse, George, was tall, lanky, and smart-as-a-whip. If ol' George wanted to get into the oat field, he would find a gate, open it with his teeth, and lead all the horses into it.

He was also fast. Every Friday night the whole community converged at the post office to pick up the mail, most coming on horseback. On the way home everybody would be challenging each other to a race. George would win every time.

However, when Nena and I raced, if Judy could get a head start, there was no way George could pass her. At the least hint of a race, she would take off and stay in the lead. George would plod along patiently, going from one side to the other, waiting for an opportunity to pass her. But Judy would kick, squeal, bite, shove him off the road, and keep the lead. So it was with Colin. He kept close to the ground, jabbing at the ball, doing whatever it took.

Colin was and is a terrific skier, a daredevil who didn't know the meaning of fear. He started skiing at 5, and at 7 joined the Nancy Green Ski Team. Eric and Haida did as well. Eric was good but his height increased his wind resistance. Haida enjoyed skiing, but not racing. The only time she came close to winning a race, I ran over to congratulate her. She replied, "I'll bet I wasn't graceful." Well, I thought, if you want to be graceful, racing isn't for you. I let her quit as soon as she wanted to. But racing smartened up their skiing so that they never hesitated skiing any hill, anywhere, any time.

I attended all races, and in fact started skiing myself. I just got tired of waiting around. The first time I went up the ski lift, it took me an hour to come down. I was 40, overweight, and couldn't even skate. With encouragement from the children, and much determination, I learned. My friend, Pat Bredl, and I would tear up the hills – sometimes snowplowing all the way – from season to season.

A few years later I joined the ski patrol. I was never a fast skier, but was strong and steady. My first day on the job, as I entered the ski lodge, an announcement came over the air, "Any ski patrol, please report to the first-aid room." I looked around frantically for another patroller. Nobody else was present. I had to answer the call. When I got there, a man was sitting on a stool with blood flowing down his face. I felt myself fainting, but willed myself to stop. I had two weeks of first-aid training, and was expected to deal with this? I remembered a doctor was in the lodge. I got him to patch the guy up.

My second memorable case was during a race. A Nelson racer, Maurice Valcourt, was determined to win. He gave it his all. He barrelled down the course, smashing into most of the poles. Just as he crossed the finish line he fell and just lay there, gasping for breath.

Well, our very efficient team of patrollers were right there, picking him up, loading him on the toboggan, tying him down before he could get his breath back. When we got him down the hill, he kept screaming at us, "I'm fine. Untie me. Damn it, I'm fine!" But we wouldn't listen. What did he know! We had him on an air ambulance and at the hospital in record time.

The next day I phoned his home and asked to speak to him. His sister said, "I don't think you want to talk to him.' I insisted I wanted to talk to him. I wanted to hear how impressed he was with our speed and concern. But she persisted, "No, you really don't want to talk to him. He is still boiling mad. He was fine, you know. Just out of breath. And because of what you did he missed the second half of the race. He's furious." I didn't insist on talking to him.

I joined every fun race held. On my first such race, I was teamed up with Rod Mcleod, a very proficient skier. The newspaper report said, "For Rod and Vera, the time keepers threw away their watches and started watching the sun." I never came in anywhere but last.

But Colin outshone all of us with his racing. At age 10 he should have taken the top trophy. However, another kid was given it because his time was very close to Colin's and, since he was 13, this was his last year in that league. We all thought Colin had three more years to receive it.

However, the next winter (1979) the federal election was called, and Lyle and I were working full out. Colin got rides with other parents to practice and to races, but he was nowhere near the top. He wasn't even close. I kept asking him if he missed having us at the races. He insisted he didn't care, but he didn't get the top award.

Next year we were in Ottawa and he never raced again. However, the kid with whom he tied went on Canada's national team. Colin said he never forgave us; he was sure he could have gone on to a world championship.

This was a lesson to me regarding the importance of parental interest in children's activities. In Ottawa, whenever any of our children had a game, we moved heaven and earth to attend. Not only Lyle and I, but I encouraged the other two kids to attend.

One night I was sitting by myself, being a lone parent at Colin's basketball game again, when a woman came in, came straight over to me, saying, "I hope you realize I am here because of you." I looked at her and said, "I don't even know you." "Oh, but I know you. You are forcing me to attend these games." She then explained. Her son was on Colin's team. One day he came home from a game and said, "Colin's mother was at the game." Later he added: "And his brother and sister." His mother asked him if he wanted her to come to his games. He said, "No." But after the next game he said the same thing. She said, "I finally realized he did want us to attend."

Other memories. There was the first time Eric lied and stayed out all night. After graduating from South Nelson Elementary, age 13, Eric asked if he could spend the night at his friend Gerry Montgomery's house. I said, "Sure."

During the evening I felt uneasy. On some pretence I phoned Montgomerys, and Skip (his father and principal of the high school) answered. I asked to speak to Eric, and he chuckled, replying, "Gee, Gerry is spending the night at your house." We realized we'd been set-up. Skip said he'd phone his network and try to trace them down and I should do the same.

There was no clue from Eric's friends. Lyle and I drove over to the north shore of Kootenay Lake, and stopped at every beach party we could find. We kept asking if anybody saw Eric and Gerry. Nobody had. Teenagers were annoyed that any adult would drop in on them, but we didn't care.

A week before, a group of high school kids held a party on the side of Kootenay Lake accessible only by boat. One group overloaded a boat and tipped into the icy water. Fortunately it was not deep and everybody walked out.

Home again, we phoned Skip. He had narrowed their whereabouts. Along with Larry Celant, they had Bunny Lightfoot (who was dating Gerry's brother) drive them to a dance in Slocan - 45 miles away. I got in touch with Larry's mother and she joined us worrying. I called Lightfoot's, but Bunny wasn't home.

We didn't sleep a wink all night. About 6 in the morning Larry's mother phoned to say Larry came home. I asked to speak to him. Reluctantly he came to the phone and told me Eric joined a group of young people at a bonfire, but they wouldn't let Gerry or him near it. So they sat for a while and watched. They saw Eric leave with some people in a black truck with steel bars across the back. Larry and Gerry then hitchhiked back to Nelson (at 4 am).

That sounded so ominous. I was seeing bodies floating down the Slocan River. We phoned a friend in Slocan and had him search around town for any clues as to Eric's whereabouts. He phoned back to say he located the bonfire, got confirmation that Eric had been there, but nobody knew anyone with a black truck with steel bars. I can't describe the panic I was going through. It was sheer hell. There was nothing we could do but wait and hope.

Finally, around noon, Montgomery phoned to say he got a call from Eric from downtown saying he wanted to come over. He advised Eric to get his butt home. Eric arrived shortly after.

He explained that he got separated from the other two (he didn't know Gerry and Larry weren't allowed to join the bonfire), and one of the guys at the party offered to have him stay at his house till morning. He thought this was smarter than hitchhiking in the middle of the night. "But", I asked, "Why didn't you phone us?" "Because I didn't want to worry you." He replied. "Didn't want to worry us? Do you have any idea what we went through all night?" He said, "Aw, Mom. You don't have to worry about me." "Eric," I said, "Tell me to stop breathing. It would be easier. Not to worry about a kid would be just as irresponsible as letting a car coast down a hill. We could say we weren't in the car so we aren't responsible for what the car does. We are responsible for what you do!"

After a long time he asked what his punishment would be. I said he was grounded. He asked for how long. I screamed "For life!" He went to his room. After a while I felt sorry for him and dropped in to see how he was doing. He was sitting, staring straight ahead, holding back tears, and said, "Aw, Mom! For life?" I burst out laughing.

Eric kept getting into trouble with Larry. We tried to get him to give up his friendship. Larry was the cutest blond, blue-eyed kid, adopted by an older Italian couple. His mother adored him and gave him no discipline. Larry was in trouble with the police constantly, and in later years, has been in and out of prison. Several people, including a policeman, advised me to keep Eric away from Larry. However, when I mentioned this to Eric, he insisted that he would keep Larry out of trouble. Fat chance!

One night around 11 o'clock, a couple of cops were at the door asking to see Eric. I told them Eric was in bed. They insisted they had to see him. Earlier that evening, Eric went for a car ride with Larry and Kevin. When I asked them where they got the car, Larry said his cousin was visiting from Vancouver. Well, it was a stolen car. I don't know if Eric knew it. The police said, it didn't matter that Eric neither stole nor drove the car. He was still implicated.

The next day, Eric and I went to see the probation officer, John Kirkhope. It was embarrassing as John and I were friends and skied together often. A few years later, his daughter was to get very drunk at a school dance. When I asked him about it, he reacted exactly like every other parent: "It wasn't her fault. Others got the liquor. It isn't funny. People are so irresponsible." I reminded him that's exactly how I felt when I saw him about Eric.

John pointed out the seriousness of the offence, and suggested we get a lawyer for Eric. I told him we wouldn't because we didn't want him getting off on some technicality, and going away thinking he could always walk away from his actions with a clever lawyer. He was under 14, so wouldn't have a permanent criminal record. We wanted him to learn from this experience. We wanted him to learn he didn't have to perpetrate the crime; just to be present or know about it and he could be held responsible.

However, John said the law required Eric to have a lawyer, and we had to see the legal aid lawyer. I attended at the legal aid lawyer's office with Eric. We went round and round again, with me outlining why we wouldn't get a lawyer for Eric.

We were advised that a lawyer would be assigned to represent Eric. He asked if I knew any lawyers, and I named someone in Castlegar whom I knew through the NDP. Thus, Stan Lanyon was appointed Eric's counsel, and a copy of a letter sent to Stan was sent to us. It stated that although we could afford it, we refused to hire a lawyer for Eric. I was annoyed.

At this time Lyle was running for the NDP federal nomination. One day I got a phone call from Joanne Partridge in Castlegar. She had stayed with us a number of times. She knew we doted on our children. She told me there was a rumour going around NDP members in Castlegar, which she was sure was not true, but wanted an explanation. It was rumoured that Eric got into trouble, that we abandoned him, refused to help him, and refused to hire a lawyer; further, that I had gone to Legal Aid and demanded a lawyer be appointed. I was livid!

It was the only time I asked Lyle to step aside from a nomination. It was hard to believe that even NDP members could get that dirty. This was a nomination for a third party, with no hope of getting power. What happened in political parties that could form governments? At least that was worth fighting over.

Lyle was very calm about it. He phoned Stan Lanyon and asked him about the rumour. Stan acknowledged he had told one person part of what was in the letter, and that the rest was added by others. Lyle told Stan that if that rumour wasn't stopped immediately, and corrected with those who were told it, we would go to the Bar Association and ask that Stan be reprimanded. It was stopped.

I phoned the Legal Aid office and told them in no way would we allow a lawyer to appear with Eric. I went to court with Eric, and laid out the situation before the judge. Having worked in law offices, I was somewhat familiar with procedure. At one stage the judge got angry with the prosecutor, and I knew it was possible to get the case dismissed or delayed because of incompetence.

However, I consulted Eric and he said he didn't want any postponements. He just wanted to get it over with and get on with his life. I stood up and told the judge exactly that, and he understood. I explained to him what I had said to the probation officer about making this a learning experience for Eric. He gave Eric half the community hours he gave the other defendants (represented by lawyers). However, unlike the others, Eric did his community work.

This might be a good time to record another experience leading up to the same nomination. Lyle was in his third term as president of the Nelson-Trail Labour Council, and had just completed a paid stint as West Kootenay co-ordinator of the Canadian Labour Congress' National Day of Protest – opposing the Trudeau government's wage (and price) control program. The protest involved a one-day general strike across Canada and, of course, all labour and protest organizers were not to be paid for the protest day.

One of the labour council delegates, Jim Conche, was determined to undermine or stop Lyle's nomination. Searching through the council's financial records, he claimed that he had found something wrong. A bookkeeping entry appeared to suggest that Lyle had been paid for working on the protest day.

Jim latched onto this and immediately, without any attempt at confirmation, told the press that the issue of Lyle's integrity would be considered at the next Council meeting. Of course, the newspaper sent a reporter to cover the meeting – not a normal occurrence.

At the meeting, Jim and a few like-minded members raised the issue and accused Lyle of dishonestly profiting from a breach of CLC policy, and demanded his resignation or censure.

Lyle was stunned and angry. He knew the charge to be false and insisted that the books must be in error. The meeting voted to table the motion of censure until the next meeting, pending an investigation of the record.

Lyle was livid. He had lived a clean life, cleaner than the driven snow, because of his involvement in politics. He was aware the least hint of impropriety could be misused to his serious political detriment. He was so honest it infuriated me at times. Now he was faced with a question raised about his honesty in the public's eye. He knew he would be exonerated in due course but, once the question was publicly raised, some stigma would remain.

Lyle immediately raised the issue with the reporter, asking that the story be withheld, at least until the inquiry was completed. The paper didn't know if they could comply, and Lyle then threatened to sue if they publicized the charge. Lyle talked to the editor, who said the paper would not be intimidated by threats. However, they did hold back publication of the story.

Lyle and the Council treasurer went over and over the accounts and finally found the problem. There was a simple bookkeeping error. A left and right column had been mismatched on one line and the resulting mismatch just carried on down the column, giving a totally false impression of later entries – including that relating to Lyle's pay. He was totally exonerated. The Council and the newspaper both agreed. The 'story' was never published.

A couple of years later, after Lyle was elected, I saw Jim at a picnic at Lakeside Park. In front of a group of his friends, I confronted him with the accusation that he fabricated the whole incident. He admitted he knew there was nothing to it and only wanted to besmirch Lyle's reputation. He laughed, and said all's fair in love and politics. "OK," I said. "Jim, I hear you work for the CIA? Is that true." He laughed at me. But a half-hour later, in front of other friends, I asked him again. He laughed again. By the fourth time he was getting agitated. Next time I ran into him on Baker Street I asked him again. This time he started telling me off. When I saw him across the street I would yell, "How's the CIA these days, Jim?" He phoned Lyle and begged him to tell me to stop.

Back to my children: Colin got involved with a bad kid in Ottawa. Eric and Haida saw him get into trouble a couple of times. One day they confronted him and told him to stop being friends. Colin laughed at them. Eric told him about his experience with Larry, but Colin wouldn't budge. Later Colin told us he looked at his brother and sister and saw them both crying. "I realized they really cared and were serious". He changed friends.

In 1987 we had a fire in our house on Robson Street, in Nelson. After returning from Ottawa, Colin set up an apartment for himself in the basement. It was not heated. He set up a portable electric heater, and promised us faithfully he would unplug it when he left the room. One afternoon, Lyle was out canvassing and I was away. Haida told Colin he had a phone call. He ran upstairs to answer it. When he got off the phone,

Haida said, "I smell smoke." Colin could smell it too, but they could not see any. When he opened the basement door, a wall of smoke met him.

I was returning home and noticed fire trucks near our place. I didn't realize until I had stopped that the firemen were all over our property. It was a thoroughly frightening experience, to think that all one's collection of things was going to go up in flames.

However, the house didn't burn down. The fire was contained to the basement. Although there was smoke damage throughout the house, the only things that burned were in the basement. Of course, everything that was no longer needed, or was broken which one intended to fix some day got put down into the basement. So we didn't really lose anything of value. Ironic part was that the U.S. flag hanging on the wall disintegrated, but the USSR flag, on the same wall, was not touched.

Our BCAA insurance company was extremely considerate and fair. We had replacement value, so could replace everything (not have it discounted according to how old it was). The adjuster agreed to most propositions in replacing some items with different ones. When I picked up Colin's T-shirts and said, "I bought this in Paris". He quickly retorted, "No, you can't get a trip to Paris to replace it."

We had six months to replace $30,000 worth of merchandise. Lyle worked at it with fervour. After it was over, he had withdrawal symptoms, and didn't know what to do with his time.

After Collin left home, he and Eric came back to visit before university started. They handed Lyle and I a tennis racket each, and said, "Repeat after us: I promise to play tennis at least once a week." We repeated it word for word.

I had taken six tennis lessons about ten years earlier. I knew enough to keep score. So - at least once a week we would look at the rackets, and say, "Well, we promised." We bashed the ball around.

But we got a little competitive. And then we were trying to win. We started going twice a week, and then three times. Before the summer was out we were out every day. We played into November, sometimes wearing gloves. The park people worried about us because there was frost on the courts and it was dangerous. We could hardly wait for spring.

It was the best thing the kids did for us. We got so competitive, we endangered life and limb trying for the impossible ball. We would be the only ones playing on hot summer days.

When the boys visited us, we would square off, Eric and I against Lyle and Colin. Although they were just as good players as Eric and I, they could not win - not one game in two years! Eric is wonderful to play with, as he is so encouraging. Even when we were down 5 to 0 (in a tie breaker), he would just keep on encouraging me, "Just one hit at a time, Mom. One game at a time." And we would catch up and win. When they finally won one game, they started to give us competition, and win many. Nothing gave me more pleasure. Haida started to play with us, too.

Same trip, I was walking with Eric and Colin, and Eric said, "Some day, Mom, I shall ask you if you want a boat, and you will reply, 'Sure', and I'll go out and buy you one." Not to be outdone, Colin adds, "And I'll ask you if you want to go for a swim, and you'll reply, 'Sure', and I'll build you a swimming pool." Did any mother have sweeter children? However, in 2007, I am still waiting for these questions to be asked.

We ran across the following poem that Mother (Hilda) had amongst her souvenirs:

> *Your children are not your children.   They are the sons and daughters of life, longing for itself.*
>
> *They come through you but not from you*
>
> *And though they are with you, yet they belong not to you.*
>
> *You may give them your love but not your thoughts. For they have their own thoughts.*
>
> *You may strive to be like them but seek not to make them like you.*
>
> *For life goes not backward nor tarries with yesterday.*
>
> *Their souls dwell in the House of Tomorrow, which you cannot visit, not even in your dreams.*

Kahlil Gibran, 1923.

I was to read this poem at Colin's wedding, with tears in my eyes.

How often I would be surprised that my children didn't know something that was second nature to me. Then I would remember that they are not me, they do not have my life's experiences. Even though I may have told them about certain things, it does not mean the same to them.

Haida began doing a lot of writing: poems and prose, sometimes getting printed in local newspapers.   The following is something she wrote as a speech to a Speakers Group that she joined in Squamish. Keeping the above poem in mind, it is quite a lesson for parents. I can't count the number of times I found my children to be like me, but yet, not like me.

"THE CHILD WITHIN"

"I want to plant a garden and nourish it from seed to sprout to full spectacular bloom, all the while weeding out the evil roots which creep through the soil inhibiting the miraculous growth of my garden.

My garden may be as big as the earth or as small as a classroom or a family. My seeds may be countries, students or my own children. But one thing is constant, absolute and for sure: my garden will flourish in the outdoors where Mother Nature can best nourish her seeds.

"I feel that to know me is to know the child within.

"During my childhood my mother always kept a garden. Back then it looked huge, like a forest. My two brothers and I complained a lot about the long hours spent with our feet dug into the soils and our knees bent low pulling out all the `wicked weeds'. It seemed so senseless. We would dig out all the weeds and the following week they would just pop right up again. Little did I know then that I would be standing here today comparing the damage of the weeds to the evils that tempt humans on a daily basis. The best thing that I ever saw - or should I say tasted - were the thin and crispy snow peas. They tasted so sweet and so fresh.

"My Mom nourished another kind of garden. Together with my Dad she planted the seeds of my older brother, Eric, myself Haida, and my younger brother Colin. Mom used a variety of ingredients in her garden fertilizer throughout our growing years, but the three ingredients that stick most clearly in my memory, and influenced me the most, were the political affairs, multicultural exposures and the outdoor activities (particularly camping and canoeing).

"At first the political affairs seemed more like fun community gatherings. Us kids would ignore the parents and find some adventurous corner to play in. Occasionally the parents played - like musical instruments, singing or acting. However, by the time I was 12, I learned what politics and government meant when my Dad ran for federal office and won.

"At age 12 politics meant making lawn signs on weekends and stuffing envelopes in the evenings. It also meant moving to the big city of Ottawa away from the only home that I ever knew, Nelson.

"So I spent most of my teen years in Ottawa. Those teen years and the big move made things quite difficult and rough, but not all bad. I did attend a great high school and I got to experience life on Parliament Hill. My Dad's office became my second home in the city. The best part, though, was I got to go home to Nelson every summer. Boy, did I ever miss the mountains!!!!

"Back to the fertilizer, ingredient No. 2: My Mom exposed us to as many multicultural events as possible, including boarding an exchange nursing student from Indonesia when I was 10 and boarding a young man from India when I was 18. The Indian fellow (Ashish Kulkarni) was part of a Canada World Youth/India Youth exchange.

"Well, most of you know the outcome of that ingredient on my life. To date I have visited 20 countries including Canada, the U.S.A. --- Well, actually only 17. We only passed through Holland quickly on our way to France, and I only spent an hour or two on the Zambia side of Victoria Falls in Africa, and I never even got past Japan's International Airport. So really only 17, but I do plan to reach 20 countries and more in the near future.

"Ingredient No. 3: Outdoor activities, is the closest and dearest to my heart. Every summer my family went camping, usually close to home if Dad wasn't with us. But when Dad got his holidays we would venture off to some place new. My brothers and I loved to go exploring. I would notice every type of moss or fungus that grew along my path. I saw the beauty within the beauty and the worlds within the worlds.

"In the first there were no limits to a child's imagination. It was so pure, simple and natural. I think this is why I am so eager to share the natural outdoors with other children today and in the future. This is also why I have grave concerns about the future of our natural environments and the evil ingredients or `wicked weeds' that we are dropping on my precious garden!!

"My greatest ambition is to plant a garden. Heck, if I can find the energy, I'll plant many gardens. And I'll nourish them, as my Mom did, through community activities, multicultural exposures and outdoor explorations. Of course politics will find its way in there too.

"I'd like to leave you with a quote which I recently came across. I feel it sums up a belief, which will guide me in my future work with children. This quote was written by Chief Luther Standing Bear of the Lakota tribe. He said: `*The old Lakota was wise. He knew that man's heart away from Nature becomes hard. He knew that lack of respect for growing, living things soon led to a lack of respect for humans too. So he kept his youth close to its softening influence.*'"

Haida Kristiansen, 1992

In June 1992, Mother (Hilda) found among her memorabilia a letter from Eric.

"May 3, 1984.   Nepean, Ontario.

Dear Grandma and Grandpa,

Thought I'd just write a few words on how things are going over here right now. I really didn't enjoy myself for the first term of school right up till Christmas break. My marks weren't what I expected them to be. I tried to spend all my free time playing basketball to improve my game so this really isolated myself from most of my friends at school. However, it really made me appreciate who my close friends were, sticking with me through thick and thin. It's funny because right around now you start to wonder who are the people that you will keep in touch with in the future and who are the ones you'll never see again. It sure is scary when I think about it. I think my choice in friends has been excellent.

Anyway, things this term are going a hell of a lot better. My grades are coming up close to my expectations so I really don't have to put as much pressure on myself the way I did first term. I try to do as much homework as possible during my spares in school so this leaves me free time after school. I got some bad news from S.F.U. It turns out now that I'll probably need grade 13 English. That means I may have to spend July here taking it in summer school. Yesterday my boss at work told me I could work there in the summer so it looks like I'll be spending at least part of my summer here. They also raised the age of that Eastern Regional Team I made last year so I'm eligible again. Mike McNeil of S.F.U. has been keeping in contact with me, which is good because I think I have my heart set on going there.

Let me now tell you about the success and failure of our basketball team. First the Carleton Board semi-finals where we played Cairine Wilson in a best two out of three series: In the first game it was a disaster. Our team played our worst game of the year and we lost by 12 points. The next night we still played bad in the first half but better in the second half. With 2:34 minutes left in the game the score was tied. At that point our team really came together and we won by 7 points. The next day in the final game it was no contest from the outset. We dominated the game and won by 14. So on to the finals against a heavily favoured St. Pius team. In my four years here I have never beat them. They are a Catholic school and recruit all the best players in the city (even if they aren't Catholic) so they're always strong. Unfair, eh? Anyway, in the first game (best two out of three) we played quite well but lost by 14. The next night would have to be considered one of the biggest moments of my life. It was the greatest win for our school in basketball in its history. We trailed by different scores the whole game until with about 2 minutes left I hit 2 free throws to tie the score. Right away we pressed and then stole the ball from them. I shot ... missed, but my teammate Larry got the rebound and was fouled. He got a bonus. This means he gets one free throw but if he makes it he gets another one. However, he missed the first but I got the rebound and was fouled. Bonus for me. There I was. 14 seconds left on the clock. The score was tied. The place was a madhouse. My whole body was shaking. That's when I knew I had to settle myself down. My conscience had a little talk with my legs and I was fine. Stood up to the line, said, "I'm no loser"" to myself and shot. Made it. Wheww. We went up by 2. Then they came down, shot but missed, but they got the rebound and put it in. However, the question was "Was there any time on the clock?" Most people I asked afterwards said "No", but the official timer said "Yes", so we had to play a 3-minute overtime.

Try to imagine the scene. The pressure was immense. Here's a summary of overtime. We won the jump ball, came down, Mark Harris was fouled and had a bonus. He made the first but missed the second, so we were up by one. They came down, missed, we got the rebound, someone shot, missed. Brian Loates got the rebound and scored. We were up 3. They came down, scored. From there it's foggy, but we never trailed again. I know that they were down 2 with 1 second left and one of their players, Jeff House (who may go to S.F.U.) shot from about half-court and it hit the rim but didn't go in. We won!!! It was crazy.

Anyway, the next day was the final game. We led for the whole first half (3 at half time), but they took the lead midway through the 3rd quarter but the lead kept changing after that. With about 1:30 left in the game we had the ball and were down by 1. The ball came to me (about 15 ft. away from the basket), I shot and missed, but the ball came right back to me. I was so surprised. I shot it again and it went in. They rushed down the court but turned the ball over. So we had a one-point lead, and the ball with about a minute left. With 50 seconds left one of our players did a stupid thing. We were planning on holding the ball and letting the time run out, but he tried scoring, shot, missed and they got the ball. Then with about 15 seconds left they scored. We rushed down but one of our players threw the ball away. We lost by 3 in the Carleton Board Finals. If we had won we would probably have won the Ottawa-Carleton finals since the team from Ottawa we've beaten twice this year. "So close but yet so far." Those are my quotes to sum up the series against St. Pius.

Anyway, our season isn't over because we can still go to the provincials but it's difficult to explain how so I won't get into it. You're probably getting bored with all this basketball talk. I guess I've got a little carried away since I was only planning on saying "a few words". Oh, well. After the final game we went to the Governor General's Winter Party. We missed dinner and were really hungry so Lisa Shreyer ordered two large pizzas for us. That was sure nice of her. There was dancing and drinking but I was too tired and depressed.

Last weekend we hosted our Grad Variety Show and it was a big success. I went into a dance skit that was by far the most popular act. I really enjoy it.

So, anyway, what else can I say. No girlfriend at present but working on it. My job's going really well. I love working with numbers. Always have. School's going a lot better. I'm kind of disappointed with my basketball season from a personal point of view. I played quite well but I thought I would dominate it more. Oh, one more thing. Did I tell you I'm taking ballroom dancing lesson? My friend Missi talked me into it and I'm glad. Who knows when I may need it. Missi's a wonderful young lady. Mom and Dad want me to marry her but I have got to be such good friends with her that she's like a sister to me.

To summarize everything I've said, things are going really well. I'm enjoying myself, realizing that pretty soon this whole facet of my life will be over and I'll be moving on to hopefully bigger and better things. So far I can't complain though. It really means a lot to me to see my mother and dad out to my games. You should have seen Dad in the Pius games. He was back in high school, playing his trombone, leading cheers, a real kid. Yes, I really love my family and you too especially. I've really been fortunate to have such a loving, caring family. I think that's what sets our family apart from most. We are special and I hope we always will be. I love you. Eric."

Colin hasn't written anything worth quoting, that I know. He put his creativity into doing drawings, paintings, carvings in wood and ceramics. In elementary school, he won the Firemen's Drawing Contest and some money. In high school he drew up a plan for a picnic table made out of one piece of plywood, which was published in a trade magazine. We have several of his paintings hanging on our wall.

My parents would have been surprised and proud of their grandchildren's achievements:

Our oldest son, Eric, graduated from UBC in Sports Administration. He had an illustrious career in basketball during university. In 2005 he helped bring the World Masters Games (senior basketball) to Edmonton, first time held in Canada. In the 20 years of existence, the U.S. teams always won. This year, after the U.S. team defeated Australia by 82 points, they were heard saying "This year we don't have any competition at all." That gave Eric's team extra motivation, and they beat the U.S., taking home a World championship medal. Eric has his own business, Advanced Athletics, selling exercise equipment.

Our daughter, Haida, graduated as a dietician. She wrote a children's book, Aida's Adventures. She is setting up an organization called Camp Uganda, which will bring young Ugandan students to a nature reserve for environmental education with a particular focus on problems facing the endangered chimpanzees. After it is set up, she plans to continue raising funds for it, and hopes to team up with the Jane Goodall Institute of Uganda to oversee its operation. She is in the process of adopting a little girl from Ethiopia.

Our youngest son, Colin, a civil engineer, is an associate of the Delcan Corporation, a private consulting firm. He has been working, with others, on designing the high bridge across the Kicking Horse Gorge on the Trans Canada Highway.

Nena's daughter, Nevenka, graduated in law. Her son, Keir, graduated from Harvard, and writes screen plays for movies. His first work was a script for the movie Hotel Rwanda. It was nominated for an Oscar, and he was nominated as the writer of that script.

Arthur's first son, David Leon Sharko, is a lawyer in Edmonton, who has just won a precedent setting case for the Samson Indian band, that will allow them to invest their millions of dollars earned from oil and gas revenue in an independent trust company, where it will result in a much higher interest rate than what the federal government paid them. (Before the case they had no choice but have the money paid into the federal government's coffers.)

His second son, Darren, is a Morgage Specialist with Royal Bank. His daughter, Janeen, is married to Jarrid Juse, and they own Absolute Power and Performance.

Neta, the first sister married, has five children, Ronnie, Angie, Gary, Randy and Cindy, who are older than their cousins, and are hard working, skilled citizens.

Anne's daughter, Roseanne, is married to Phil Oatway, who owns a company called Altrac, that has heavy construction equipment that is used in the oil and gas industry. They have four daughters.

Haida with her packed backpack, ready for a six
month tour of India and Africa.

Eric and Colin one-on-one.

PREJUDICE

Everyone has some prejudices. Whether they recognize or acknowledge them it is another matter. My family had loads of them.

In 1990, talking to my mother, she said, "Audrey McLaughlin and Brian Mulroney are the same kind of people." I was stunned. The same kind of people? I couldn't imagine two more different people. Then it came to me: she mistakenly thinks they are both Scottish and, by definition, are stingy, selfish, and bad tempered.

It's too late to argue with my mother. She had everyone pegged into a category. I simply replied: "Yes, Mother. Audrey and Brian are the same kind of people. His mother and her mother were both mothers."

So many times I had explained to her that prejudice is unfair because it stigmatizes everyone in a certain ethnic group with certain characteristics, without exception. Lord knows, we were discriminated against because we were Russian, and I considered it unfair.

I should explain why I refer to our family both as Ukrainian and as Russian. My father gave me this explanation. Ukraine and Russia was one large region, with Kiev as its capitol. Someone drew a line and decided it was two countries. Peasants' sons would then be called upon to defend the border. The language is so close one can find a common root for every word. And the word "ukraina" means "the edge". So, father would not accept the division and considered everybody to be Russian. And we belonged to the Russian Greek Orthodox church.

I searched the internet and found this: In 1169 Kiev was the capital of the whole region (Ukraine and

Russia). In the 13th century, Ukraine, Poland, and Lithuania (as well as many other countries) were overrun by Genghis Khan and his Mongols and remained under their control for the next 300 years. At this time Moscow became the dominant city of the upper part of the region.

In the 16th century the "Rus" attacked the Mongols and slowly but determinately cleared them out – out of Lithuania, Poland and the Ukraine. It was natural for the "Rus" to feel they were simply re-uniting the previous territory, by restoring former boundaries and liberating the region from foreign control.

Not all Mongols left the area, some intermarrying with locals. These would have pressed to keep the Ukraine as a separate country. Occasionally a family will pop up, who are black haired and dark complexioned, which may be descendants of the Mongols. I am thinking, in particularly, of our neighbors, the Zachodas, who fit this description. It would be interesting to know.

The most prevalent prejudice in our area of Alberta was against Canadian Indians. They were considered lazy, drunks, unreliable, liars, and dirty. During a visits to Edmonton, my niece, Rosanna, told us this joke: "A man told me he saw two miracles today – he saw one Indian working and another Indian sober." Everybody at the dinner table laughed: her husband and children; my brother Arthur and family. I stared in amazement. This was funny? When I repeated it to friends in Nelson, they said "Where's the joke?"

The joke stayed with me all through the summer. 1989 was a summer of great native discontent. First, Donald Marshall, a native Canadian, was released from jail, after spending 11 years for a murder he did not commit. Another man confessed to the murder on his deathbed. On close examination it became obvious

Marshall should never have been charged, and likely would not have been if he had not been an Indian. There was gross prejudice throughout the police force and justice system in Nova Scotia. The length of time it took to get an apology and compensation suggested the prejudice was ongoing.

In Regina, a drunken native activist was walking down a back alley, when he was approached by a policeman and asked for identification. He refused, got belligerent, and was shot dead. At first the policeman said it was in self-defense. His superior covered for him. Under pressure, an investigation was undertaken. The superior who did the cover-up committed suicide. The cop was arrested.

Throughout these news broadcasts I kept remembering Rosanna's "joke". I was feeling guilty because, in a way, I had contributed by listening to *that* stupid joke and saying nothing.

I wrote Rosanna a letter saying that a river could never exist without the thousands of little streams, creeks, and rivulets that go together to form one big river. In the same way, intolerance could not exist and manifest itself in such ugly ways as had happened all year, if it wasn't supported by stupid jokes like hers.

When I moved to Vancouver and met the Kristiansens, I became aware of my Indian prejudice. I worked consciously to rid myself of it. One day I saw a photograph of a beautiful young Indian woman. I said to Mother (Hilda), "Isn't she beautiful. She doesn't look Indian at all." Mother smiled and said, "What you are saying is that she is beautiful BECAUSE she doesn't look Indian. That is not a compliment to Indians." I realized that was exactly what I was thinking, and knew I had a ways to go.

I have prejudices. Mine are against Catholics and Germans. I know why I have them. I try to control them but they creep up without notice.

My prejudice against Catholics stems from a childhood experience. One cold winter morning Mother and I walked seven miles to attend Catholic mass. We weren't Catholic, but because a minister came to our part of the world so seldom, all denominations attended whatever service was held. After all, we were all Christians who worshiped one God. I listened to the priest say all Catholics would go to heaven and everybody else to hell. My mouth dropped open. I whispered to Mother, "He's talking about us!" Mother agreed. I think we walked out.

There was a raging controversy within the community over the incident. Catholics apologized for his comments, saying they should have informed him that other denominations attended these services. I thought, "Thanks for nothing!" Nobody apologized for the comments themselves. People stopped going to each other's services.

In fact, Catholics, as well as some other religions, have deteriorated to the point of saying, "God will forgive anything as long as you believe in him." This has removed the emphasis, which I believe is in the bible, that you have to live a good, clean, sharing and caring life to enter the kingdom of heaven. Instead, the bible's quotes such as "It will be harder for a rich man to enter the kingdom of heaven than a camel to go through the eye of a needle" or "Love thy neighbor as thyself" are seldom mentioned, but some obscure statement is used to justify their campaigns against homosexuality and against abortion.

When I attended the University of Montreal campus in 1964, we were all older students attending the Canadian Labour College. Every Saturday night, while most of the non religious students stayed in their dormitories, studying, playing cards, and going to bed early, most of the Quebec Catholic students were out drinking and whoring all night. I'd hear them stumbling in around 3 or 4. Then I'd hear their alarm go off at 8, and they were off to mass.

One Saturday night I asked, "How is it that we atheists are here and the Catholics are out every Saturday night?" One student said, "Because as an atheist I have no-one to forgive me. I have to live with what I do. There is no-one to wipe my slate clean." What a sad commentary on religion.

In the 1990s Lyle was at the United Nations conference of the International Labour Organization in Geneva, when Pope John II was present as a guest speaker. Lyle phoned home and told me that he shook hands with the pope. I told him to have his hand amputated before coming home.

That pope, in particular, was a reactionary leader who stemmed the tide of progress on contraception and women's rights. He reversed the earlier, though short-lived, tolerance of revolutionary theology, which allowed local priests and bishops to endorse militant and progressive movements for change, especially in poverty-stricken countries. At that time the NDP had a Catholic priest, Father Bob Ogle, elected in their caucus. He was ordered not to run for re-election.

The Roman Catholic Church has caused hundreds of millions of deaths, especially in Africa. Its injunction against artificial birth control has resulted in monumental birth rates and resultant death, starvation and deprivation. Yet, it is simply edicts from Rome by a pope that is responsible. Nowhere in the bible is birth control or abortion forbidden.

The condemnation by the Catholic Church of the use of condoms has made AIDS a pandemic. In fact, that church has condemned millions to life-threatening and life-ending diseases.

Furthermore, it was Rome that was responsible for the crucifixion of Jesus. Rome used crucifixion as a method of keeping a conquered people in line. The whole idea of crucifixion was to cause suffering to discourage anyone rebelling against Rome. Romans were known to crucify hundreds of people in a day and line them up on a roadway into town - so that troublemakers fermenting a revolt against Roman occupation - coming to town would see what fate awaited them.

My German prejudice developed, of course, during World War II. Since then I have diverted my anger from "Germans" to "Nazis". When I travelled in the Soviet Union in 1985, I noticed that nobody there ever said, "When the Germans bombed..." It was always "When the Nazis bombed..." When I asked our tour guide about it, she said that it was purposely and consciously referred to that way, because so many Germans suffered and died under the Nazis, and fought them inside and outside the country.

Lyle re-enforced this by reminding me that Willy Brandt was elected Chancellor of West Germany, even though he had fled his country, joined the Norwegian armed resistance, and fought against German forces. Not many countries would later elect such a person to their highest office.

When I was between 8 and 12 years old, my father would receive his Ukrainian News through the mail every Friday and read to us about the war. I felt deeply and suffered with my kinfolk in the Ukraine. Vivid images would stay with me and I would dream about them.

The story that shook me the most was about the time the Nazis were trying to get women in a village to reveal the whereabouts of the local partisans who were causing havoc for the German army. Someone in the village had to be providing these partisans with food. No one squealed. The Nazis saw a mother and a newborn baby. They snatched the baby from her arms. "Talk or we'll bury this baby alive!" She was silent. The baby was thrown into a hole, and then buried alive. The mother didn't make a sound; didn't shed a tear. She suffered silently for her country. This haunts me still.

Easter Egg Hunt: Grandsons, Nikolas and Kai.

TAMARA

Lyle wanted a dog of his own. He had had several family dogs as a child, which he loved, but they were not his choice. He wanted either a Great Dane or a St. Bernard. We agreed to a Great Dane. To me, dogs were working farm animals who lived outside or in the barn. It would take a lot of getting used to, having a dog in the house.

When Haida was born and I was still in the hospital, Lyle, with Eric and his mother, drove to Kaslo to see a kennel raising Great Danes. He fell in love with a particular puppy. She had undershot teeth so could not be sold as a show dog.

When we picked her up a few weeks later she had had her ears trimmed and bound to a frame so that they would stand straight up. She looked a mess. We named her Tamara.

When I got home from the hospital, I had a two year old, a newborn baby, and this very boisterous, very expensive puppy. She had huge paws and was forever jumping up on Eric and scratching him. Eric loved the neighborhood dog who was old and serene. But this pup, try as he would, he could not love!

We were living in Balfour (20 miles from Nelson), in a small summer cottage. Whenever I had to drive to Nelson, I had to keep these three apart. If Eric sat in the back, Tamara would scratch him to bits. If I had to get out of the car, I had to take the baby and Eric with me, or Tamara would jump all over them.

It was a hot, sultry summer, and our doors were always wide open. I worried about where the pup was. I found myself wishing she would get killed.

Tamara loved to roll in rotting fish (the local Dolly Varden, travel upstream when they reach four years, spawn, and then die). These dead fish lined the shoreline. One morning I stepped out of bed and onto a rotting fish. Tamara had brought a gift for the family and left it at my bedside. I hated her.

In August we moved to Nelson, to the first house we owned. We loved that old house. It had been a grand old family home that was converted into three apartments. (It has now been restored to its original grandeur as a "heritage home").

Lyle fenced in the small backyard to keep Tamara in. This didn't always work. If she wanted out she would pull herself up to her full length, lean on the fence, which would either give way, or she would leap over it. Many times I had to chase her all over the neighborhood. When I was pregnant with Colin, this was quite an ordeal going up and down those hills.

One Sunday we took a trip to Creston, over the Skyway and through Salmo. We were cramped in our little red Volvo. On the way home we stopped along the way to smell the country air and stretch.

When we called Tamara to pile back into the car, we found she had rolled in some fresh cowslip, was covered in green dung, and smelled to high heaven. There was not a drop of water to wash her down. We used some newspaper to wipe her down. This just smeared it over her. We had to drive in a hot, stuffy car, with Tamara and two of the three children in the back seat, for many miles all the way home.

Tamara was such a happy dog. She would bounce up to people. The neighbors loved and hated her. The first time the dogcatcher saw her, he just opened the door and she hopped into the back of his van. But she did not like being caged in a pen until I bailed her out. The next time he arrived she wouldn't go near him. He just sent his ticket to us through the mail, because he knew exactly whom she belonged to.

When Colin was one year old, I knew we couldn't put off buying a new home much longer. We had two bedrooms, our own and one very small room for Eric and Haida. And Tamara needed confining.

When I mentioned it to Lyle he would say, "Let's wait till spring. We'll have more money." I knew that house prices are always higher in the spring. We had to do it then. I contacted a real estate agent and got him to show me a few houses.

There was one house at 821 Robson Street that was made for us. It was a big, two-story house with four bedrooms, a big yard (three lots), and a tree house. There was a full basement and a large patio at the back overlooking Kootenay Lake. It was a house that would change to accommodate the children at different ages. Besides which, there was room to hold a meeting of 100 people in our organizational undertakings.

I asked the realtor to let me keep the key. On the weekend I asked Lyle take a ride with the children. I took them to this house (which was empty) and let them roam around the yard. I could see everyone was impressed.

Then I took them inside. I knew Lyle was thinking exactly what I had: what a place to hold meetings. He loved it. The children loved it. We bought it (with help from parents and 3 mortgages) for $17,000. Next spring it would have cost $30,000. For years Lyle told people how we saw this house that he had decided to buy but wasn't sure how to convince me. I finally asked if he remembered we had gone inside the house, although nobody was home. "HOW DO YOU THINK WE GOT IN?" He said, "Hmmm".

Here, Tamara had lots of room. Lyle fenced in part of the yard, with a wire fence. This would not hold her if she decided she wanted out. She would lean against it until it gave way, and then she was gone. All our Italian neighbors had big gardens, and they knew whose dog walked through their garden - nothing else left such big tracks.

One day I was on the phone to Ruth Hufty, a friend from our old neighborhood. Suddenly she let out a scream and said, "My table is moving around the kitchen." Tamara had gone to visit her old stumping ground, walked in the open kitchen door and, when the phone rang, ducked under the table. When she decided to leave, she stood up and the table stood up with her.

She was in the newspaper as often as the children. A reporter who came from Toronto told me he thought he would give some kids a thrill by taking their picture as they were played in the snow with their dog. After taking some photos, he told them, "This will probably be in the newspaper tomorrow. Won't that be exciting?" "Again?" Colin responded, "That will be my 8th time." The reporter was amazed. In Toronto, this would be a milestone in a child's life.

Tamara loved to chew on spear grass. Sometimes, in the fall, when this grass was brittle, it would pierce her cheeks and get infected. One day we saw this huge lump on the side of her neck. We rushed her to the vet, thinking it was cancer, but were told it was spear grass. They sedated her and clean out the abscess. When I picked her up she was just coming out of sedation and stumbled about. Going up the stairs in the yard she looked like a drunk. I want to assure anyone who has ever looked at a Marmaduke cartoon that it is not an exaggeration – it's for real!

When we prepared to leave to spend Christmas with the grandparents she would us the run-around. Lyle seemed to be on nightshift every Christmas Eve. We would pack and wait for him to return so we could head out immediately, driving all night.

Inevitably, Tamara would feel the excitement in the air and would bounce around the house. If anyone opened the door the least bit she would push past them and be gone. She would then bounce around the yard with the kids and I trying to catch her. We would leave her alone, hoping she would come into the porch, or maybe one of the neighbors would grab her. She made me so mad so often.

If she wanted out in the middle of the night she would run around the house, keeping me awake. I would finally get up and let her go. Then she would want in. Scratch, scratch, scratch. I would try to ignore it. Scratch, scratch, scratch. I would finally relent and get up. No sooner I opened the door, she would decide, "Nah, one more run." Off she went. This would be repeated three, four, five times. I could have killed her. Our front door was gouged out. I painted it regularly, but it became an eyesore.

The rest of the family always said: "Oh, our dog is no trouble at all. She is so good." There were times, however, when the children complained. When they went tobogganing down the back alley Tamara would run alongside and pull them off the sleigh. They would scream and hit her, but she persisted. When they built snow forts in the back yard with benches and a barbeque pit to roast wieners over, she would pounce everywhere, smashing everything. They were not amused.

But the day came when she grew old. Great Danes are known to have short lives. At nine she slowed down, got arthritis and hobbled around on sore limbs. We started giving her meat instead of canned dog food. The children hand fed her. She was getting thinner by the day.

The summer of 1976 we took her camping with us to Lazy Lake, near Cranbook. We knew it was her last trip with us. She had stopped eating altogether. At night she paced up and down, unable to lie down. The last day at the camp, she couldn't even control her bowels. We lifted her into the back of the station wagon, and drove to Cranbrook. Lyle dropped us off at friends and took her to a vet to be put to sleep. It was the first family funeral. She had really been a member of the family. To me a very annoying member, but a member. When Lyle returned and we headed home, everybody was in mourning.

DISNEYLAND

In 1973, after we sold the old house and had some extra money, I took the children to Disneyland. My sister Nena was living there and said she and her family would be moving before long. It was our last chance to experience Disneyland.

We planned it for spring break when Eric was 7, Haida 5, and Colin 3. I phoned Amtrak to reserve seats, but was told no reservations were necessary. The children talked about the trip all the time. Excitement kept mounting each day.

With Lyle left behind working in Nelson, we were on our way. Leaving Nelson in March, we took the bus to Vancouver, spent the night with grandparents, and at 5 a.m. next morning, caught a train to Seattle, where we would board an Amtrak train for Los Angeles.

On the way to Seattle I started a conversation with the conductor, trying to get some idea how to get the right train. We didn't have much time between trains. He asked me if we had reservations, and I told him I had been informed it wasn't necessary. "Aw", he said. "That must have been some time ago. Since the oil embargo, train travel has increased considerably in the U.S. You definitely need reservations now."

That put a crimp into our plans. As I watched the excitement of my children, I couldn't imagine how we could turn around and return home. I kept badgering the conductor every time he passed for some suggestion. Finally, he told me, very quietly, to bluff my way through. "Run to the cashier, get your tickets, and run for the train as if you were in a panic. Find an open gate with nobody guarding it, get on the train, and keep walking until the train pulls away. Once the train moves, they won't put you off."

Well, it wasn't much, but it was all we had. And that's what we did. We got off the Canadian train, and ran, I mean ran, to the cashier and told her to hurry with our tickets. I handed her the money, and she handed me the tickets. As I turned to leave she said, "Oh, please wait, what is your name so I can cross you off my reservation list." Not being a good liar, I said, "We didn't have reservations." She gasped. Her face started turning colours, but I didn't wait. I said, "Come, children, run." And we all ran; me with suitcases and bundles, the children half dragging theirs. We ran to the gate and waved our tickets at the guard who was busy talking with someone and hardly acknowledged us.

We ran alongside the train until we found an entrance with no guard on it. We boarded and started walking. A black porter stopped us and asked what car we were looking for. I hemmed and hawed, and when nothing came to me, I blurted out the truth. He said, "Quickly, give me your luggage. You can pick it up later." Without luggage, we continued walking through the train.

On the second car, I looked ahead and coming straight for us, blocking our way, was a big conductor. "What car you lookin' fer, lady?" I opened my mouth. Nothing came out. I looked from side to side. There was no escape. I was about to blurt out the truth to him too, when suddenly, beneath my feet, I felt the train lurch. We were on our way! I broke into a broad smile. "We're not looking for any particular car, sir. We have no reservations." His eyes bugged out, he puffed up and turned red. "No reservations!" he yelled. Lady, do you realize what you are saying? We left people behind who had reservations?"

I didn't care and couldn't hide it. We were on our way and they couldn't put us off. I'd put up with anything to complete this trip as promised my babies. It was a feeling of super human determination mothers get sometimes, as my mother told me.

The conductor said, "Follow me!" He walked ahead of us through several cars, announcing very loudly to all porters, "This woman does NOT have a reservation. She will have to be shifted from one seat to another all the way to Los Angeles." We ran across our friendly porter who gave us a wink and we smiled. Finally the conductor took us to the bar where people lined up for the dining car, and told us to sit there. Here, too, he announced our plight for all to hear.

We sat down quietly on one chair, with the children sitting on my lap and at my feet. It was embarrassing. I handed out books, and they sat quietly. When the conductor left, the guy behind the bar came over and handed us soft drinks and bar nuts. We must have looked like refugees. We were grateful because of the humiliation we were put through. Shortly, our friendly porter came through and whispered, "Don't worry. I'll get you a seat soon." And he did.

We settled in our new seats and relaxed. It was wonderful. We were on our way. There were friendly people in the USA. We hauled out our cards and played games, laughed and talked.

But not for long. Along came grouchy conductor. "Aha", he said. "Don't expect to be here very long. This seat is spoken for at the next station." He was right. We shifted back to the bar. Again we were plied with nuts and drinks. An hour later we were given seats. And again displaced. This time when friendly porter saw us in the bar he whispered, "Ol' grouch is finished at 10 o'clock. After that I'll find you permanent seats"

True to his word, friendly porter came for us after 10 o'clock and led us to two facing seats. He then collected our long forgotten luggage. "There now," he said, "Ain't nobody goin' to move you now. Just stay put." He said Amtrak was unable to keep reservations straight. They just were not set up for the increase in business.

We turned the two seats into a bed and, with pillows and blankets supplied us, we snuggled down for the night. It was actually comfortable

When we woke, palm trees were blowing in the breeze, and the ocean looked so nice. It was exciting. The children were happy. However, when they started getting rambunctious, I called them together and pointed to the elderly couple across the aisle. "Look, kids, you don't have the right to let your fun interfere with other people's holidays. You must not upset that couple by making too much noise." This worked. If any one got loud, the other two would quickly say "Shhh. Not so loud." I was so proud of my babies.

We finally got to Los Angeles. Nena and I had been very close when we were younger. In fact we were like twins in looks before I got fatter and she taller. We had spent 25 years together off and on. We had two wonderful years in Vancouver with nothing to do but entertain ourselves. Then marriage broke us up, and later distance separated us. She had a daughter five months younger than Eric and a son four months older than Haida. We saw them occasionally in the summer when they stopped on their way to Edmonton to visit our folks.

Nena had her children enrolled in a "free school", a phenomenon of the 1960s. At that school, children did whatever they wanted: if they felt like classes, or artwork, or drama, that's what they did. Each day they chose what to do. Nevan blossomed in this atmosphere. Keir didn't seem to enjoy it. I worried what it would do to them when they hit the regular schools. However, it didn't hinder them. Nevan graduated from law school. Keir attended Harvard. He was a member of their rowing club when they represented the U.S. in the World Olympics in Spain.

We went to Disneyland for a day and took in every ride available. We then finished off the day with a second ride on our favorites. At the end of the day we stopped to buy souvenirs, and Colin got lost. It wasn't for long, but this is the only thing he remembers of the trip.

Next day we took in Universal Studios, saw burning buildings, the façade of a Western town, saw how the Red Sea was parted, saw Jaws jump out of the water, and limbs falling from trees. We even partook in a movie shoot and bought a copy to take home. This was the highlight of our trip. Everyone was thoroughly impressed.

We also took a trip to Marineland and took a boat to see the whales. I saw them. But, it seemed whenever we approached a whale, I would say, "Look over this way"; the children were either vomiting, asleep, or very sick. I don't know if any of them saw anything.

And then it was time to go home. There was no way we could get train travel. No planes, either. We had to take the Greyhound bus back. It was a good trip.

WOMEN'S LIBERATION

In this 21st century I look back and see the great changes that took place in the last century. There were technological changes, environmental changes, and major social changes - especially in women's lives. It started during the World Wars when young men were sent off to fight, and women stepped in to do the jobs left behind. There were women in every mill, factory, farm - everywhere. After the war women didn't want to give up their jobs. At the same time the birth control pill was freeing women from having "all the babies god willed them."

Women fought back. They demanded, cajoled, pushed, prodded - they wanted to have choices. For every inch won, a price was paid. The fight for abortion lasted over 20 years, and was ugly and vicious. It is still not over. Token women were hired for some jobs. Excuses were made. In construction, the excuse was that separate toilets would be needed (women asked "Do you have separate toilets at home?")

On radio talk shows there were comments such as, "Women shouldn't be allowed to drive cars. Their minds don't work that way." But slowly, changes were taking hold. Mind-sets were changed.

Charlotte Whitton, the first woman mayor of Ottawa, said "Whatever women must do they must do twice as well as men to be thought half as good. Luckily, this is not difficult."

In our own family changes were happening, but resisted unconsciously. Mother (Hilda) was at the forefront of all progressive political change. She helped set up kindergartens in Vancouver. She worked on all fronts, improving women's lives. Within the CCF/NDP she held leadership conferences for women, arranged public speaking lessons, gave parliamentary procedure and group development courses. She encouraged and supported women candidates.

However, she was furious when women went to conventions and demanded that some nominations be reserved for women. She – and other women her age and experience – felt insulted: they said they believed women were equal to men and could do anything men could do – as long as they were given a fair opportunity. To set up separate criteria meant that women could not compete with men on an even playing field. I agreed with her.

However, in her own life she could not change. She was brought up at a time when there was a division of labour - men went out to work; women took care of home and children.

We had big family dinners about six times a year, which included the grandparents and Mother's sister and family (the Williamses). The women worked all day to put on a feast, served the meal, and then washed the dishes.

The overstuffed men would retire to the living room where coffee and liqueurs were served them. I would be so tired. But this is how it was done.

When Lyle and I married, he really tried to make the transition to equal partnership. Not always successfully.

After the children were born, I became a full time homemaker, by choice. I tried very hard, very consciously, to bring up my children to accept equality between the sexes

However, Mother could not change. One morning when we arrived from Ottawa, she phoned and invited Eric to join us for breakfast. It was a cold, windy, rainy day. I noticed she was putting her coat on, and asked why. She said she was out of cream and would just run down to the store. I told her Eric could pick it up. She replied, "Oh, no, I couldn't ask him to do that." I picked up the phone and asked him.

Other times I would hear her say, "Haida, help me set the table and make lunch. Your brothers are coming over." No amount of bringing this to her attention would change her.

I finally demanded that the "boys" wash dishes after the women made the meal. It took a shouting match between Lyle and his mother to get her to let them. From then on, she grudgingly allowed them to help,

On the other hand, I could not accept the sexual promiscuity of the late 20th century. As Archie Bunker was to describe it: "Hello. How are you. And before they even know each others name, Zap! They are in bed." To have sex just because it made one feel good, without any commitment, is just unacceptable. I did not see that people were happier. Promiscuity was not admirable.

Today I visit my sons' homes, and watch them pitch in helping with cooking, cleaning, and child rearing, without hesitation. It flows so naturally it is easy to forget what used to be. Haida has a husband who does the same. It's wonderful.

Mother made her contribution in so many ways. In 2006 I watched Kai (4 years old) taking skating lessons. Alongside me was a young man watching his 4-year old. We started to talk and I asked him where he lived. He said in the West End. I murmured "Bringing up a child downtown." He replied, "Oh, you have no idea what a child friendly city Vancouver is. It's wonderful. It has so many amenities. It is so safe. No speeding traffic. I don't know who put so much thought into it, but this is a wonderful city to raise a family in." I smiled and said, "You can start by thanking my mother-in-law."

I told him about some of the campaigns that Mother led or participated in. Starting in the 1950s, there was a movement to close West End schools, leaving the downtown with only commercial buildings and expensive upscale residences for swinging singles and executive apartments. Linked with the above was a push to follow the California example and riddle the city with freeways and ramps – which is such a disaster in Los Angeles.

Mother led the campaign against closing schools. She participated in the fight against freeways, and having the West End as a through-corridor for traffic from West Vancouver. Instead, a few streets were assigned to carry through-traffic, and the rest had traffic circles or little parks installed to block such traffic on cross streets: so good for local traffic, but so frustrating for others.

As chairman of the West End Community Council she worked at setting up community centres and services to establish a sense of community. Active in the B.C. Parent Teachers Association (PTA), she involved that organization, not only in stopping school closures, but in advocacy for social and community planning generally.

Forestalling the razing of Robson Street with its small shops and international flavour and its replacement with mega stores, she chaired the Robson International Village Corporation, a co-operative housing project mixed with ground floor, small scale commercial space, which was geared to take advantage of federal and provincial government funds.

She worked to establish the Vancouver Seniors' Network and spearheaded the building of Haro Park Retirement home, to which she would retire in 2002. The day we were driving her there, she said, "I never thought the day would come when I would need these facilities."

In 1972 when the NDP formed the provincial government, it was just in time to stop two more huge high-rises being built as the new downtown courthouse. Instead, Premier Dave Barrett had the world famous architect, Arthur Erickson, design a beautiful, low rise, tiered building with trees growing on each tier. The below-ground level has a skating rink where workers can get exercise at noon and families can enjoy in the evening. Around the skating rink are small ethnic food outlets with outdoor dining. I read articles in international travel magazines praising these buildings and saying, unlike other big cities, there is sunlight downtown instead of the usual wind tunnels blowing around tall buildings. At Christmas the place takes on a magical aura with all the twinkling lights on the trees.

While I was relating all this, the young man (at the skating rink) just stood there with his mouth open. He didn't know any of this. A Vancouver newspaper carried a full-page story on Mother and her battles. I wished Mother could hear how a young man appreciated her contribution to the life of his family.

Mother was involved in every provincial and federal election, working for the NDP. She helped elect Mike Harcourt as mayor of Vancouver. Harcourt was mayor when the World Expo was held in Vancouver in 1986. He refused to sign the enabling Expo agreement until the B.C. government agreed that any deficit resulting from the event would be borne by the provincial government. Many cities were stuck with debts after such expositions. Montreal took about 20 years to pay off their debts. The same would have happened in Vancouver. Most official histories will choose to ignore this fact.

Hilda,in her 90's, with Haida.

Kathy (Telford) Coffey with Hilda.

LAST YEAR IN ELECTED OFFICE

1993 was our Nordic year. In the spring, before Lyle was to attend a NATO conference in Copenhagen, we flew to Denmark, took the ferry to Oslo, Norway, and rented a car. We took in the Viking ship museum, a period village in Oslo, and visited the Winter Olympic sites. We spent the next ten days touring Norway, seeing the mountains, fjords, and valleys.

At Songfjorde we saw the recreated Viking longhouse, museum, and boat building display. Watching the clouds and fogbanks roll down the mountaintops, it's easy to understand why the Vikings believed that the gods lived there.

Their farms are small, scattered between the mountains, in the warm, moderate, mini climates of the fjords. There has existed for about a hundred years, a social contract between the various social groups, whereby the city folk earned a good wage (minimum wage in 1993 was $14 an hour), and farmer's products which were heavily subsidized. This is one reason Norway is holding back from joining the European Common Market. There were no beggars or hucksters harassing tourists. Good housing. No sign of poverty. It is such a sane, calm society.

Norway is very much like British Columbia. It has many ferries and hundreds of tunnels through the mountains. One tunnel was 16 miles long. These are very costly for a population of only four million.

In the city of Bergen 14th century wooden buildings, converted to modern, stylish offices and living quarters. They preserved their heritage beautifully.

Later that year, in the summertime, Lyle attended the Nordic Council in Reykjavik, Iceland. It was a meeting of all nations and indigenous peoples bordering on the Arctic Circle. He was impressed with the on-going studies and cataloguing of traditional health practices and medicines of northern peoples.

He took a few days to drive through the volcanic areas, went for a ride on an Icelandic pony, and visited Thingvillier – the site of the first parliament in the western world. The "Thing" valley is located over the fault line which divides the European from the North American tectonic plate.

The speaker of the parliament, who was called the "lawgiver", stood on one side of the fault line, while the assembly gathered on the other. Of course, a thousand years ago they didn't know this. It is an interesting coincidence that this was the meeting place of the first people who sailed from Europe to North America.

As the result of the location over the fault line, Iceland is rich in geothermal resources which provide the electrical power and hot water which heat all the buildings. They have large water tanks which cool the water before distribution.

I could not attend this conference, so spent the time with Nena Perepolkin in Thrums. It was a hot summer, and we went swimming in the Slocan River every day. Not being a good swimmer, I loved to swim to the middle of the stream and let the current carry me down for a mile, with little effort on my part.

In October, before the election was called, Lyle and I flew to Newfoundland, rented a car and drove out to view the Viking ruins at Lance aux Meadows. This is at the northern tip of Newfoundland where Lief Erickson landed on the North American continent. It took a long time for history to accept that it was not Columbus who discovered America.

Newfoundland is somewhat of a dreary province; Lyle calls it beautiful, rustic and rugged. Its old forest along the highway consisted of short, gnarled trees. None could be cut into lumber. There is very little black soil, so people plant vegetables wherever they can find it. Every now and then along the highway we saw potatoes growing in a patch of ground.

Everywhere we went we asked for lobster, and learned the season was over, just days before. Finally one restaurant told us they had one left: a five-pounder! We took it, along with half a pound of butter and a loaf of bread. It was great but I haven't wanted lobster since.

By the time we got back, the federal election was called. The Tories were very low in the polls, and would be reduced to two seats.

In our riding, we had expected Gerald to be nominated as our candidate. However, just before the nomination, he dropped out of the race, saying it was time for a woman candidate and Heather Suggit was the NDP nominee. The NDP executive was complacent, saying the seat was safe as there was no one to challenge us. In the 1988 election, Lyle had received 49%.

However, Lyle and I could see that the Reform Party, made up of disgruntled Conservatives and Social Creditors, was rising quickly across the province. There were letters to the editor from their members every week, in every part of the riding. We tried to warn our people, but they could not see it coming.

Lyle and I canvassed hard, as usual, but the writing was on the wall. The Reform Party candidate won in Kootenay West, as they swept all but two NDP seats in the province.

RETIREMENT

After ten years in parliament - with "four years off for good behaviour" in the middle - we were out of public life and retirement looked soooo good. In fact, I realized this was the first time in my life I was FREE! No school, no job, no children, no public responsibilities: this was indeed Freedom! Every day I would wake up and say, "What do I do today to entertain myself." Wow! So this was what the leisure class did their whole life!

We stored our furniture and headed west. We had a dog waiting for us, which we acquired from a policeman. He was a six-year-old black Labrador, and his name was Dane. He was destined to be ours, with a name like that. He was such a comfort and companion for me when I lived alone while Lyle went back and forth to Ottawa for the next six months until our condominium was sold.

What a difference from our previous dog! Dane was well trained. One day, I was about to jump into our truck when he came bounding over, eager to go with me. I couldn't take him, and said, "Stay". He froze in mid-step, and kept the one leg lifted, not moving a muscle - only his eyes followed me out of the yard.

First thing we had to do was build an addition to our home at Madeira Park. We had bought a small house on the property next door to the cabin which we had purchased in 1989. Colin designed and drew up blueprints for our new house. We hired an excavator to prepare the ground for the addition.

We kept Dane in the house until the excavation was completed. When we finally took the dog outside, he looked panicked at what he saw. Dane was a habitual bone-burier. He now ran around as if saying, "Where are all my bones?"

Shortly after, we were walking down the road behind the house discussing where the contractor should place the excess fill from the excavation, when Lyle pointed to a hollow above the road, saying, "He can put more fill here." Dane looked at us, and immediately started digging up bones and moving them to another site. It seemed he not only understood what Lyle said, but understood its implication.

We hired a contractor to frame the house. One day I was taking a puff of Lyle's cigarette, when one of the carpenters asked why I didn't have my own cigarette. I explained that I quit smoking while the children were growing up, but never stopped wanting to smoke. After the last child left home, I started taking a puff of Lyle's cigarette. I said that as long as I didn't light up my own cigarette, I wasn't smoking.

One afternoon when Lyle was away, I sat down for a break, and thought to myself, "I'd like a puff." Having no recourse, I lit up my own cigarette. Suddenly, I heard a loud voice from above say, "Aha, smoking again!" I jumped. Looking around, I thought to myself, "It's god. No, it's my dad." Then, a carpenter up on the framework, laughed. After being an atheist for forty years, my first thought had been, "It's god ."

For several months we lived in the original dwelling, with one wall missing, and much of the roof off, while the contractors tied the old and new construction together.

After the trusses were installed, and roof framing completed, another contractor shingled the roof. The roofing was finished on a Sunday morning. The rains started two hours later, after a hiatus of some months. Not bad for a couple of heathens! But, then again, maybe Thor (the Viking god of thunder) was on our side.

Once the roof was on, it was time to put up the drywall. Cousin Bob Williams and his son, John, along with another cousin's son, Tommy Jenkins, did most of the work. Lyle and I did the sanding, which was a most unpleasant job.

When it came time for the cedar siding, Colin and Eric came over and, along with Bob, put the siding up on the highest peak, over the deck, facing the water. I had previously painted the boards with 3 coats. Lyle and I finished putting the siding up on the other sides ourselves. After each section was done we gave it a last coat of paint, filling all the cut edges and nail holes. And then there was the trim, and the windows, and the doors!

As soon as the outside work was done, we started laying the hardwood floor in the living room. Before we were finished we got a phone call from a trucker saying our furniture was on the way. *"No way. You can't do that. We didn't ask for it yet. The house isn't finished!"* "Too bad" he said, " I am just crossing the border into B.C. and should be at your place tomorrow." I begged him to delay coming a couple of days, which he did.

The furniture arrived in December and it was so nice to have familiar things around. I had to unpack and immediately prepare for Christmas, with the family. That year there was a new member in the family – Colin had married Cindy Gee in July.

My feet were burning hot after I stood on them for a couple of hours. Realizing I needed help, I phoned Haida and begged her to leave her job on Salt Spring Island, and come home to help. She came and took over Christmas preparations.

When my feet continued to burn after Christmas, I went to see a doctor. He listened, shrugged, and said, "Guess you'll have to stay off your feet." I phoned a naturopath in Sechelt, but she couldn't see me for three months. I said, "Never mind. I don't think you can help me anyway."

She asked what the problem was and I told her. She said, "I can help you. This is tied in with menopause. Your thermostat is out of whack." With this information, I read everything in my Natural Health books on menopause. And there it was: "When your hands or feet are on fire." It listed three vitamins and the dosage. I took them, and three weeks later I was cured. And I haven't had a hot flash since then, either. The doctor didn't know what to do.

This wasn't the first time I had to find an alternative solution to a "medical" problem. Two decades earlier, during the seven year period when I had 3 children, and nursed them for ten months each, I found myself eating every two or three hours. After I weaned the last, I found I had to continue eating the same way. No matter how hard I tried, I could not go longer than 3 hours between meals. For example, one day Lyle and I were shopping, and we postponed eating until we got to our favourite restaurant. It was four hours since I ate, and I was literally ill. When I got there I had to run to the washroom to vomit.

In Ottawa, while attending a Natural Health School, taking a course in Swedish massage and reflexology, I was encouraged to read books on natural healing. In one of these books, I read about my problem. It suggested one should not eat carbohydrates together with proteins. I followed instructions, and when I ate meat, cheese or eggs, I did not eat pasta, potatoes, rice or bread. I did this for three days.

On the fourth day I had porridge in the morning, went to Lyle's office and worked all day. It was an especially busy day. At 5 o'clock our secretary said, "Vera, you haven't had lunch yet." *I DIDN'T HAVE LUNCH YET! Eight hours since I ate, and I was not even hungry!* I shut down the computer, took the bus home, made dinner, and when we sat down to eat at 7 o'clock, I was nicely hungry. For years, I had told doctor after doctor about my problem and not one had any suggestion for me. People put their faith in doctors thinking they know everything about health, but they don't. If I had searched for answers earlier, I would not have gained so much weight.

Back at our house construction, the hardwood flooring was finished and the outside completed, but all the molding and finishing remained to be done. Lyle worked at this over the next ten years. He had to learn every step of the way, but did a marvelous job on laying ceramic tiles in front of the front and back doors, laying new linoleum in the laundry, tiles in the kitchen, installing showers, putting down baseboards, and covering beams.

He went on to build me a greenhouse and an arbor by my flower garden. For someone who hardly knew how to hold a hammer, he learned well.

We were so looking forward to living on the ocean – and we do enjoy it. What we didn't know were all the challenges that the ocean presents: the tide going in and out plays havoc with docks, particularly when our salt water bay ices over because of the numerous creeks. Boats and docks are exposed to mussels growing on the bottom and need constant scraping and painting. Salt water erodes dock railing.

Every morning it is wonderful to look out on the water. Every day is different. Even in the rain, and with a mist, the view is wonderful. We have an abundance of wild life around us. Not only ducks, geese, cormorants, herons, and eagles, but also squirrels, raccoons, bears, elk and deer.

The latter are not always welcomed when they eat my vegetables and flowers. Every September a black bear would strip my grapes, just before they were ready to pick. The last one I watched tried to climb the arbor to get at the grapes on top. I shoo-ed him away. Then I pulled the vine up. I was not getting any grapes anyway, and stood the chance of having the arbor demolished.

However, we do enjoy watching hummingbirds and other birds on our deck. One day we were watching a hummingbird feed, and a small bird sat on the railing watching as well. When the hummingbird flew away, the small bird jumped up, flapped his wings as fast and hard as it could, and tried to eat the seeds in his feeder in the same way as the hummingbird. He could only peck twice, and then flop down on the railing. But he continued trying to emulate the hummingbird for quite a while. It was so funny.

We have a small island in front of our house. Our friends said it is a big rock; an island has a tree on it. We considered planting a tree, but twice a year, when the tide is high, it is completely under water. Every year a pair of geese have a nest on it. One year we saw the proud parents take their goslings out for their first swim. The little goslings were cavorting in front of their parents, ducking in and out of the water, over each other. Suddenly an eagle above them tried to dive down to grab one, but because he was directly above them he had to weave back and forth. This gave the parents enough time to scatter their babies and avoid the eagle's talons

After the eagle flew away, they lined their goslings up between them, and went on swimming. Shortly after that, Lyle was sitting in the livingroom, when he saw two eagles with their talons locked, falling, tumbling from the sky, heading straight for our deck. They broke off about eight feet before disaster. One flew off towards the bay, and the other headed directly towards our large glass doors, literally scraping against them as he peeled up and away from under the eaves. Lyle actually ducked, expecting him to crash straight through.

Our home at Madeira Park on the Pacific Ocean.

Early one morning, Lyle shouted at me that a bull elk was eating our apple tree. He towered above our 8-foot arbor. I grabbed a broom and went screaming out of the house. A cow elk was grazing just outside the door. Fortunately I frightened her, and she took off down the road, followed by five other cows and calves. The bull then loped casually after them. Neighbors have had much more difficulty shooing elk away, and some dogs have been killed trying. I was glad I didn't stop to think. These are the stories that make living here so wonderful. I can't imagine living anywhere else.

PEACOCKS

In 1995, Haida brought us two peacocks from the Salt Spring Island children's camp where she was working. We hoped for a male and female, but they were both males. We kept them penned up for three weeks before releasing them. Then the fun began.

They roamed up and down the community, with us constantly chasing after them, trying to keep track. One neighbor said, "If I see a peacock I'll think I have died and gone to heaven." However, his wife, who had a garden, had quite the opposite opinion.

They were hard on gardens, picking off buds and flowers, scratching around plants. Many times I cursed them, asking if they were more of a nuisance than pleasure. Pleasure always won out. I started putting fishnet over my garden plants. This also protected my plants from deer and other birds.

Every evening they would come up on our deck and fly into the big cedar. If we were in the hot tub on the deck, they would sit on the railing and watch us. Whenever we were away for a couple of days, when we got home I would go out on the deck and give a call similar to the one I heard from them when they were apart from each other. I would immediately get their "answer" call, and they would be home in five minutes. Every autumn they lost their long tails, and the house is full of peacock feathers.

In the spring they would make the most urgent calls, searching for a mate. We finally bought a very young female. It was a comedy act, watching them fuss over her. They scratched in the dirt for her. They urged her up on deck and tried to get her to fly up into the tree with them. She tried but found she couldn't and had to settle for the roof of the carport. Before long she disappeared. The two boys were alone again.

Shortly after, I heard an awful racket from one as he came flying home from the direction of the woman with the garden. He sat on our deck and called but there was no response from the other one. He called late into the night until he was hoarse. We heard through the school grapevine that our neighbor caught him and released him 30 miles away.

This poor bird (whom we named Big Bird) had the most distressing squawk, the most mournful call, which he emitted until 3 in the morning. Lyle described the call as a combination cougar's scream and jackass' bray. One evening we saw a flock of geese land in the water in front of the tree where Big Bird sat. Among the gray geese was one white Canada goose. The white goose and Big Bird called to each other for hours. After the gray geese left, the white one stayed. We were expecting to have a new pet, but sometime during the night she flew away.

We bought another pea hen. In the wild male and female peacocks do not hang around together. However, there wasn't much choice here. The first few weeks a female appeared, Big Bird would act most servile. As soon as she came in view, he would drop his head to the ground and walk timidly around her.

One day I watched as he approached her, but as soon as she saw him he would turn away. When she went back to scratching, he would again look at her, and again turn away if she caught him looking. It was like watching awkward teenagers in their earliest encounters with the opposite sex.

But she too disappeared. And another. And another. Not all the neighbors were unhappy with our peacocks. Most found them enchanting. Finally, we got an "older" female and, after the first weeks of coyness, we saw them running together, flying up to the same tree at night. She became "Ladybird".

Spring came, and the rituals of courting and mating took place. She went off to build a nest and lay eggs. We were told from the start that peacocks will not nest in enclosed spaces. When we bought her, she was in a long covered "dogrun" wire area, and was laying eggs. However, not in a nest – one was in one corner, another dropped in the middle. She would not sit on them. So we expected her to go off into the woods. Every second day she would come running home, squawking loudly, demanding to be fed, go to the feed trough, eat quickly, drink water quickly, eat again, and then run out of the yard.

A couple of weeks later a neighbor phoned to say he saw her with chicks. We found her with seven babies. Big Bird stood around nearby. The next day, I went back to the same place and found one dead chick on the road, looking like it had been trampled to death. I said the evidence pointed to Big Bird, but Lyle said the evidence would never stand up in court. However, when she approached him, she would give him a wide berth, leading her chicks around him.

Within a week she brought them home (by now there were only four) and led them up onto the deck to feed in the trough. After they got their fill, she flew up on the railing and stood there, clucking away, "Fly up here. You can do it. Come up here." The chicks ran around, "We can't fly, Mommy." But she continued, until one chick found that if he jumped up on a flower pot, he could then fly up onto the rail. The other three followed suit. She then flew down into the yard. Again she clucked away, "You can do it. Just spread your wings. Fly down here." Again they ran up and down the railing. "We can't do it, Mommy. We're scared. We'll get hurt." Again, one of them spread his wings and flew down. Two more followed. But the fourth was absolutely petrified. Finally, he spread his wings and flapped so hard he flew over the mother and a long distance into the yard. What a mother!

THREE DAYS LATER, a neighbor, Stan Barker, phoned to say, "Come and see. She has them flying up into the tree already." We walked over and watched as she led them from branch to branch, up and down, and then over to a neighboring tree. Then she spread her wings and all four huddled together under them. She knew they were vulnerable as long as they were on the ground and she had to get them flying into a tree as soon as possible. Some human mothers don't put that much effort into teaching their children.

Through the summer we didn't see them for weeks. The population of our area increases dramatically in the summer months, as cottage owners, their children and their dogs and cats come to spend their vacations.

Ladybird obviously thought it a good time to remove her brood to safer pastures. Neighbors up and down our community would report seeing them from time to time. In the fall they came home, but now there were only two chicks. They looked like straggly teenagers. And just as noisy. One day I heard the mother make an awful commotion, from the direction of the neighbor with the garden. Ladybird called late into the night. One more chick had disappeared. Now there was one.

By the next spring we could see "Junior" was a male. Mother and son were close, and Big Bird "tolerated" him. Ladybird went off to build a nest again, and performed the familiar ritual of running home squawking, eating and drinking, and then running back.

However, Junior would attach himself to her, literally placing his head on her body, murmuring. When she had to leave, she had a terrible time getting rid of him. She obviously did not want him following her to her nest and endangering her life. She had to work very hard to lose him. Then one day she came walking back and didn't return to her nest. Something had taken her eggs.

The next spring Big Bird tried to chase Junior away. He chased him all over the yard, flew after him into the neighbor's yard, harassed him for weeks. He was obviously trying to get him to leave home – to found his own colony. Ladybird nested and Lyle saw her with four chicks one day, but alone the next. She lost them overnight. Big Bird continued to try to get rid of Junior long after summer set in.

One morning Lyle and I were standing in the window, watching Big Bird chasing Junior, when Junior turned on him. They swung at each other, with wings and feet. They kept leaping over each other, trying to strike, panting heavily. They fought for so long, we gave up and left the window. However, Big Bird obviously lost the battle. He left the yard. He had been deposed. We could hear him in the neighborhood, and occasionally we would see him during our walks. We left food around for him.

Early one morning he came back onto the deck and was eating as fast as he could. Junior walked onto the deck, and Big Bird walked off, with Junior walking alongside him to the edge of the yard. Then Junior came back, and Big Bird never set foot in the yard again. If we hadn't observed the fight we would not have known what happened. Big Bird was deposed, de-throned, cast out.

Ladybird joined him in exile for a couple of months, although she would come back to eat now and again. Late in the fall she came back and stayed. We didn't hear him again. We don't know if he walked away to live elsewhere, or if he fell prey to a coyote.

This year (2006), Lady Bird was seen with three chicks, one being all white. When the summer crowd arrived, she walked her brood quickly through our yard, to an isolated point. They didn't come home until the summer crowd left, with their children, dogs and cats.

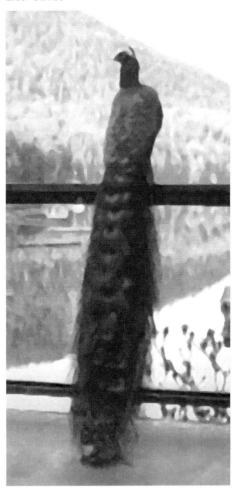

Lyle took food and water to them all summer. Junior was very much part of the "family", eating with them, walking with them. This was never the case with Big Bird. He would watch them, but he was never part of the group. We – and the neighbors – are anxious to see if the white one is male or female. The male would be beautiful with the blue-green "eyes" on the

AFRICA

All our married life we talked about taking a trip to Africa. Finally, in 1997, after the house was built, we did it.

We flew to Johannesburg, via Hong Kong, in early May. We joined a safari made up of two Mercedes safari buses carrying 15 people each, that took us through northern South Africa, Zimbabwe, Zambia, Malawi and Tanzania (including the island of Zanzibar), and ending in Nairobi, Kenya, stopping at wild life reserves along the way. We put up tents every night and camped outdoors; sometimes in campsites and sometimes in the open bush. The driver cooked tasty meals for us over an open fire, and everybody took turns at cleanup.

Victoria Falls was fabulous. We took a helicopter ride over the falls. One evening, on the Zambezi River above the Falls, we took a sunset dinner and booze cruise on a boat, maneuvering among the many hippos and crocodiles in the water. After eating, we joined in African dances, and had a great time.

In South Luanga National Park, in Zambia, we were camped near the water, and felt our tents shake at night as hippos tripped over the tent ropes. We took a night ride in a jeep outfitted with powerful spotlights, and watched a leopard stalk an impala. The leopard appeared annoyed with us.

We pulled into our campsite on Lake Malawi just in time to see two dogs facing off with a six-foot long black mamba in the middle of the campground. After a few minutes the snake slithered off into the bush. Needless to say, our fellow campers competed with each other to get the dogs to sleep outside their tents that night.

Next morning, we took a tour of the lakeshore, watched the fishermen bring in their catch, and the women and children spread the fish, in their thousands, to dry in the sun. We spent a couple of days, relaxing and swimming in the warm lake.

Malawi is one of the poorest countries in East Africa. The highway was atrocious. Our vehicle travelled most of the way with one set of tires on the shoulder to cushion the potholes. At times children lined the roads, making an attempt to fill in the potholes, and then stretching out their hands for tips.

When we crossed the border from Malawi to Tanzania, we were impressed by the lush green countryside, the tea plantations, and the rubber trees. We were told there was a great effort put into attempts to get the nomadic tribes to put down roots. As soon as they started planting gardens, the government built schools nearby, encouraging the children to attend. There was no way this could be enforced, just encouraged.

At Dar-es-Salaam, we left our buses, and took a fast ferry to the Island of Zanzibar. This was an early centre of the slave trade. We toured several slave-holding building. We also toured a spice plantation.

Leaving Dar-es-Salaam, we headed straight north for Kenya. I knew we were going north, but the sun was there. It took some time for me to realize we were south of the equator, putting the sun to the north.

At Arusha, we left our buses again, and used local, smaller vehicles and guides. Before entering the Serengetti, we toured a nomadic Masai village. These people are constantly on the move with their cattle. Entering one grass hut, it was clear to see how they could do this. There was not one chair, table or bed.

Camping that night, we watched our new guides prepare dinner on an open fire. One of the guides placed tea bags on a table and went away. A big baboon loped over casually, grabbed the tea and took off. The other baboons started cheering him on, as the guide grabbed a machete and took chase. It was several minutes before he came back with the tea. We were warned, "If you have to go in the middle of the night, DON'T. Keep a plastic bag handy." There were hyenas hanging around the campsites.

We took tours of the Serengeti plains for several days, seeing herds of buffalo, zebra, gnu, impala, giraffes, elephants, lions, vultures and wart hogs. One morning we took a balloon ride over the Serengeti and watched thousands of animals stirring as the sun rose over the horizon.

Upon landing, Mameluke-clad waiters served us a silver-service champagne breakfast on linen-covered tables, on the Serengeti plain. Our safari ended in Nairobi, Kenya.

After the safari we took a bus to Uganda to visit Anna Amaliak's family. We met her (along with her three children and her sisters) in Ottawa when she was High Commissioner to Canada. She had since died. Her children returned to Uganda and were living with her sister, whose husband, Abbey Ongom, was a Member of Parliament

Our first day in Kampala was a Sunday. Walking through downtown Kampala we saw a tourist office open and went in. The man that waited on us wasn't able to do what we needed. He said, "Are you sure I couldn't do anything else for you?" I told him we wanted to meet someone but that would have to wait until the next day when Parliament opened. He asked who, and when we told him, he said, "Not only do I know him, but I know exactly where he is right now.

Wait a few minutes and I'll drive you there."

He drove us to the golf course where Abbey and Dorothy Ongom and their son, were playing in a tournament. I was glad to see this place, otherwise I would have left Africa thinking it consisted of beggars, hucksters and shanty-towns.

At the golf course we saw the middle class, where beer flowed freely, and free cigarettes were passed around. Ongom's son won a trip to New York during the tournament.

The next day we went to Parliament and watched the session. Uganda holds elections, but prohibits political parties. They reasoned that their country had several tribes, and parties in Africa were always divided on tribal lines, not ideology. Everybody in that tribe was encouraged, prodded, cajoled, forced (if need be) into voting for their own tribe. Whoever won had jobs and goodies for their tribal members.

To encourage cross tribal voting, parties were disallowed. Candidates ran as individuals. Parliamentarians sat together – not opposite each other. Rather than confrontational sessions, they tried cooperation.

They had appointed 30 women to sit as MPs. Then in the last election 15 more women got elected. There was a real effort to include women in government. In fact, in several countries we saw huge billboards saying, "A government without women is like a pot sitting on one stone." I might mention, also, there were billboards saying, "Please don't make beggars dependent on you."

We flew to South Africa from the Entebbe airport. This is directly under the equator, but at night we had to put sweaters on because it was so cold. At the airport in Johannesburg we rented a car and headed for Kruger National Park.

Thankfully we immediately entered a divided highway and had time to get used to driving on the left hand side. Driving for a week slowly through the park helped. This is when our holiday really started. It was so nice to travel when and where we wanted. We had to sleep in the car as we had no reservations. But it was no hardship. We had sleeping bags with us, and the car was comfortable. And cheap!

Within the first hour in the park, we had our first "adventure". Travelling along a river we watched the crocodiles lined up, lazing in the sun. Then from behind a big tree a huge elephant came up from the river, and, startled us - and him. He started stomping his foot and waving his ears back and forth. He was so big we could have driven the car under his belly. He could have flipped our car with his tusks and rolled it into the river. Lyle slowly backed the car up. The elephant lost interest and walked off into the woods. That got the adrenaline flowing.

From then on it was one adventure after another. We watched the animals coming together to drink at the waterholes. At one such station the zebras and impalas were drinking at the low troughs, and the giraffe drank at the tall water tower. The giraffe lifted his head and saw a big elephant lumbering towards him. The giraffe galloped away.

At a river we watched the hippopotamus and crocodile swimming and eating near each other. A group of six more hippos came floating down the river. The crocodile walked out of the water and waited for them to pass, and then went back in.

We had to be inside the campgrounds by 6 each night. Within each compound there were grocery stores, butcher shops, and restaurants. We hadn't come prepared to cook in the campsites. We did, however, have plates and utensils. Before long various people gave us pots, pans, and cutting boards, and we were cooking all our meals on the propane stoves.

In each kitchen there was a small tank of boiling water, which gave us instant coffee, tea or soup. At 6 o'clock each morning, we would make our coffee, and pull up to the gate, along with a dozen others, waiting for the gates to open.

During the night we would have heard lions roar, or hyenas fighting, and would have some idea where there might have been a kill. Everybody headed off looking for action. As cars passed, people would tell each other, "Lions feeding on a carcass about a mile back." Or "Watch out for an irate female elephant." "Two gemsbok to the right." "Herd of elephants ahead with two babies."

By ten o'clock the animals would be less active and people headed back for breakfast. Sometimes we would pull into an "off the beaten track" campsite, where we could refill our coffee. The attendant would pull out a gas-fired "wok" on a stand with wheels, and light the propane. We would make bacon and eggs and sit at a "blind" where we would eat and look out over a valley teaming with wildlife.

We walked along pathways on marshland between "blinds" to observe birds. Someone had told us to forget Serengeti and go straight to Kruger, and they were right. Here we had more close at hand animals and action, in a very congenial surrounding.

After a week we exhausted all the side roads, and had to head out, driving on the left side of narrow highways. We drove along the border of Lesotho, through replanted forests, and down to Durban. We didn't stop as it was known to be the most crime-ridden area in the country.

Further along the ocean was Umtata, where Nelson Mandela was born. There were no hotel rooms to be had. We pulled into the city campsite and slept in the car again. The countryside was beautiful. It was rolling countryside. Farms were obviously prosperous. We stopped at Ado Elephant Park.

Just before leaving on this holiday, Lyle watched a TV program about elephant dung beetles, and he was curious to see them. In fact, at the entrance to this park, it warned people to avoid riding over elephant dung lest they crush the beetles, which were so necessary in disposing of the dung. However, for all the piles of dung we saw, we did not encounter any beetles. But there were many elephants. In one spot we counted 43, of various sizes and ages.

Capetown is a very beautiful city. We had a friend there who vacated his apartment and left it for us. From here we could explore markets and museums; drive down to the southernmost point where the Indian Ocean meets the Atlantic. We saw many animals (like the bonteboks) that could not be found anywhere else in the world – not even in other parts of Africa. Took a boat ride to Robbin Island where Nelson Mandela was imprisoned.

Then we headed back to Johannesburg. We stopped at Kimberley with its diamond mining history. Near Johannesburg, we took in one more park, Palenesburg. We rented a tent, all ready set up, with beds and blankets.   We saw the usual animals, including leopards, gemsbok, and hartebeests. On the very last day, we a saw a sable.   We did want to see one, and now we felt we could go home happy.

Back to Johannesburg and back to Canada through Hong Kong. On our way to Africa, Hong Kong was British. On our way back it was part of China. From the newspaper we learned that, for the first time, a pension was provided their seniors, but, the editorial complained, it should have been larger. But the grass was still green, the sun still rose in the East. No great changes happened with the switchover to China.

What a trip! What a holiday. It was worth waiting a lifetime. Loaded with adventure, new experiences, fun, and interest!

BACK TO MADEIRA PARK

We saw the new millennium, 2000, come in, sitting with Mother in Vancouver. We wondered what new things this century would bring.

In 1998, Eric married Maki Haruno. a landed immigrant from Japan. Colin had married Cindy Gee in 1994, who had immigrated from China when she was ten years old. We told Haida if she married an Indian we would have Asia covered. She didn't. In 2003, she married Blair Bolton, ethnic origin English and Swedish.

Our first grandchild, Kai Levonti (his second name after my father, which pleased me so much), was born September 14th, 2001. In 2004, Colin and Cindy's son, Nikolas, was born.

The family at Christmas 2001.

VISIT TO INDIA - 2005

Ever since Ashish Kulkarni and Mark Dixie stayed with us in 1986, as participants in the Canada World Youth exchange program, we talked about going to India. When Ashish got married we talked about it, but didn't go.

When he had a daughter, we talked about it, but didn't go. When Ashish was in Hollywood in 2002, as one of the judges at the Emmy award ceremonies, judging animated film (he is in the film-making business), he came to visit us. Again, he urged us to come to India, and we said we'd think about it.

In 2004, I got a computer, and one of the first emails I received was from Ashish, reminding us that we were going to think about a visit. It was so thrilling: an email from India! Shortly after that Haida got an email from Mark Dixie in Toronto, telling her that he and his mate applied to work in India, and they both got assignments in Bangalore. When he found out that Ashish lived there, Mark said that we now had to come to India.

We decided to do it. Ashish was so happy to hear it. The earliest flight we could get was December 25th to Toronto, then to Dehli on December 30th.

We spent Christmas Eve and Day with the family in Vancouver. After Christmas dinner, we flew to Toronto and stayed with Eva Cargill, my hitchhiking-through-Europe friend.

On Boxing Day, we heard about the big Indian Ocean earthquake and tsunami. However, as we were heading to central and west coast India, we didn't expect it to affect our plans. It took 17 hours to reach Delhi, flying over Iceland, Russia, Kazakstan, Afghanistan, Pakistan and then India.

We were met at the Delhi airport by Ashish's brother, Ankoor, his wife, Sujata, and their 10-year old daughter, Disha. We stayed with them in their very nice, second story, 3-bedroom Delhi apartment.

The next day, New Year's, we went sightseeing together, visiting several temples, including a new B'hai temple built like a lotus flower. Every tourist spot we went to had enormous line-ups. We found the bright-coloured saris that women were wearing stunning, especially as they flowed behind them on their motor scooters.

I knew India had a dense population, but was unprepared for the sight of so many people. India gets monsoon rains for about a month. Then there is no rain for the rest of the year, and the dust settles on everything. People must sweep and wash their floors and sidewalks every day just to keep the dust in check. The ever-present dust mingles with the air pollution to cause a major air quality problem in many of the big cities. To make matters worse during our visit, there was a major air inversion in Delhi, which caused an airport closure for several days. I got a chest infection that had me gasping for breath.

The next day Ankoor arranged to have a car and driver pick us up at 6 a.m. to take us on a 3-day trip. We went to the city of Agra, which has the famous Taj Mahal monument. Every picture I saw of the Taj Mahal had this glistening white marble against a blue, blue sky, surrounded by very blue water. It was a cloudy day so nothing looked quite like those pictures.

After seeing the Taj Mahal, we started to head out of town about 2:30 en route to Jaipur where we were to meet another friend, Anil, at about 9 o'clock, after stopping at Sikri, another tourist sight. The driver didn't have a map, and got lost. As a result we did not get out of Agra until almost 5:30. The side trip was cancelled and the trip that should have taken four hours lasted for almost seven.

The road to Jaipur! There were camels pulling carts, elephants walking, bullocks pulling wagons, men pushing carts, every kind of tractor, some looking like they were home made, three-wheeled motorized rickshaws. Cars and trucks darting back and forth passing these slow moving things, together with motor scooters, bicycles, donkey carts and thousands of people, cows and dogs milling about on the road. There were men holding chained bears alongside the highway asking if we wanted a photo taken with them. I was told it was illegal; that there would be a crackdown; then a little time would pass, and the bears would come out again. Now and then the pavement would disappear all together for a distance.

If this drive had lasted for an hour or two, one could simply chalk it up as an interesting, if hair-raising, experience. But seven hours was horrendous.

Anil is another one of the Canada World Youth exchange kids from 1986. He was Ashish's best friend in Nelson, and visited our home many times. He insisted that we visit him and his family in Jaipur when in India. He was now an electrical engineer with his own company.

When we hit town we phoned him, and he met us within minutes. Together with his wife Geeta, son Akul (10) and daughter Apoorva (13), he took us out for a very nice vegetarian dinner.

The next day Geeta and the children took us sightseeing. We saw the Amber Palace, which was marvelous. It was on the side of a mountain, with stone walls running up and down the mountain ridges as far as the eye could see - a smaller version of the Great Wall of China. We then toured city museum and former maharaja's palace. Anil joined us for lunch.

That night they took us to a very large cultural tourist park which depicted past and present life in the state of Rajastan. We watched a variety of dancers and entertainers. Then took a ride on an elephant.

We wanted to ride a camel. Lyle and I told everyone that one of our priorities on this trip was to take a day or two ride through the desert on a camel. Here was our first taste of riding a camel. As I got on, the camel went "uuuhhh", and then Lyle got on the back side of the saddle, with only me to cling to, and the camel went "uuuuuhhhhhh". The camel brought his back legs up, tossing us forward, and then his front legs, tossing us back. I jostled back and forth with only a tiny horn to hang on to, and Lyle was in a worse situation, sprawled across the hump, hanging on to me for dear life. It was distinctly uncomforable. As soon as we got off we both declared the desert ride on a camel was off our agenda.

We were taken to a bullock-pulled wagon. We sat on the front seat, with nothing at all to hold on to. It was a narrow seat with each of us having half a cheek overhanging. When we turned corners the driver in front of us would extend an arm so we wouldn't go flying off. I sat there thinking what the security inspectors back home would think of these rides.

We were off to have a 15 course dinner at a very big restaurant. We had to take our shoes off and wash our hands. People sat cross-legged on a platform at a very short table. Anil spoke to a waiter who arranged for two chairs to be placed beside the platform in order that we could sit on the same level as those sitting cross-legged on the floor.

The meal was served on a huge plastic sheet which was probably disposable. There were lots of chapattis to pick up the food. With each serving we got an explanation of what part of the state the food came from. Everything was good. It was a lovely evening - something that was not duplicated anywhere else in India. Next morning Anil, Geeta and Akul came to see us off, back to Delhi.

Lyle wanted to re-pack our luggage, so Sujata and I went for a walk. As we passed a school, I asked her why Disha didn't go to that school, instead of taking a bus at 7 a.m. and travelling 45 minutes. She replied, "Oh, we could never afford this school. This is a business class school." So what were they? "We are the service class. We are all Brahmin caste, but Brahmins are divided into three classes." Government pays each school the same amount of money; parents pay extra money to their children's schools. These fees vary greatly.

I was amazed to learn that Ankoor, who is a chartered accountant, and had worked for a bank for around 15 years, worked from 9 to 9, six days a week. Six months earlier he changed jobs and began working for General Electric. He now works 9 to 9, five days a week, and half days on Saturday - the half day being from 9 to 6. He gets no paid holidays. He can take a day or two off, now and then, for special occasions - weddings, funerals, religious days. But at no time can he take a whole week off.

Sujata complained bitterly that there is no time for family life. Disha leaves for school at 7 am, before Ankoor gets up, and is in bed before he gets home. This was like England during the Industrial Revolution a hundred years ago.

Later, I read about some "techies", who work in the data processing industry, complaining because they had to work from 7 am until midnight. They signed a two-year agreement, got trained on the job, but had part of each pay cheque paid into a bond which they forfeited if they quit before the two years was up. The company, of course, said only a few techies were complaining.

However, we did get to speak to a manager at a tractor factory about working conditions there. He said the workers had a union and worked five 8-hour days a week. We understood him to say that they get 30 days off a year that could be taken in whatever fashion they wanted. The 30 days could cover all funerals, weddings, religious days, and holidays. He didn't know what the wages were but thought they were pretty good.

I suppose that Indian white-collar workers will have to wage their own battles if they want to improve their lot.

BANGALORE

We flew to Bangalore – called the Garden City and the site of India's "silicon valley". Ashish met us at the airport with his driver, and took us home to meet his wife, Suvarna, and 11-year old daughter, Awani. They live in a beautiful four-storey apartment building that looks like everything is made of white marble. My lungs felt better immediately. This was a much cleaner city. However, they do have their problems. There is a population of 8 1/2 million people. Once there were 200 lakes in the area; now there are 50.

Ashish had arranged for us to be guests of honour at Awani's school, and for Lyle to be speaker at their "annual awards" night. The principal told us that he had located the Gir School, which is a very progressive private school, outside of city boundaries in the middle of what was to be a green belt. Now the city was selling green belt lots to accommodate more homes and development, and he was fearful of it all disappearing. He wanted Lyle to touch on this in some fashion and perhaps offer some advice.

Lyle felt distinctly uncomfortable. He was a foreign tourist, in one of the oldest civilizations in the world, being asked to give public advice on a complex subject, after only a few days in the country. He didn't eat any dinner. He tossed and turned all night. When I woke in the morning, I asked, "Have you got it yet?" He said "Yes, it came to me in the middle of the night. I know what I have to say."

Mark Dixie came with us. As Lyle spoke, Mark kept saying, "Wow. He is pulling all the right strings." "He is saying everything that needs saying, tactfully." "What is he running for?" Lyle did deliver a brilliant speech. He was applauded throughout.

The day before when we met with the principal, he said, "We don't know what to do". I blurted out, "For heaven's sake. You brought the British Empire to its knees. India taught the world how to protest and win." Speaking to the assembly, Lyle said something like that, only much more tactfully.

Lyle then presented certificates to half the students, and I presented the other half. There were about 700 students. Awani was one of them. They had a concert program with each class representing a different Indian state and culture. It was tremendous.

Next day we picked up Mark and his mate, Shaleen, and took a trip to the countryside south of Bangalore, to a high mountain station which Awani loved. The air was refreshing and clear, and the view of the countryside was wonderful.

We travelled through farmland and watched farmers ploughing their land with bullocks in time-honoured fashion. In several places we saw farmers spreading what looked like straw across the highway. Ashish explained that this was a grain called "ragi" and is used by the lowest castes to make very dark bread. I tried to buy some but to no avail, as it was not available in uptown stores. Cars driving over this grain "threshed" it. In the evening when we were driving home, people had removed the straw, and were sweeping the seeds off the highway.

On Monday, Awani had a day off from school. Ashish's driver drove us to a zoo and wildlife park. It was supposed to be the driver's day off - he works 7 days a week, but can take a day off whenever he has a reason. This was such a day, but he agreed to drive. When we got there we asked if he would join us on the safari drive. He said, "no, no, no". We said since it was his day off, we wanted him to come. Suvarna encouraged him, too, and he did.

He had never been there before, and it was a pleasure watching him enjoy the animals. The bus travelled through the park, amongst a variety of animals, including bears, white tigers, and eight other tigers lazing in a pool of water.

The highway to the zoo was bad. Each state places different priority on roads, and the state of Karnataka gives roads a middle priority. The main highways are good, but the side roads are miserable, but not as bad as the road from Agra to Jaipur.

KERALA

We flew from Bangalore to Cochin in Kerala state. Our trip was all carefully arranged by Ashish. At Cochin we were met by a driver and car and taken to a posh hotel. Within minutes of arrival, we had a phone call from Ashish, checking that all was well.

After lunch the driver picked us up and drove us to the Arabian Sea. It was lovely; moist, warm air, with all kind and shapes of boats plying the waters. We watched some fishermen casting their nets from the shore. I bought Kai a puzzle box which I later filled with "treasure", telling him I got it from a pirate.

Cochin is a city sitting on islands at sea level with man-made dikes and canals all around. There are very long bridges spanning the canals.

The State of Kerala was formed in 1957 by combining several small states. In the election of 1958, the Communist Party won, and stayed in power until the last election when the Congress Party won.

The state has 100% literacy and practically no unemployment. Quite unlike the rest of the country, I saw only one beggar. There was an orderly and relatively calm atmosphere everywhere we went. We saw no piles of garbage nor shantytowns, and no cows wandering within the city. However, no matter whom I asked about these observations as compared to the rest of India, they immediately and invariably replied, "It has nothing to do with the government." Really?

In the evening we were urged to see a Kerala cultural presentation and dance at a beachfront theatre. We picked up the tickets, went to a bar overlooking the Arabian Sea, and enjoyed a beer and the atmosphere. I could have stayed there all evening, but headed for the theatre at 6, where we sat and waited. The show was unique and skillful but very formal and traditional in style – really not our cup of tea.

The next morning we left early to drive across the width of Kerala to a major forest and natural wildlife preserve. The scenery was breathtaking as we traveled through mountain ranges and deep valleys.

Many of the mountainsides were covered with tea plantations and we watched women at work in the fields. They had long scissors with a bag attached, so as they snipped the tea leaves they fell into the bag.

Our resort was owned by Ashish's friend which was located in the midst of a spice plantation. I took the spice tour. In the evening I took an Ayurvedic treatment massage. Warm oil was poured over me, from head to toes, followed by an invigorating massage and a thorough wash. What a feeling!

As I stood in the office I lamented that we were scheduled to take a two hour boat trip in the forest park the next day, with nothing else planned. The clerk said, "Why don't you take this 8-hour bamboo rafting trip". She handed me a pamphlet which I showed to Lyle. He agreed it sounded ideal. "Eight hours of quiet poling by your guide as you watch the animals come down to drink in the lake." Wow! We agreed to take it.

Early next morning the resort made us an egg omelet to take with us, and we arrived at our jumping off point by 8 a.m. We found eight others pulling on canvas gaiters over their legs. We did likewise and headed out.

There was a short ride on a bamboo raft to cross a small stream. Then we climbed up a bank and started "trekking". I asked how far we would be trekking, and was told "not far". We walked through a rain forest, filled with birds, monkeys, squirrels, interesting trees and plants, and tiger tracks in mud.

Two hours later we were still walking. The others hadn't had breakfast and were getting hungry. Four hours later we arrived at our first destination. It was now noon, the tarps were laid out, and breakfast was served. I was pooped. While eating, we watched two rafts pull up. We were divided into two groups.

When our guide arrived, somebody asked in jest, "Where are you going to get a motor to move us?" He said, "Heh, heh, heh" and handed each of us a paddle. Well, the roar of laughter reverberated in the forest. We didn't mind the paddling. It was better than walking but it was not what we expected.

We rowed for an hour before we spotted a gaur, which is a very large blue-black buffalo – the largest in India. We landed our rafts and sneaked up to watch him. After 15 minutes he got up and walked into the woods. The guides had, in the meantime, laid out the tarps again.

Before lunch was served, one of the guides asked if anyone wanted to go for a short walk - about half a kilometer. I said, "Forget it" and promptly laid down on the tarp and went to sleep. Several other women did the same. I woke up just as the gang was returning. Lyle looked hot, sunburned, exhausted. He said he enjoyed it but it was the longest half kilometer he ever walked. A good lunch was served.

We packed up, returned to the rafts and headed back to our launching spot. When we got there we saw a herd of elephants, including a baby and a big tusker. We all piled out to get closer to them. I was tired, but was reassured by someone that we would be taking a motorboat back to where we started. Not so. The guides informed us we would be walking. "But it is not as far back. We walk along the waterfront."

I must admit if I had known what the day would consist of, I would not have gone. But I'm glad I did. It was one of the most enjoyable days we had in India. The group we were with, including people from Vancouver, was a lot of fun.

We were still tired the next day, and sunburned. We headed back to the coast. Again we stayed in a very posh resort, in a cottage with a surrounding water-filled moat. There were huge fountains and a large swimming pool that looked like it was spilling over into the Arabian Sea. The food was great: buffets for breakfast, lunch and dinner. The waiters were very congenial and wanted to practice their English.

The next morning we found our houseboat. We were alone on the boat, with a chef, a helmsman, and an engineer. We travelled slowly through the canals, motoring through vast farms and agricultural communities. All the farms were below sea level. The canals were dredged, and the soil used to build up the dikes and raised areas where the houses are built. Beyond them are flooded rice paddies. We felt like we were looking into people's backyards, watching their lives unfold. Residents were washing clothes in the canals, bathing their kids, going about their business with no apparent regard to us.

That night our chef served us a traditional and tasty Kerala dinner in our forward dining and living area. We slept in a nice bedroom amidship, complete with mosquito netting - although we saw no mosquitoes.

Next morning after breakfast we traveled for a few hours along the canals, passing a multitude of varied vessels, carrying children to school, delivering freight, materials to building sites, and generally doing the business of any community.

By noon we were deposited in another small town where our car and driver awaited us. He drove us directly to the Cochin airport and we flew back to Bangalore.

If I had to do it over again, I would plan a longer backwater cruise. The memory of Kerala brightens my memories of India. The biggest mystery about India is how each state retains its identity. It is like a group of separate countries tied together. They share a common currency, but everything else - language, religion, culture, food, clothing - is unique to each region.

MYSORE

A few days after we returned from Kerala, Ashish and family took their annual holiday and joined us. We headed south to Mysore by car.

On the way we stopped to see one of the biggest trees in India – a large banyan tree that covered some four acres. This tree reproduces by having its roots drop down from branches until they reach the ground, then travel underground before breaking the surface again as a new trunk.

At a bird sanctuary we took a boat tour around the waterways. It was filled with birds, fruit bats, and crocodiles. The birds migrate here for the winter, many all the way from Siberia. My mother talked about storks she saw as a child - these might have been descendants from those very storks.

Then on to Mysore. We toured Tipoo Sultan's palace. Though different in style, it rivals Versailles for beauty, which I had thought was the world's grandest. Tipoo Sultan was the last holdout against the British takeover of India. When they couldn't buy him off - like they did the other maharajas - they attacked, four times, before they conquered and killed him.

The descendants (Weysards) still live in the palace. One had been elected to Parliament for several terms, but had just been defeated in the last election by a Congress candidate (Indira Ghandi's party).

We headed for Kabini Forest and wildlife reserve. Ashish knew the chief guide and asked to be assigned to his jeep for our safari. Within an hour we sighted a tiger, walking ahead of us on the road. The driver sped up, but the tiger veered into the woods before we came very close. Nobody else in the other nine jeeps saw one. There were also many other animals; a gaur, elephants, wart hogs, and monkeys. We had dinner around a campfire in the evening.

Next morning we had the same guide, and again saw a tiger. Awani spotted him as he walked on the edge of the bush. We backed up, and he continued to walk alongside the road, then turned, hidden by a thin screen of trees, he looked at us. We could see him clearly about ten feet away. People and tiger just looked at each other.

Arriving back from our second safari, we proudly told the other visitors that we had again seen a tiger. Nobody would believe us. The nine other jeeps had not seen a tiger again. They were sure we were making it up. Next day, after breakfast, we headed home to Bangalore. During the trip Lyle and I were fine healthwise, but both Suvarna and Ashish got diarrhea. It seemed ironic. – who were the tourists?

When first discussing our trip to India, Ashish had "guaranteed" that Lyle would get his wish and see a tiger in the wild. He delivered on his promise and beat the odds.

On our last day with the Kulkarnis, they took us shopping and bought us gifts. There is something about gift giving in India that is either cultural or inherent. People would not take "no" for an answer. Ashish bought me a beautiful silver necklace, and Lyle a blue silk shirt.

The next morning we were on the move again. We had enjoyed Bangalore and the wonderful hospitality. Plus, it was nice having a maid and a driver. Now I knew what I want for Christmas. Suvarna was great and made our stay very pleasant, seeing to our every need. Awani, a lovely girl, will be a beauty.

En route to Ahmedabad, we had a four-hour lay-over in Mumbai (Bombay). Ashish arranged to have two of his friends pick us up at the airport and show us around town. We would see one of them again, as he was marrying a girl from Abbotsford, and invite us to his wedding.

We flew to Ahmedabad, which is the capital of the state of Gujarat. There is a sense of stability here and it is the richest state. Its highways are good; even side roads. We took a cab to see the ruins of one of the paramount port cities of the Haranad nation which dated from about 2500 B.C.

There was an excavated, artificial harbour with canals to the sea, from which they had traded with nations from Persia to Arabia to East Africa over 4,000 years ago. Sea levels have changed, and the ocean is now nowhere in sight.

Returning to Ahmedabad, we went to see Mahatma Gandhi's ashram, which is beautifully preserved, and as simple as one would expect. There was such a serene feeling about the place.

We stayed with Bibek Banerjee and Sejal Dand, both of whom were also in Nelson with Canada World Youth. Bibek had visited in Bangalore, and insisted we should stop with them en route to the Gir Forest Lion Reserve. Sejal was a great help to us. She made travel arrangements and phoned for reservations in a lodge. In fact, she handed us a note to give the bus driver on our way back, telling him where to drop us off. I half expected her to pin labels to our coats.

On the train we had a compartment, so were very comfortable. Just before reaching our destination a smartly dressed young man joined us and asked where we were going. When we said Sasan Gir he got all excited, "But you can't get there from Junagad. You have to go to the next town, and then wait for a bus tomorrow. You will need a hotel. I can help. I know everything about this place. My daddy works for the railway." It sounded so much like what our book on India warned against. We just kept saying, no, no, no. Finally I remembered Sejal said someone from the Lodge would pick us up at the station.

We were indeed met at the train, by the manager of the lodge. He said that Sejal had told him that he was dealing with very important people, and was to take good care of us, which he did. After a 3-hour drive, we arrived at the attractive Maneland Lodge, which was conveniently located in the park.

Next morning we piled into a jeep with a couple from France, and went looking for Asian lions. The French couple said they were jinxes and never saw animals on safaris. And it was true. We didn't get a glimpse of lions when we travelled with them. That afternoon the French couple left for Junagad.

The evening safari saw us alone in the jeep with our guide. Before long we left the main road, parked the jeep, walked through the forest, and came upon three one-year-old cubs eating a spotted deer. The mother was probably around but not visible. We watched for quite a while. When we headed out we were thoroughly satisfied with our sighting.

Just before dusk, we were called off the main road again, and were met by two guides, watching a pair of male lions eating a water buffalo. One looked too stuffed to move, while the other kept on eating.

Next morning our safari jeep wouldn't start, so we took a forestry jeep. We stopped at a crocodile farm where they are raising crocs to release in the wild. They told us that many species are dying off in the park, including crocodiles and vultures. There was some suspicion that this was happening because of what local farmers were feeding their buffalo.

We saw a lion and lioness, courting and mating. There are only about 400 wild Asian lions left in the world - all of them in this reserve. At one point they were down to less than 20. There are currently attempts to mate them with some that are in zoos in other parts of the world in order to strengthen the gene pool.

We finished this leg of the trip in a very satisfied mood. After dinner, the manager said he would drive us back to Junagad. He was an interesting character. He said he was a lawyer, as was his father, and his brother. However, he didn't like law so undertook to run this lodge and put together programs for young students to view animals. He was in his 40s, but had just got married. He was of the Jain religion and, as he told me this, I noted that he was eating onions. Knowing that Jains do not eat any root vegetables, I pointed at his onions. He laughed and said, "but I like onions". He said his mother had never eaten a carrot or potato or onion in her life. I asked how his mother agreed to his marrying a Hindu woman. He said, "If you wait long enough mothers will agree to anything. As long as you get married!"

When we got back to Junagad he took us out to dinner at a pleasant outdoor restaurant, next to a large, historic Muslim mosque. Then he took us to his home. Expecting a posh home, I was surprised to enter a huge, dark, stone and concrete building, with simple furniture. It appeared as though the living quarters were simply appendages to the great hall of a medieval castle. They were very hospitable and it was a pleasant evening. His older brother came over, and neighbors kept dropping in.

At midnight we went to the bus depot. We handed the driver the note Sejal gave us, telling him where to drop us off in Ahmedabad. The trip would have been all right if it wasn't for the movie that was played very loud until 3 a.m.

We rested at Sejal's, and then it was time to take another train - at midnight - for Ranthambhore - the park where Project Tiger was started. We had a good night's sleep on the train, and were met by a jeep from our lodge.

Our hotel was a former maharaja's hunting lodge. It was beautiful, a little tattered but full of character, located at the top of a long hill. We had the 3-room "Panther" suite. Just off our suite was a huge common room, which could easily entertain 25 people. Five steps up was a large balcony. Up on the rooftop, we could scan the countryside for about 25 miles, in all directions. From here the maharaja, with a good telescope, could see where the game was amid the forest and ruins of far off temples.

We took a safari on a 20-person open bus. Our book on India said, "No self respecting animal would be seen within 20 miles of that bus." It was noisy and ugly. We were miserable, cold, and bruised from being knocked about. We saw nothing but a few deer. We were told the only way to book a "gypsy jeep" was to go to the forestry office in person.

Next day we walked down the long hill, across a farmer's field, and up the road to the forestry office. Lyle got in the lineup an hour early - he saw the shamozle the day before as people shoved each other around to get a jeep. This time nothing was going to stop him getting a jeep. As the young men, who are sent down by the private hotels to book jeeps, arrived, they tried to jostle Lyle out of the way. But he latched on to the windowsill and wouldn't budge. We booked a jeep which we shared with an Australian couple. Then we had to walk back up that looong hill.

We were happy in our gypsy jeep. The Australians were good company and we had many laughs. With the news that there might not even be 20 tigers left in the park we didn't really expect to see one. We saw langur monkeys, a small jungle cat, spotted deer, nilgai, a chital, but no tiger – although there were enticing tracks on the road.

About three hours into the safari, we rounded a corner, and walking towards us was a huge tiger. The glow of its striped coat, powerful unhurried silent walk, confidently strolling down the middle of the road, was a sight to behold! Power and sheer beauty. The tiger turned and walked into the jungle.

We told the driver, "Now you can turn around and head for home." We were all satisfied. But a mile down the road there he was another, bigger tiger, crossing the road. He stopped to sniff a rock, left his scent behind, snarled at us, climbed up a hill and out of sight. I can now die happy.

The next morning we went to the train station at 7 am. A redcap came to get our luggage, and told us he needed another redcap to help. We tried to carry some of the bags, but he wouldn't let us. We meekly walked behind them. When they deposited our bags Lyle gave him 50 rupees. He shoved the money back at Lyle and said, "pay me when I put you on the train. It will be 100 rupees for each of us."

We were a bit taken aback, but said, "So they are asserting themselves. No problem." They got us on the train, but found two women in our seats, told them to get out in no uncertain terms. The women shrugged and moved out.

But, when the conductor came along and looked at our tickets, he said we were in the wrong seats: instead of 1 and 2 it was actually 101 and 102. By now the train was moving and we had to pick up our many bags and move down the length of the car. So much for assertive redcaps!

Back to Bibek and Sejal's. Rest, wash, did some sightseeing. Sejal took us to a "vessel museum". Lyle thought it was a boat museum, but I knew it would be cooking vessels. It was interesting. Then Sejal ordered some finger foods in the restaurant part of this museum, and we enjoyed some very different but tasty Indian morsels.

Sejal was a marvelous person. She had stayed in Rossland during her Canada World Youth exchange days. Later she and Bibek lived in the U.S. for a couple of years. She was well rounded in several cultures, but they couldn't stand living in the States, saying even poverty was better in India. In the States poor people blamed themselves for their state and were more desperate and unhappy.

Back in Delhi, we took a cab to Ankoor's. Ankoor took a day off work, and we, and his whole family toured the National Railway Museum. India has the biggest railway system in the world. The displays were quite fascinating.

We toured the museum home of former Prime Minister Indira Gandhi and the garden where she was assassinated. This was followed by a visit to the museum dedicated to her father, Jawaharlal Nehru, India's founding prime minister.

Another former Canada World Youth participant invited us to tour their Parliament Buildings where he was deputy chief of security.

I said, "How can elected Members not be inspired to do good deeds when they see this statue." The guide was pleased to hear that because it was on his recommendation that the statue was erected in that spot. Others had wanted to put it in the inner courtyard.

Sugata and I took a motorized rickshaw home, while Lyle went out to the historic Red Fort for an evening sound and light show. He later took a bicycle-pulled rickshaw to view the cremation site of Indira Ghandi on the banks of a river.

Then it was back to Canada. Vancouver looked so beautiful. Nobody was at the airport to meet us, so we piled up our luggage on a cart and headed out the door. Seeing a taxi, we headed for it. But the driver waved us away, pointing to a lineup waiting for cabs. We stood in the lineup and waited our turn. This was

Canada.

Our cab driver was a young Indian man. When he heard where we were coming from he wanted to know what we saw and how we viewed India. How can one explain in a short time what we had experienced. When he was making a left turn, I burst out laughing. I told him in India five cars would have turned in the time it took him. As I looked out at the streets I could understand why Ashish told us what had been his first impression of Vancouver. He had said, "All I could see was cars, cars, cars everywhere. But no people." And he was right. But now I know why he was so shocked.

Our son in India, Ashish Kalkarni, his wife, Suvarna and daughter, Awani.

EPILOGUE

On November 28th, 2006, Mother (Hilda) died, at the age of 94. She had had a long and fruitful life. The last five years spent at Haro Park Retirement Home saw her deteriorate slowly. She had many visits from us and the children. She especially enjoyed having the two great-grandsons visit.

On hearing the news, Haida wrote a parting letter to her grandmother, which I quote, in part:

"What I appreciated most about you is how you lived your life by example, not by lecture. You were the change you wanted to see in the world. You were the example of unconditional love, of giving all that you had to give, of welcoming all people into your home and treating them with the kind of respect you wanted to be treated with. You were strong, independent and loving without ever really using the word 'love'. During my years living with you, you were as much my friend as my grandma, in fact you were my best friend. I have missed your friendship lately, but always knew it was still there in spirit.

"All breathing life comes to an end, but your memory, your example, your love and my love for you will last an eternity. This I know in my heart."

She won't see my book published. She leaves behind many friends, and people whose lives she has touched. To me she was the best mother-in-law. There, when I needed her, but never imposed.

After receiving the news of Mother dying, Lyle and I took our new dog, Rex, for a walk around our neighbourhood, and saw, for the first time, a swan in our bay. It seemed to be there to cheer us up.

The next day we got a picture by email of a little girl in Ethiopia, that Haida is hoping to adopt. Life goes on.

Thinking back to the sixties, it's hard to believe how hopeful we were. How determined we were that we could build a new world, a better world. Everything was unfolding so well. Colonialism was on its way out. Young people in North America were getting very political, casting off trendsetter styles and opting for plain clothes. Revolutionary songs were making the hit parade. I had so much hope.

However, I don't think it is a better world. The problems facing future generations are enormous. But that will have to be tackled by other generations.

Good luck!

ISBN 1425114024

9 781425 114022